Limey

Smokejumper

Fighting Wildfire in the Rockies

by

Robert D. Hubble

ISBN-10: 1480129259
ISBN-13: 978-1480129252

DEDICATION

Firstly, to Bill Yount and Geno Bassette, without whom I would never have visited these magnificent places or worked alongside these many wonderful people.

And also:

Walt Smith; for excellent training. The organization lost a stalwart and the heavens gained a prize.
Tim Eldridge; a great friend who shared his space, enabling me to retain some sanity through the years of trial.
Walt Currie; just for being there. Nothing more need be said.

In Memory

Don Mackey | Jon Kelso | Sonny Soto | Richard Garcia
Ken Heare | Walt Smith | Todd Stamm | Darrel Wittke
Tim Eldridge | John Murray

There are too many to list all. These I knew.
Thanks for the opportunity.

Cover design by Christina Voyles

Introduction

In a situation where the consequences of wrong decision are so awesome, where a single bit of irrationality can set a whole train of traumatic events in motion, I do not think that we can be satisfied with the assurance that "most people behave rationally most of the time."
– Charles. E. Osgood

F irst of all, without question and to this day, I still consider smokejumping to be *the* best job in the world. All those fortunate to have done it, currently doing it, or doing it in the future are, indeed, some of the luckiest humans. The problem with having such an immensely satisfying, worthwhile, stimulating and adventurist job, however, is the inevitable balance that must, according to the Law of Administrative and Managerial Bullshit (LAMB), be paid by those on the fireline, at the warm and toasty end, to compensate for all those rousing complimentary adjectives. It is a law much like gravity, designed to bring even the hardiest of souls crashing to earth with frequent regularity, just like a jumper seeing his canopy torn to shreds above his head.

But what is smokejumping? In German it roughly translates to Feuerspringer; fire jumper, which is basically what smokejumping is. That does not, however, make it a circus act, as some German friends once assumed it to mean while visiting them in Cologne. "Robert doesn't look like a circus performer," they said, being a relief to me since I've never much liked circuses. They thought we jumped through rings of fire, on bikes perhaps, in tight pants or leotards, next to elephants under a big tent maybe, who knows? The thought alone is quite uncomfortable. In reality, though, smokejumping is a national wildland firefighting resource. Its primary purpose being to deliver personnel and equipment to remote wildfires quickly and effectively using a fleet of fixed-wing aircraft and parachutes. We jump fires. Not circus hoops.[*]

However, due to the LAMB, jumpers *are* routinely forced to jump though a myriad of hoops, administrative hoops, designed by experts just to remind us of which in the latest of a long line of swivel-chaired slugs is in charge. The last time jumpers governed their own destiny was in the early '90s, though older vets will say independence was lost long before even then. Since that coup, for it was a coup, seizure of power is a coup, hordes of self-righteous administrators and managers have cocooned the once independent organization and precipitated virtual insanity onto one of the most valuable, respected, professional, skilled and yet underutilized resources in all of America. It is no coincidence, and probably no surprise, that just about every single one of these administrators have been desk-jockeys with no association or understanding of the sharp-end whatsoever: where metal meets meat, where pulaskis meet rock and dirt, and where heat, fuel and oxygen burn. Female administrators are excellent at organizing, brilliant at it, even just for the sake of it they do it. But therein lies the problem, because smokejumpers never needed more organizing, never needed more paperwork, never needed anyone to teach 'cohesion,' never needed anyone to lecture on the latest fashionable oxymoronic buzzwords: 'diversity,' 'ethics,' and 'equal opportunity.' We jump from planes to fight wildfires. Not too difficult in itself, apart from the physical effort, but neither is it like baking a bloody cake, so leave us alone.

To some, 'insanity' might seem like a harsh word to describe this encroachment of bureaucracy, but bear me out: during the last few years of the twentieth century the smokejumper organization, Missoula in particular, underwent some very disturbing changes at

---

[*] Smokejumper History (abridged), p.335

the hands of unskilled managers either unwilling or incapable of reining in entrenched, egocentric, power-hungry, administrators. Instead of experienced fire people – base managers, trainers, squad leaders, etc. – determining who could become a smokejumper, based upon prior experience and credibility borne from word of mouth, desk-bound, non-jumping administrators became directly involved in the hiring process, actively going out to recruit people (women and minorities mainly) from all across the country. In effect, forcing people into the organization who had no purpose being there while eliminating others who did – and who were very literally lining up and waiting in the wings. For example: in one instance a woman who should never ever have been hired, routinely warned as being unsatisfactory by senior trainers, was very nearly killed and several of us watched in horror as our fears became reality before our very eyes. Other more woolly instances of heavy-handed administrative incompetence emerged when jumpers were forced to sit in circles and tell others their bloody secrets like some inane hippy candlelit vigil shite of the '60s. A handful of veteran jumpers left the room in disgust. Others, under the perceived threat of sanction, no doubt, stayed to endure the abuse and embarrassment. Such is the power that one entrenched administrator can wield when allowed to do so. Further examples could fill a large book, cover to cover, with insane sordid tales of the LAMB.

The best years, though, are always the busy years. Years that real money can be made, the big earner years. But more to the point, when years are busy, when you're out in the wilds of nature, miles away from roads and the hustle-bustle of civilization, baking hot, worn out from working a 36-hour shift, covered in soot from head to toe, bleeding, blistered and desperate for a cold beer, those are the best of times. Those are the years jumpers live for; up to their elbows in dirt, swinging an axe, tugging on a crosscut, eons away from the three ring circus of bullshit.

That's what it used to be like anyway. Maybe now, doing the best job in the world, they secretly wear tight pants and leotards, hold hands round the fire, and chant. Bleeding shoot me if that is so! I think not, however. From what I see the organization in many ways has finally undergone a change for the better, and about time. Morale has revived. Recent years have been busy and jumpers are more frequently used outside of their more traditional role. But it has to be asked, like the elephant in the room, why *that* airplane, that wonderful "collection of parts flying in loose formation," the Turbine DC-3,* has not been seen in the red skies of Montana this year (2012)? Someone quietly told me it was politics. It's a damn fire organization! What has politics got to do with anything?

As I write I am exactly 55 years and 9 months old. "Strange," you might say, to be so specific. But wait, because exactly 18 years and 3 months ago it was determined, without question and without remorse or opportunity for recourse, that I was no longer qualified to be a primary firefighter, despite having been a smokejumper for the preceding three years. An administrator somewhere decided that should a person reach that mysterious age of 35 they were all of a sudden underserving and unqualified to get a full-time job in primary firefighting. That unnamed administrator, hiding under a rock somewhere amidst the bureaucracy, not only forced me, and countless others, out of an occupation that we loved, but cost us untold thousands of dollars in lost earnings compared to everyone else who were not yet, simply, 35 years old, for doing exactly the same job. Exactly two years later the government, in its infinite wisdom, out of the goodness of its little heart, arbitrarily raised that

---

* Missoula's DC-3 is rumored to have evolved as a result of drug money. The DEA already had the plane on its radar but waited for the cartel to upgrade it to turbines before confiscating it on its next drug run. Someone was thinking ahead.

limit to 37, to save on its dwindling retirement funds, no doubt. By which time, of course, everyone caught in this trap was still too old. Nevertheless, I remained a smokejumper for as long as I could afford to, forced to subsidize my firefighting career by writing inane computer code, and finally leaving the organization (strange term isn't it, for what is dysfunction) in 2002 to get that elusive real job that I hated. Not surprisingly, I now unreservedly despise any person who would agree to this egregious, quite abhorrent, willful process of discrimination. If you are that person or, indeed, even if you agree with that person, you are a fucking idiot – so put this book back on the shelf and scurry back under the rock from where you came. Leave the real work to people you know nothing of: those who don't mind getting dirty, don't mind getting broken, don't mind getting old, don't mind doing tough physical work at any age, don't mind prostituting their bodies on an annual basis to put out fires in a job they love, despite incessant bullshit. That, in a nutshell, is smokejumping.

Finally, a good friend, with far loftier ambitions than I, now a preeminent professor at the University of Montana, once said of smokejumping, "the best job to have ever had." Me? I just wanted to work hard, get sweaty and dirty in beautiful places, jump from airplanes and enjoy my job, all the while trying to maintain the old ethos and spirit of smokejumping. If in this book I come across as harsh, it is deserved, for I want no more than the organization to prosper and be the best it can possibly be, with the best people trained to the best of human ability, given the best tools for the job and, moreover, be run by the best of the best. When such simple things are hindered by bureaucrats or inept managers I don't much like it. I loved the job. I loved it while I was doing it and I never once lost that perspective, which is why I would so readily tear the verbal heart out of anyone who was ignorant enough to damage the credibility of the organization or disregard the unrelenting efforts of those at the toasty end.

Throughout the text I have not used anyone's last name. It's completely unnecessary to do so; those who know, already know, and those who don't, never need to; and because it simply doesn't matter. But also because there are individuals among the jumper organization who frequently get involved in the more clandestine aspects of parachuting. Winter occupations that see them in far-flung fields doing things that would make most people cringe. For them anonymity is compulsory and, as such, is being respected in these pages, hence the use of an occasional alias. Such occupations made necessary due to the seasonal nature of wildland firefighting; being laid-off each September until April. Or, as in my case, *Catch 22*; being too old. Though not old enough not to be hired by other sections of the government for equally risky work. Also known as Joey Rule #2: 'They can do anything for you or anything to you.'

Footnotes have been used solely for added explanation or to further include facts to the associated text which may, or may not, be of interest to the reader. They are not intended as citations.

It was never my intention to write an accurate account. I shall leave true history to those far smarter and far more patient than I. In fact, it was never my intention to write this book at all, but for some reason it was suggested that I should, almost expected that I would. So with that, I started to scribble, unconcerned for specific dates, times and places, which these days tend to merge into one anyway, coming and going as they please like spooks in a smoke-filled mist. Though now and again, a spark, a vivid memory, would emerge to the fore, completely out of the blue, for no reason, only to vanish as quickly as it arrived if I did not write it down. So there are stories mislaid due to procrastination, lethargy even, in not wanting to rise from slumber and reach for my keyboard. Those I shall leave to others. Those scribed here come alone from memory, without research, just as I remember, warts and all. Continuity may be inexact, but that is simply due to merged thoughts, forcing two or three fires into one maybe, years perhaps, into months. I suspect for those who also never kept a journal it is the same.

Smokejumpers fight many things during their lives: fire being the obvious and, for the most part, probably the most sensational, the most exiting and rewarding. But those sky-scraping 100-foot flames are not the greatest of foes. Financial worries, family issues and job prospects all play a part just like for anyone else. But with the addition, year after year, of reaching that perfect level of physical fitness to avoid the burden of an injury that can mean the end of a season or even the end of a career. That fitness made all the harder by those niggly injuries, always acquired in physical activity, that make fitness that much harder to achieve, young or old. But the greatest, most consistent, and most insidious foe comes from outside the confines of the smokejumper enclave, but inexorably and inextricably seeps into it. That is why this book is not just about fires, but about what else firefighters endure to keep the job they love – and do so not just for their benefit, but for the benefit of the nation. Because these great sweeping forests are one of this nation's greatest resources, and greatest of all treasures. Not just for their timber, but for the public pleasure, for recreation; hiking, hunting, fishing, camping, climbing, even just to sit back and look at it in awe, for nature's sake, admire it, wonder in it. For the main subject and star of this book is not the smokejumper or the fire, but the land on which both live. A land smokejumpers are fortunate to call 'jump country.'

Chapter One

— First Fire Jump

The American way of life consists of something that goes greatly beyond the mere obtaining of the necessities of existence. If it means anything, it means that America presents to its citizens an opportunity to grow mentally and spiritually, as well as physically. The National Park System and the work of the National Park Service constitute one of the Federal Government's important contributions to that opportunity.
– Newton B. Drury, NPS Director (1940-51)

T HE SECOND I ENTEERED OBLIVION I knew my mistake. But it was too late. No vigor. I had stepped when I should have leapt and the blast from the powerful turboprop just feet from my head sent me into an immediate uncontrollable spin. When I focused my eyes at a little over 1,300 feet I first saw mountains, then water, and then mountains again, with a brief glimpse of the disappearing aircraft on each blurry rotation. The spotter's white helmet still visible in the open door as he looked back in what must have been utter bewilderment. So it went as I corkscrewed towards earth a little faster than is healthy.

The parachute cords were twisted so tight that my neck felt as if it was in a vice, and I couldn't lift my head to see if the canopy was fully inflated, or, more importantly, if it was even there. Then, finally managing to wiggle my head forward, I peeked up through the cage of my helmet and saw the reassuring sight of red and blue ripstop nylon above me. The parachute was inflated at least, but it was spinning rapidly anticlockwise and making me quite dizzy.

This faster than usual approach to earth, and hasty overtaking of my jump partner – who I managed to glimpse on each rotation – was becoming increasingly alarming. The problem was obviously humorous to someone, though, because at 800 feet I heard a laugh.

Despite the incessant spinning my canopy was, in fact, quite stable, even if not fully inflated due to the cords being completely twisted from the base of the parachute right down to my neck. The problem in the whole process was the rag doll dangling beneath it.

Somewhere below me was the jump spot. A meadow in which I was supposed to land and where everyone else was, I assumed, watching my descent in comedic amazement, and no doubt taking bets if I would ever make it in.

Certainly, if I didn't control the spinning soon I would never reach it. Instead, I'd crash into another part of the planet; either the water on the other side of the mountains or the mountains on the other side of the water. Or that big bloody tree in the middle of the meadow, motioning me ever closer. Its ugly outstretched branches beckoning like a giant flytrap.

As I neared the end of the twists the spinning slowed, and for one glorious but excruciatingly brief suspenseful second it stopped, before starting up again in the opposite direction. With the ground rushing closer by the second it was no longer funny. It was both foolhardy and dangerous and threatened to smash me to pieces.

Finally, at 300 feet, I managed to pry my risers apart to stop the spinning and quickly surveyed the dizzying scene below. I was lucky. The wind had been strong but, remarkably, I had remained within the wind cone. So with no help whatsoever from me I was exactly where I was supposed to be; directly above the meadow with the small stream meandering just off to the right. All nicely surrounded by 70-foot pines and Douglas-firs.

At this point the ground was just a little bit closer than I'd anticipated. But finally able to do what had been drummed into me during weeks of training, I turned into the wind to reduce my bone-shattering forward speed. But now going backwards, I could only see where I had been and not where I was going. Remembering that the stream was off to my left, and knowing that I didn't want to end up on the wrong side of it, I pulled on my right toggle to quarter the canopy and steer away. Happy to be in control for the first time during the entire descent, I gloated over my regained confidence and prepared myself for a perfect backwards parachute landing fall. Just before slamming into the dirt like a sack of shit.

There was nothing pretty, safe, or remotely enjoyable about my landing and I impacted like a Napoleonic cannonball. A fitting end to a dismal performance. But being resilient I was relieved not to have heard anything crack. My feet had hit first, thankfully, then my backside, followed by the back of my head. My feet would have hit again, completing the somersault, had the canopy not re-inflated and unceremoniously hauled me across the meadow on my back. Enabling me to pick up a delightful assortment of wilderness fauna, mud, and buffalo crap along the way. Most of it, of course, embedding deep down my neck. I reached for the parachute cords above my head, grabbed a couple, and reeled them in until the canopy spilled air and collapsed, which, after what seemed like a 100 yards, left me supine, motionless and exhausted. Yet I was unhurt – except for a severe case of damaged pride.

I jumped up as though everything had gone exactly according to plan, and to my great relief everyone seemed to feign ignorance to the drama, the others busy gathering their gear in various parts of the field, or pretending to. Then I heard a yell and looked up to see another body fly over my head at an alarming rate and thump into the ground a few feet away. My jump partner (JP) had arrived. In better circumstances he should have landed already, being a good thirty pounds heavier and having left the aircraft a couple of seconds before me. But my twists had given gravity the advantage and I had overtaken him as Newton predicted.

Nevertheless, my JP was here, and he landed with an almighty thump that only weight and added wind velocity can provide. To better see where he was going he hadn't fully turned into the wind, as is generally considered advisable, so on impact I heard air being involuntarily expelled from his lungs and even thought I felt sod shudder. He had four points of contact: his feet, ever so briefly; his head, uncomfortably; his knees, painfully; and finally his head again as it embedded itself into the grass in an inglorious face-plant. Then, just as he started to get up, probably thinking it was all over, the wind re-inflated his canopy, yanked him off his knees and hauled him face first across the grass, only stopping when hitting a log in an elk wallow. But it gave him time to release his canopy by unclipping one of his mud encrusted Capewells.[*]

This newly arrived form rose from the mire like some strange mythical creature and, like me, made an attempt to look as though nothing untoward had happened. (Such actions are a common trait among resilient young rookies looking to emulate youthful, though often foolhardy, invincibility, even in the face of extreme trauma and injury.) Once sure nothing was broken he looked towards me and started to laugh, waving his arms in delight. He told me later he'd been laughing the whole way down because my unorthodox descent and abundant use of English profanity had amused him considerably. It was fine with me, because watching him extricate himself from the muddy mire was equally amusing. Our laughter was a natural response to the grateful realization that after landing like two sacks of shit in a shallow pond neither of us was broken.

---

[*] A manual mechanism initially developed for the military during WWII which allows jumpers to quickly detach the canopy from the parachute harness.

The recent arrival's helmet cage was plastered in a colorful selection of summer foliage, but it was still easy to tell who he was. At a lean six-foot something it could only have been Steve. Being my rookie bro and frequent jump partner I was thankful that he wasn't hurt after hurtling into the planet so fast. Many wouldn't have escaped injury so easily. I was, however, selfishly reassured that someone else had endured equally as bad a landing as me. Not that it at all detracted from my dismal performance, for which I was certain to receive a good bollocking in due course.

We both later discovered that everyone had experienced an uncomfortable landing. Partly because the jump spot was perfectly flat, and unusually long in the prevailing wind direction, allowing us plenty of leeway to jump with the wind vastly exceeding normal operational conditions. We all agreed to jump, however, because the spotter had thought it worth a try, and for some reason we had trusted him. Being new to the game my JP and I were more than willing to prove ourselves in front of the more experienced veteran smokejumpers who we generally looked up to, trusted, and didn't want to disappoint. In other words, we knew squat and stepped out of the door of a fast moving aircraft at 1,500 feet, like sheep to the slaughter because we didn't know any different.

The spotter and squad leaders in charge of us that day were apparently equally willing to see the results of brand new rookies in high wind behaving little better than crepe paper streamers. That quickly infused the notion that trust had to be earned, not granted unconditionally because of seniority, position or overt confidence.

There were exceptions to this rule however. There were some in the organization that gained everyone's confidence and respect by instinct alone. But that stemmed from credibility, not position; from experience, not seniority; and from quiet stabilizing earned authority, not overt brashness. For one person in particular it was because he was built like the proverbial brick shit-house and could crush a rookie's skull with his bare hands. And given my recent performance that's no doubt exactly what he was going to do at his earliest convenience.

Despite the excitement over the windy jump we knew it had been the easy part. All it had entailed was falling out of a perfectly good airplane under a few yards of silk and being fortunate enough to stay in one piece – even though little I did that day advantaged me in that regard. Now, however, we had to fight the wildfire that was raging in the woods a few hundred feet from the field we had just cultivated with our bodies.

As we gathered our gear from various parts of the meadow the jump ship came roaring over the treetops and began delivering cargo. At 200 feet the spotter was easily visible in the door as he threw out the first of many cardboard bundles – I think he was also giving us the middle finger salute. Containers of food, water, tools and chainsaws floated down on flimsy eight feet 'splat chutes' and thumped in all around us. A few boxes didn't fare too well beneath some of West Yellowstone's test parachutes, causing their contents to be strewn across the meadow like a lazy mid-west garage sale.

After ten minutes the plane did one last low pass. The spotter waving from the doorway as he left the meadow littered with little orange parachutes, brown boxes, crushed cans of fruit cocktail and splattered remains of Beany Weenies, looking like pavement pizza after Friday night in Missoula. After circling overhead to relay fire information and radio frequencies the ship turned to head back to base, its engines getting steadily fainter as it disappeared into a dwindling dot between the white-capped mountains in the distance.

Silence. The drone that had engulfed us for the past two hours was gone and we became accustomed to a new sound, reminding us of a more immediate role. Loud crackling in the woods signaled increasing fire activity and we could see flame lengths growing rapidly as they reached the tree canopy on the edge of the meadow.

An odd Doug-fir was igniting and torching brilliantly, first one and then another. Then two and three, as several became one massive 100-foot flame licking at the sky, preheating more in its path in readiness for the same treatment. The fire was bright, hungry and growing. As trees torched, hot burning embers rushed high into the atmosphere on the updrafts. If they fell back to earth too soon they would ignite more fires hundreds of yards ahead of the fire-line.

We were thankful that we had jumped into a natural firebreak. The long, wide and lush meadow would stop the fire from burning anything further in that direction. However, there was plenty of forest yet to burn in the other three directions, and it was a forest ready to burn, just like the Yellowstone fires of 1988. Only this year extraordinary efforts were being made not to have a repeat of that devastation. The political backlash from those fires had halted temporarily the park's normal let burn policy for natural fires and managers were still a little edgy.

#   #   #

ONE OF THE BEST THINGS ABOUT jumping into the wonderful Yellowstone National Park that day was that few people, smokejumpers or not, ever get to parachute into America's, and indeed the world's, first great National Park. Yellowstone is a majestic place and everyone wants to visit, urged by a deluge of documentaries that examine its unique geology, and by an impressive array of nature shows that follow the lives of its many inhabitants. And in visiting, being enthralled by everything about it: the splendor of the landscape with its boiling pools of mud, spouting geysers, deep canyons, pristine rivers and high alpine lakes nestled among vast mountain ranges; the remarkable and fortunate history from its inception in 1872 to become the peoples' park;[*] and the enduring survival of its many lowly critters and imposing beasts.

Yellowstone may no longer be the extreme hidden wilderness it once was when small pockets of Shoshone made it their home, or when the first white fur trappers arrived. Nevertheless, it remains a significant place amid an expanse of splendor. One where ordinary people are fortunate to have the opportunity to get up close and personal to the magnificently beautiful wilds of nature.

To be lucky enough to be there on my first fire jump was indeed a privilege. It was befitting compensation for starting at the bottom of the list and made the effort of the preceding year and pain of the previous weeks worth it. And, as Drury's chapter quote so aptly said, that effort, and these wonderful and wonderfully wild places, had enabled us to "grow mentally and spiritually, as well as physically." At thirty-four I knew I had truly found a job I would love. This really was the best job in the world.

---

[*] In 1871, geologist and explorer Ferdinand V. Hayden, along with other equally concerned, forthright individuals, were the first to propose to the U.S. Congress that the *Great Geyser Basin* be forever preserved "for the public good." On March 1st, 1872, President Ulysses S. Grant signed The Act of Dedication into law, whereby protecting these great lands from "the vandals who are now waiting to enter into this wonder-land," and who, "will in a single season despoil, beyond recovery, these remarkable curiosities, which have required all the cunning skill of nature thousands of years to prepare." – Hayden.

Chapter Two

— North Fork of the Clearwater

I'm in love with Montana. For other states I have admiration, respect, recognition, even some affection. But with Montana it is love. And it's difficult to analyze love when you're in it.

– John Steinbeck

I T WAS THREE MONTHS SINCE our dairy barn burned to the ground. And with characteristic corporate lethargy on behalf of the insurance company in effecting their end of the bargain, Anne, my wife, and I now had no farm. With the onset of winter we were forced to sell our herd of cows in November. Then, on the last day possible, the insurance company compensated us at a fraction of value. But by then it was November and too late to do anything. We no longer had a choice because it was impossible to keep dairy cows outside during a long cold Minnesota winter, not if we expected to make a living. In Minnesota the snows continue for months and temperatures frequently drop to minus 30 degrees Fahrenheit – sometimes even considered a warm day to the Finnish inhabitants during January or February – making running a modest dairy herd difficult at best and constructing a new barn virtually impossible. And without cows the farm was nothing.

The whole episode was thoroughly depressing. Watching the best of our herd being sold was a heartbreaker. Since the fire Anne and I had long run dry of tears and we stifled emotions in the cold November morning as the last of our herd boarded the truck. Even they seemed to sense the misery that had befallen them. It was one of the worst days of our lives, and probably the worst of their short lives too.

Yet they boarded the truck in their own inimitable way. A few fought the experience because that's what cows are supposed to do. Others were clearly nervous about the commotion but could see their herd mates onboard and left anyway. A few were totally nonchalant to the whole experience and strolled about oblivious to anything; a testament to their contentment in some, a testament to dumb stupidity in others. Petra, the youngest of the herd, had all the flighty characteristics of a high maintenance blonde and kept glancing over to where her calves had been housed. A mothering instinct concerned about the whereabouts of her latest twin heifers.

She had routinely escaped the confines of the barn to peer over the calf pen door, just to make sure they were being looked after properly. But all that remained was a charred, pitted piece of concrete. No door. No pens. No warm straw-filled comfort against the fresh northerly wind that signaled the arrival of another winter. She wandered around in confusion, as any youngster would when not understanding what had happened or what was going on. Her skittish eyes seemed to plead for explanation.

All the animals had been our extended pets. Each had a name and a distinct character, some good, some bad. After six years of relentless back-breaking work, through hard-fought misery brought on by drought, blizzard, torrential rains, stray voltage and, at times, abject poverty as a result of frequent milk price reductions, these cows had finally started to earn their keep and make us money.

But now, as the truck drove away down the drive, with a row of warm wet muzzles breathing steam through the slats, all we had to show for those years were three old vehicles, an assortment of farmyard pets and a heap of oily old railroad ties. Time had come to rethink a life that had never been easy. Such things are but a chapter of life and this reevaluation was but the consequence of risk. We had lived a little of Aeschylus' "reward for suffering is experience." It may not have been particularly easy, life rarely is, but it was, had been, at least, a very real way to live, a life at the productive end. A necessary one for people to survive. It provided a true perspective and a valuable lesson on the quirkiness and often unforeseen uncontrollable fortunes and fates of life.

After the insurance company finally settled the claim they had the unmitigated gall to continue billing us for the preceding three months for a barn that they clearly knew no longer existed. At first I thought it was a simple mistake, a clerical error, but then another bill arrived, and another. I was finally forced to go to the office and yell at a desk-ridden Fryer Tuck who tried to say that we "hadn't cancelled the policy" – for a barn he knew no longer existed.

But that didn't work either, because the company continued to send us ever-increasing bills over a period of months, even finding us in Montana six months later. I eventually stopped them coming by attaching one to an eight-inch rough chunk of two by eight and giving it back to the postman Elvis-style; *Return to Sender*.

The barn fire, however, was not the catalyst to my later choice to fight fires. Indeed, Anne and I had absolutely no idea what we would do after leaving the farm, although the choice to move west, into wildfire territory, was in part initiated by a previous journey:

\#   \#   \#

THAT JOURNEY UNDERTAKEN in the early summer of 1988, when we had driven though the vast unchanging dry plains of North Dakota to the mountains of Montana, Idaho and Wyoming. Being from the 'burbs of London I had never seen anything like it, finding myself saturated in the Wild West I had only seen on television. The country was magnificent, awe-inspiring and endless and I imagined legendary cowboys standing tall behind every rock and burned up twelve rolls of 35mm film in six days on scenery that I never envisaged existed except for on revolving celluloid. The mountain ranges fascinated me. One after another they appeared like distant ghosts on the horizon; subtle, grey, obscured by haze, steadily growing more massive mile after mile. Until finally, after countless more miles, they would tower above us to block the sun as their baldly white tops pricked holes in a crystal blue sky. The panorama was spectacular, monumental and ruggedly beautiful. To a lad from London it was a delight for the eyes and a thrill to the senses.

Flanked by mountains the valleys were green and lush. Made so by sparkling pristine rivers providing drenching irrigation. Ranchers herded cattle on horseback between immense open-range pastures, just as they had for generations. Nearby, monster machines cut endless fields of hay and filled the valleys with the sweet dusty aroma that lifts a farmer's heart. Deer were plentiful and roamed in unconfined freedom. Solitary moose sauntered undisturbed along riverbanks. Lone black bears roamed the hills in search of early summer huckleberries, and contented Angus and Herefords grazed, fat, in the hundreds, head-down and oblivious to the magnificence of their backyard.

They have a term for this vast open Montana landscape: 'Big Sky.' Although the term doesn't fully compliment the vastness of this land. One has to see it, feel it, smell it. Seize it into the senses to fully experience what is one of the most awe-inspiring, freedom-inducing, romantic and exciting places on earth.

We stayed in a cabin owned by the Pillsbury family just outside of Jackson Hole, Wyoming. Anne's aunt was the cook and to test the amenities before the dignitaries, celebrities and general wannabes arrived she was allowed to invite a few friends and family. We stayed in an immaculate old log cabin – as one would expect with many famous names in the guest book. The ranch was located right on the banks of the Snake River, in the shadow of the Grand Teton. The place names were all recognizable from my childhood and seeing them for the first time held an almost surreal fascination. To discover that these places really existed thrilled me. Yet I felt I had been there before. Everything seemed strangely familiar, and comfortable.

On our second day I decided to go for a run. I was told that guests often tried but because of the altitude rarely got very far. Of course, I was determined to prove them wrong and headed out along the long drive to the main highway, then on toward the Jackson Hole ski area. It was over 6,000 feet and 85 degrees. The air was thin and warm, and full of floating cotton from the river-bottom trees. On my left was the Grand Teton, to the right the ranch, and just beyond, the impressively wide meandering Snake River. I started to get a feeling of déjà vu and as I ran I vaguely remembered a dream from childhood where I was running along a road bordered by mountains and a ranch where Olivia Newton John lived – being the if only star I always lusted after during those awkward teen years.

Continuing on towards the airport I briefly stopped to watch a few obviously very rich people arrive in their lavish private jets. Soon heading back along the road and yet all the while trying to make sense of that strange feeling of having being there before.

Anne was ready waiting for me and once I'd showered we all went to the cookhouse for dinner. Just inside the door was a guest book that we were all expected to sign. We hadn't noticed it earlier and sifted through the pages to see if we recognized anyone. I just about fell flat when Anne pointed out that Olivia Newton John had stayed there the same week the previous year!

We left the cabin the next day to begin our long journey home to Minnesota and it felt as if I was leaving something behind. I had never felt such a connection before. Being in the mountains with countless new scenes unfolding at every turn was incredible. The car's windows were open the whole time, the air so fresh, sweet and invigorating. I couldn't inhale enough of it.

But of course we had to return to the cows and the life we had chosen in the winter-frigid, summer-sweltering, mosquito-bitten flatlands of Minnesota.

#   #   #

A FTER LOSING THE FARM later and reconsidering our options it wasn't hard deciding in which direction to go. While still in Minnesota Anne found a position on a Forest Service (FS) wildlife crew in remote central Idaho, based on a veterinary qualification she had gained at college. She drove west in April and I stayed behind in Minnesota while a replacement was found for my milk testing job, and eagerly waited to hear if Anne's FS district would hire me on their fire crew – digging ditches being about the only thing I thought myself qualified to do after slinging cow shit most of my life.

I had recently heard of these summer fire crews while milk testing for a neighbor's dairy herd. John, one of the more energetic young farmers in Becker County, had earlier told me about a local teacher, Chuck, who headed west each summer to fight forest fires during the school holidays. Apparently a few weeks before Chuck left he could be seen running the roads to get in shape. He would then disappear in June after school finished and return exhausted, battered and bruised – but happy and much richer – in September. Rumor had it that the children in Frazee, Minnesota, didn't learn much English at the start of a new term, but did hear a lot of jump stories about firefighting in mountains most of them had never seen. John's was a casual conversation initiated by his desire to hunt in Idaho and I never really thought much about it at the time. But it must have embedded in my subconscious because it was to return to the surface later, and change my life completely. Yogi Berra once said: "If there's a fork in the road take it." I was about to run headlong up that fork with all the naivety, exuberance, hope and vigor of a determined adolescent.

Anne eventually called to let me know that the North Fork District of the Clearwater National Forest would, indeed, hire me and keep me working until September. I was thrilled, packed in a day and immediately headed west. After the misery of the fire, and living in limbo with the in-laws for a few months, life had begun to improve. It took 18 hours on a mostly deserted highway to reach Missoula, Montana, and four more to reach Canyon Work Center, right in the middle of the massive Clearwater National Forest.

Anne was in the middle of nowhere. The nearest town was an hour away and barely surviving on a beleaguered logging industry. The majority of vehicles I'd seen for the last three hours from Missoula were logging trucks, all careening down narrow roads as if possessed. They weren't of course. At least I don't think so. I assumed it was more because they knew the roads like the back of their hands and, since their wages were determined by how many trips they could make in day, they drove fast. My Minnesota license plates were a dead giveaway and they let me know it. They didn't know the half of it.

On the first morning I awoke early, full of anticipation and introduced myself to Chuck, the district Fire Management Officer (FMO). Gleaming with excitement I was crushed when he told me that he couldn't hire me after all. This was such a disappointment after the anticipation, the weeks of waiting and the long trip. He explained that only United States citizens could be employed with the Forest Service, even if it was only a temporary seasonal job. No one had thought to tell us and we had never thought to consider it. Anne had mentioned that I was English but there seemed to be no way around the bureaucracy. It was a problem, and a big one. But without anything else to do I stuck around to watch, listen and bide my time while figuring out what to do next.

After talking with a couple of Anne's new friends on the wildlife crew we learned that I could volunteer my time. For this I would get an allowance of $7 a day for four 10-hour days, plus, graciously, the use of a bed. Seeing as I was already there, Anne was there, and since I really had nowhere else to go, I decided to push for it. I asked around to see who needed people for certain types of work and ended up approaching the silviculture manager, explaining that he could save some money on his budget by taking me on. For $28 a week it seemed like a bargain on his behalf, because I hadn't been paid that little since working an agricultural 60-hour week in England when I was 16. He was a little skeptical at first, he didn't know this Limey from Adam, but he eventually agreed to try me out. I was greatly relieved, even though I would remain greatly broke.

Over the next few weeks I planted trees, marked cutting boundaries, surveyed old boundaries, mapped roads and inspected cut banks. Then I inspected other contractor's work while they cut poles, killed moles and planted trees. It seemed as though the FS was all about checking up on how other people were working FS land, and then building the roads that allowed the companies to do it and cleaning up the crap they left behind. The time, money and effort expended so that companies could tear up the mountains was anomalous to me. It was ultimately anomalous to others as well because it gained the attention of a host of environmental groups who were forcing the whole logging industry, rightly or wrongly, ignorantly or arrogantly, toward a major upheaval. The silviculture crew had a lot to do with making that upheaval less dramatic in the '90s, although few in the logging industry were impressed by their efforts. It was a damned if you do, damned if you don't kind of job, stuck between the longstanding timber industry paying local wages on one side, and city environmentalists with easy access to politicians on the other. But hell, to me it paid $28 a week – and I got to use a bed!

On my days off – those when I got paid seven dollars less – I went out with Anne on her wildlife tasks. Her job was to document all the plant species in pre-designated, satellite-selected areas of the forest. We would drive out in a putrid green FS truck to some remote logging road, walk a few miles up mountains and across meadows before finding the specific quarter-acre spot. Then, once on a horrendously steep slope Anne would write down all the plant names in Latin, literally hundreds of them. I have no idea how she managed to learn them all in the time she was there. She picked it up amazingly quickly. Latin to me was, well... Latin.

If anyone asked, we always said that I drove my own vehicle because as I wasn't being paid for those days I wasn't supposed to be riding in a FS rig. This was just in case some grizzled old office fart wanted to blame someone for anything – the FS is like honey to such people. It was a cover your ass (CYA) policy that I soon learned proliferated, like the holes in Swiss cheese, and just about as useful, all aspects of this once noble institution.

Those days with Anne were wonderful. Once finished with work we would have lunch on top of a remote undisturbed peak: two flatlanders mesmerized by the endless, unspoilt, velvety green vistas in one direction and appalled by the nuclear-like devastation of clear-cut logging in the other. Once back at camp our newfound friends would harass us with whistles, catcalls and innuendo. But they were only jealous.

The snowline on the mountains surrounding the camp rose as summer approached and the fire crew soon needed extra help for their prescribed burns. To get that help they asked for volunteers –

the FS simply loves volunteers, even more so than the army. I had been waiting for this opportunity and jumped two paces forward like a Gurkha volunteering to parachute for the first time, uncaring of the consequences. Chuck initially gave me an 'are you still here' look but reluctantly, or in fascination of persistence, nodded his head anyway. He had probably thought the hard work and lack of wages in silviculture would have made me quit. But during years on the farm we'd often earned far less for doing far more and I hadn't thought much about it. Now, however, although still poor, I was having more fun than I'd had in years.

So, at the start of the fourth week I was provided a pulaski[*] – a long handled axe with an adze (a hoe-like tool used to hollow out logs) opposite the axe, like a mattock – and found myself digging dozens of firelines in 90-degree heat on excruciatingly steep south aspect slopes in the middle of Idaho. It was bloody wonderful! I was having the time of my life!

Chuck stared at me rather quizzically when I showed up the next morning looking for more. I had a handful of blisters from no gloves; torn feet from useless boots; but unequaled ambition from having... the best time of my life!

"Glutton for punishment?" I think was the question Chuck posed before sending me back into the hills for more of the same.

The work was physically demanding but was little more than we'd done for years on the farm, except for being on slopes that I, and especially my legs, had never seen before. Minnesota doesn't have anything worth calling a mountain and my legs screamed every time they met another 30-degree incline. But it was all new

---

[*] Originally introduced to the U.S. by Collins Tool Company in 1876, but reportedly 're-invented' in 1911, at Ed Pulaski's request by Joseph B. Halm, Pulaski's assistant, both U.S. Forest Service rangers based in Wallace, Idaho. Largely as a response to what Pulaski saw as a need for better firefighting tools after being credited with forcibly saving (under gunpoint) 45 lives during the *Great Idaho Fire* of 1910, which burned 3 million acres over 2 days and killed 87 people, at least 72 of them firefighters.

and exiting and in some strange masochistic way I even welcomed the daily exhaustion and cuts and bruises. I clearly wasn't doing it for the money, though, because the food bill alone was more than I was earning.

Many of the crew were in their second or third year and had developed a comfortable routine; pacing themselves throughout the day. Some routinely fought for the privilege of driving the engine. Whereas a small group of us would thrive on just doing the down and dirty hard graft. I was becoming an anomaly. Not for wanting to work, or even volunteering to do the hard work, but for doing it for 7 bucks a day.

"It's not even beer money!" They said.

It didn't take long to realize that a few of us were routinely putting in a lot more than our fair share of work. It's easy to tell when you're digging miles of fireline day in, day out, up, down and across almost every mountain in the forest. Even with the back aching, hands ripping, feet tearing and legs burning there is still plenty of time to think. So although I was thoroughly grateful for having the work, I was, nevertheless, growing frustrated at doing more than a fair share for a gross less reward. With encouragement from Pete, one of the brilliant squad leaders, I explained this rather succinctly to Chuck one morning. But word had preceded me.

My basic approach, never accused of being diplomatic, was: "Com'on, gimme a job. I can do this!"

Slowly but surely I was wearing Chuck down and unknown to me others were also helping my cause. I'm sure Chuck had more important things on his mind but after a few more days he decided to hire me as a contractor. Apparently the government had released some fire emergency funds under a severity clause to make this possible. After that, I started getting real wages. It wasn't a lot, but at least I could now live on it. I don't know which of us was more relieved, Chuck for not having to deal with my daily harassment or me for finally getting paid for work I was already doing.

The whole crew was earning a lot of overtime now that we were doing more burns: slash burning; setting fire to the trash left over after logging operations, smaller diameter trees and branches, often several feet deep on the hillside. And whether out-of-touch, desk jockey, middle managers choose to accept it or not, for every seasonal firefighter, it's the overtime that makes it a livable wage.

We were now starting at six in the morning, going until dark, and getting 14 to 16-hour days on a regular basis. Overtime (OT or Oats) was a wonderful thing, even if mine wasn't time-and-a-half like the others. But with the nearest town so far away there was nowhere to spend it anyway, so it grew rather nicely as there was no longer any feed, fuel or veterinary bills to pay.

These burns were incredible. There's no other way to describe the wanton destruction of setting huge tracts of land alight littered with so much brittle-dry fuel. This summer Chuck had more than the usual acreage to burn and he needed to use up his funds for the year or he would lose them. So we would set one 50-acre clear-cut alight and move to the next to set 80 acres alight, then move again to set 100 acres alight. These massive ugly clear-cuts were where logging companies had removed all the valuable timber and left the rubbish (slash) behind for us to clean up by burning before replanting could occur. During the season we dug miles of fireline around the clear-cuts and pre-positioned hose-lays to prep them. Then, once the weather obliged and fuel conditions were right, we would ignite the slash in strips during the early evening in an attempt to draw the heat to the center. If it was done right the air would be sucked in from all sides and, hopefully, stop the fire from escaping the perimeter and burning the surrounding healthy forest. The technique was very effective and remarkably successful most of the time. Chuck seemed to have a knack for it. It was grueling hard work but immensely exciting.

North Fork clear-cuts are nearly always steep and brimming with brittle slash, loose stumps, downed snags and rocks, making traversing through a slash unit extremely difficult, especially when carrying a drip torch and a five-gallon jerrycan full of fuel mix. We would strip off the top of the unit in few tight rows to provide a good burned buffer and then work down, widening the rows as we went. All the while watching for rollers – logs or rocks dislodged by the fire that could bounce down on us – with only our wits and flimsy plastic hardhats for protection.

Stumbling through three feet deep brittle slash with fire above and behind us while carrying a flaming drip torch often provides a good test of Darwinism. Dropping an unintentional glob of burning fuel while climbing over piles of slash can be an enlightening experience to say the least, and it frequently initiates that intrinsic surge of adrenaline needed to get the hell out of Dodge. Lighting behind you without a suitable exit can also be awkward when carrying an extra five gallons of incendiary fuel. Either way, such mistakes can be the makings of a kebab, much like an immolated monk, and are usually followed by a loud "OH SHIT!" and a rapid departure from the vicinity.

Everyone wore green Nomex[*] pants and yellow Nomex shirts, designed to protect against occasional direct flame but not heat. During burns we'd invariably have flames lapping at our ankles that would scorch our trouser legs. While we didn't care too much about burning our trousers, which were issued, we did care about our boots, which weren't. And although issued we also cared about our hard to find, old-fashioned, cotton Nomex shirts.

---

[*] A synthetic flame-resistant material, somewhat resembling cotton, developed by DuPont in the 1960s that does not melt, ignite or drip.

Having a traditional cotton Nomex shirt was like owning gold dust and we hung onto them no matter what state they were in. It was quite normal to see people wearing more patchwork than shirt, especially the sawyers, who would rest the blade of their long Stihl chainsaws on their shoulders. The type and condition of a yellow shirt was used to signify experience. And in many cases provided a better gauge of fire experience than the later mandated pieces of paper claiming a myriad of superior classroom fire qualifications.

By ten o'clock in the evening we would have three or four 80-plus acre fires raging on various aspects of the forest, turning darkness into a bright orange glow. The crew would then split up between each unit to monitor the fires and extinguish anything that escaped the boundaries to threaten the forest. With the night sky ablaze smoke columns could soar up to 20,000 feet, allowing the smoke to diffuse over a larger area instead of sinking to the closer valleys where it would annoy the local residents and attract even more animosity towards the Forest Service.

Forest smoke management is a contentious issue among the large burgeoning communities of Montana and Idaho. Most of the understory prescribed burns close to these communities are done solely to provide firebreaks for their protection, and yet complaints abound, especially after being subjected to several days of settling smoke. Such complaints often originate from newer inhabitants, however, rather than the longstanding residents who have already experienced the disastrous effects of wildfire and are, therefore, more inclined to accept a few days of smoke in order to safeguard their livelihoods.[*]

---

[*] As I write, we have only now, after almost two months, seen clean fresh air. With 49 consecutive days of no rain, the large summer fires have been smoldering away and filling the valleys with smoke. But that's life in the northwest. On a recent drive from Missoula to Seattle we didn't get relief from the smoke until Snoqualmie Pass; that's 427 miles of constant smoke.

As the dirty dark smoke from our infernos billowed upwards, burning hot firebrands rose into the night sky to be whisked away on the prevailing evening winds. It was still early in the season and atmospheric humidity would extinguish them long before they ever fell back to earth. Later in the season it would be different. During the long hot summer months embers of wildfires cause constant problems as they are carried on the wind to ignite countless more fires in the tinder-dry timber far ahead of constructed firelines – spotting is a serious hazard to firefighters and firefighting.

Occasionally the massive heat and flames in the burns would escape the boundaries and surge over the fireline in search of fresh fuel, causing everyone to jump into action by digging more fireline around the spill – or slop-over. Pre-positioned hoses were efficient in laying down the flames so that we could dig line more directly. But the steam caused by this was always horrendous, almost worse than the smoke itself. Our eyes and nostrils took an absurd level of punishment from steaming hot ash and other airborne debris. Eyes would sting, streaming with tears, while lungs rebelled by hacking up dust and mucous. If it got too bad we'd step out of the smoke to inhale fresh air in a moment of respite before submitting ourselves back to the task. We never had breathing masks and relied, instead, on simple cotton bandanas, which weren't very efficient but they at least kept the larger particles from being inhaled.

After a session in these conditions our mouths were bone dry, caked with so much dirt and dust that we could feel grit between our teeth and taste dry wads of desiccated ash on the tongue. Tears from irritated eyes created rivulets that left pale vertical streaks on otherwise sooty faces. The nose and sinuses would get so clogged that it felt like flu. Headaches were commonplace. All we could do was maintain fluid intake to combat the symptoms of dehydration from working so close to the heat of the fire. The slightest moment of fresh air was a godsend and when available we inhaled it by the gallon.

Due to the varying conditions on these burns there was always discussion about who would ignite and who would hold it. Those holding the perimeter were destined to eat smoke and spend hours in misery. It was a dirty thankless task, but unquestionably vital. The glory, though, was all in the ignition. As was all the fresh air. Once Chuck knew the fires were secure, usually midnight, we'd drive back to Canyon to shower, grab some late dinner, a few beers and fall sleep. At five o'clock the next morning we'd be up again, putting on our stinking clothes and heading back to the burn to check the perimeters, cooling any hot edges so the fire didn't creep over, or under, the fireline. Without rain the burns would smolder away all summer, always threatening the line. So until it rained it was a daily chore to check the miles upon miles of line we had dug. It went on for weeks. By the end we were so incredibly fit. The once excruciatingly steep slopes no longer fazed us. We were each now volunteering to go down into the depths of these units and would even, on occasion, jog back up because it seemed easier. Some of the firelines were so steep and rocky that we would hold onto the hoses and almost abseil down. When it came time to remove the thousands of yards of hose we would hook one end to the back of the engine and haul it up to a road – not an officially sanctioned method but an efficient one nevertheless. To stop the connections from snagging on rocks and stumps we would hang onto the hose and have the uphill ride of our lives. It was like being on a rope tow, except that we had to run alongside it, jumping over logs and rocks along the way. As long as we kept our feet moving and knees high we were okay. Otherwise we'd catch a limb or a stump, trip up, and cultivate the mountain with our backsides.

It wasn't all work, however. We would take regular breaks throughout the day to keep hydrated and fed, and we used the free time to get to know each other. After work on shorter days I would run halfway up the Black Mountain trail before dinner, just for the hell of it. When feeling especially ambitious I'd occasionally do it with a ruck full of rocks. On the way I'd see deer, a few mountain goats, if I was lucky to get high enough, and even a solitary black bear rummaging for bugs under a rotten log, its large paws tossing it aside as if it were kindling. The views were amazing, looking over the slopes and meadows of the Mallard Larkins, instilling a sense of complete freedom and solitude that I had only felt atop the craggy tors on the barren moors of England. The air was fresh, raw and invigorating, and crystalized snow still lingered under shaded overhangs and inside crevices among rocks well into the summer.

The running, the volunteering for everything, and the sheer enjoyment I got from the job was gaining me a reputation and with that came a level of credibility to match that of the rest of the crew, Limey or not. So when burning season ended and the real wildfires started I automatically became an integral part of the crew on the fireline. Like the others, I was now gaining real fire experience. Fires became like a drug; addictive, we couldn't get enough of them. We would each vie for position and argue over who would go out on the next one. Then we would argue who'd go on the next one while we were still on one. We spent days and nights camped out on the fireline in the mountains and meadows of Idaho eating countless 'Meals Refused by Ethiopians' (MREs),* sleeping in the dirt, in the ash, filthy, unwashed and working every daylight hour and many nighttime hours. When we finally relaxed around the fire at night, totally exhausted, sometimes in pain, we drank copious amounts of coffee and hot chocolate to keep us awake, never in a hurry to go to bed. Caffeine and youthful adrenaline kept us up and

---

* Meals Ready to Eat were developed by the Department of Defense in 1981, becoming standard issue in 1986 with 12 available, and quite delicious, entrees. The successor to the Long Range Reconnaissance Patrol (LRRP) Rations developed for Special Forces in Vietnam (Lurps).

we had a never ending supply of both. Firefighting campfire stories abounded, revolving around fires, heroes, successes, failures, bears, old firefighters, snags, injuries and, of course, *Big Ernie*. In the morning everything would start over with renewed vigor, that which only emanates from youth. Being older I guess mine came more from the coffee, the little green Ibuprofens, and the pressure to succeed in front of more youthful peers who, without exception, I greatly respected.

I was fifteen years older than most of the others and obviously a little slower. Years of kneeling to milk cows and running roads with a ruck had worn my knees and my back had seen better days. I was envious of others' youthful joints, lack of any serious pain and their seemingly limitless adolescent playfulness. When the old niggardly pains became too much of a hindrance, while working or when trying to sleep on a rock, I'd break out the Ibuprofen again. And after a couple of green pills with my morning coffee I could forget my age for a little while longer and wonder who the hell *Big Ernie* was.

Chapter Three

— Early Fires

After an 18-hour shift, sore, dirty, thirsty and hungry, tired for rest, the best help is nature: it doesn't steal effort, it enhances it; it doesn't steal overtime, it adds to it; and it doesn't take credit, and it disappears as readily as it arrives, on the cool morning air.

– Author

U P TO NOW MOST OF THE FIRES had been small, a quarter to half acre at most. To get to them we would drive as far as the road would take us and then walk the rest. This often involved spending four hours driving in cramped pick-ups on little used logging roads ridden with washboards, followed by hours of hiking through acres of almost impenetrable Clearwater alder brush. It was not a quick exercise. Before heading out we would estimate the equipment we were likely to need based on the terrain, likely fire activity, fuels and weather in the area, and take enough food and water, radios and sleeping bags, together with heaps of motivation. The smoke-chaser packs could weigh upwards of 90lbs, which isn't considered a terrific amount in such occupations, but hiking blind though alder brush for hours on end, not getting very far and unable to stand upright or see in which direction to go, can be quite detrimental to a person's motivation. Tempers sometimes got frayed, especially when popping out of the brush, torn, bruised and exhausted, only to see that the fire was still a couple of hours and two ridges away, in another direction.

Despite the complaints, however, and the associated profanity always inherent to such a group, not once did anyone ever give up. Many would say these individuals would put the youth of today to shame. But they were the youth of today. They were the youth of any generation determined to do something worthwhile in a job they enjoyed. Which is all that anyone really wants.

But there's always a pompous prat in every group. They are everywhere, in all lifestyles and all jobs. It was no different among the crews we met while at Canyon. Some of the knuckleheads we would encounter were quite frightening, because they clearly had no clue and could easily have gotten someone hurt. Thankfully, though, this was very rare and everyone knew who these people were and avoided them like the plague. The major problem was that these idiots would often get promoted. It was ironic, but promotion seemed to be a tried and trusted, but useless, method of removing people from a role where they couldn't otherwise be fired. To do so, supervisors would provide them a good reference, which inevitably passed the burden of incompetence onto another poor sod. It was utter madness and very efficient in fragmenting the management structure and lowering the morale of everyone else. Smaller fire crews are usually somewhat protected from the worst offenders, but on larger fires these lifetime parasites can still be found roaming fire camps stuffing their fat faces in the canteen and high-grading the best equipment – with no intention of ever using it – from supply. All we could eternally hope was that they never became operations chief of any fire we were on.

After climbing ridge lines and the odd tree to try and see the smallest whiff of smoke it's a great relief to actually spot the fire from the ground. New fires generally don't give off much smoke unless conditions are right, in which case the fire will probably run and need more people. After ignition the smaller fires can smolder away in the undisturbed litter layers for days on end without ever being seen. When the smoke is visible it's often wafting above the trees like a fine mist some distance away from the actual fire. But it provides a direction, and when close enough a person can smell it. Some firefighters get remarkably good at smelling the smallest whiff of smoke, like a solitary pine needle smoldering in a charred forest. American Indians are renowned for the skill. There's rarely much flame with smaller fires, but if not suppressed there likely will be. But this is dependent on a variety of things: available fuels such as litter, twigs, logs, trees, etc.; weather being consistently the most important; as well as topography and who is actually fighting the fire, or not fighting it.

After spending the better part of the day reaching a remote fire the firefighter then has to have enough remaining energy to put it out, and do it, more often than not, without access to water. The water we've expended so much effort in carrying is possibly the most valuable item in our pack (although some would say toilet paper). Wasting water on the fire can quickly lead to dehydration, a common problem in the heat, especially among inexperienced young firefighters where, if left untreated, it can be incapacitating, or fatal. Discarding water due to its weight is especially foolhardy. There is never a guarantee that resources can be replenished and a 20 mile hike out from the woods with no water in 100-degree heat can be disastrous, and places others at risk.

Wildland fire suppression is not rocket science, although there are plenty of scientists who attempt to make it so. Fire survives because it has three essential elements – the fire triangle; oxygen, heat, and fuel. Take one away and there is no fire. Without access to large amounts of water removing the fuel is obviously the most efficient method of fire suppression. So when on a fire, wildland firefighters spend most of their time either removing available fuels, stopping the fire from reaching available fuels, or removing the heat and oxygen from available fuels, by burying them.

To accomplish this a variety of hand tools are used depending on terrain and fuel type. The most common in the western states is the pulaski, but also shovels, rakes, flappers, spruce boughs and variations of each. Chainsaws are invaluable and are treated with the utmost respect. Explosives are also used in some areas and provide for a wholly different level of efficiency, and a certain amount of excitement.

Initially the firefighter needs to stop the fire from spreading, so they dig a shallow trench around the fire down to mineral soil level, thereby encircling the fire inside un-burnable dirt – this is containment. The depth and width of the trench largely depends on fire activity, soil conditions, roots, fuel density, and weather, etc.. It also depends on experience, and whether or not the squad leader is a practical fellow or by-the-book. (Show me a firefighter who hasn't been told to dig line through a rock-slide at some point in his life.) If flame lengths are reasonable crews generally build the fireline directly next to the fire. This is also considered the safest tactic with 'one foot in the black.' However, on larger more active fires distance can provide for greater safety and the fireline can be built some distance away – indirectly – employing topographical features to advantage, such as ridges, roads and rivers, etc.. The fireline, then, very simply, is an attempt to stop the fire's lateral spread. If the fireline is direct and effective it will stop the spread immediately. If it is indirect it will take longer and might be susceptible to other elements: weather changes, locally specific winds or spotting. The time it takes for a fire to travel depends on distance, weather, topography, fuel type and firefighting efforts. All affecting the fire's ability or inability to prosper under a variety of constantly changing conditions. This is all encompassed in what firefighters call fire behavior.

Removing available fuels is also an attempt to control the fire within the fireline to stop its vertical spread, which would enable it to jump the fireline by spreading first vertically through the ladder fuels – low hanging branches – and then laterally through the tree canopy. For this, all the unburned fuels – branches and logs – are either removed to outside of the fireline or, more easily and great for cooking, burned in controlled piles within the fireline – bone piling. Ladder fuels are removed, trees can be removed but are usually best left standing if not burning or in imminent danger of igniting or falling. It's a long laborious and dirty process, and further saps the energy of the firefighter after having spent most of the time up to now reaching the fire and vigorously constructing the fireline, often continuously for hours, if not days, on end. On average the digging firefighter can drink a quart or more of water each hour, while burning 8,000 - 15,000 calories a day. The work causes blisters, bruises, abrasions, cuts, and numerous aches, pains and strains and sometimes even severely debilitating injuries such as herniated discs, torn ligaments, broken bones and even death. Pain is a constant companion to any active firefighter and for many Ibuprofen the constant remedy companion to pain. It's demanding work but immensely satisfying when successful. Especially when accomplished alongside good people on a good crew.

Despite good people on good crews firefighting is not always successful, however. Unforeseen variables can quickly materialize to ruin even the best of plans. Inexperience, fatigue, conflagrating fires, accidents, negligence, administrative incompetence, sudden weather changes and, of course, plain bad luck are but a few of the causes of failure. Millions are spent on weather forecasting but it remains an unpredictable science for pinpoint accuracy in specific areas of remote forests. Predicting localized mountain weather is monumentally difficult. Delicate variations in topography cause a plethora of weather situations that are never going to be precisely predictable. But having said that, firefighters still need to study the forecast, update it continually throughout the fire's lifetime, taking into account local variations and assimilate everything within the immediate vicinity's idiosyncrasies. And then always look out for and be prepared for the unexpected. Because although it might not happen this time, shit will happen. That part is predictable.

These days good effective communications are of paramount importance to firefighters. That wasn't always considered to be the case, however, mainly due to early equipment being excessively cumbersome as to be impractical in quick mobile situations. Once smaller handheld devices were developed firefighters finally had a way to communicate with lookouts, each other and aircraft easily, which would, in turn, relay information to district offices where it was needed. Abundant forest communications had arrived to stay. Although it's only since 1995, and as a direct consequence to the South Canyon Fire,* that individual firefighters have been issued personal radios. Previous to that tragedy it was thought only crew leaders needed them – incident ICs, foremen, and squad leaders – for receiving elementary weather reports and requesting resources. But that was before it was realized that personal radios would save lives, or the funding of radios would save lives. It came too late for some, however.

The firefighter in charge (IC) always checks in first thing in the morning and last thing at night, with updates throughout the day depending on fire activity, weather, crew requirements and the district's communication protocol, keeping the district informed on how firefighting efforts are progressing and giving them an idea of resource needs, such as more people, water, food or equipment. Or for the district to notify firefighters on the ground of a change in the weather – or if there's a fire on the next ridge waiting to gobble

---

* The July 6th, 1994, fire on Colorado's Storm King Mountain that killed 14 firefighters; 9 Prineville Hotshots, 2 Helitack crewmembers and 3 Smokejumpers.

them up. The radio is invaluable if someone gets injured, as people invariably do while working in steep terrain with an assortment of sharp tools. Radios have even been thrown at bears as a last resort. Although I think it just pissed them off even more.

Today this new fire was about five miles away, but the smoke was clearly visible above the ridgeline in the foreground. It was significantly larger than any we'd seen so far and we were keen to get stuck in. We were lucky in that it was just off the road so we could almost drive right up to it. It also had a good water source in the bend of the road where a creek flowed through a large culvert, so little effort was required in building a sump by damming it with a few rocks and some plastic. That was the engine crew's domain and they were tasked with arranging that while the rest of us gathered our personal gear (clean socks, rain gear, water, food, etc.), personal protective equipment (gloves, hard hat, fire shelter, etc.), and tools (shovels, pulaskis, chainsaws, etc.), and clambered up the rocky embankment before bushwhacking though the dense Clearwater brush up the incline toward the fire.

Within minutes we were lost in a sea of alder brush and could only just see the person in front. Smaller branches slapped at our faces and bigger ones knocked us flat. Tools got tangled, clothes were ripped and shins got bruised. We sounded like a platoon of soldiers with all our profanity, on all fours for much of the time as we bent, twisted, and wiggled our way up the hill through the brush. Alder brush is like a natural medieval barrier that returns its tugs and thrusts with thrice the vigor and vengeance. And, just like a medieval barrier, broken branches can spear an eye in an instant.

Somewhere behind us the chainsaws started to cut a line up because eventually we would have to put a hose-lay in place and the line would provide an escape route. A bear might be able to run through this stuff but a human would just bounce off it.

After fifteen minutes we found the tail and the sawyers started flanking it, followed by four diggers on each side. The saws ripped through the brush easily but digging with one foot in the black was immensely difficult with roots so tough that pulaskis just bounced off. Then, after getting mad and swinging extra hard we would hit a buried rock and it would feel as if every hand bone had shattered.

Digging uphill is generally considered the preferred practice for safety, because fire also tends to go uphill, but it's a lot more difficult than digging down. Everything moved from above comes down. Then it has to be moved again. The same dirt gets moved repeatedly. The idea is to scrape the debris to one side but that's easier in theory and less in practice on steep slopes, so a downward angular stroke seems to work better. Being the lead digger I made an initial scrape and others steadily improved it until it was wide and deep enough to stop anything rolling out. This process would continue for however long it took until the fire was completely contained; whether it be 2 hours, 4 hours, 12 hours or 36 hours.

Every fifteen minutes or so we stopped to replace fluids lost in rivers of sweat, and to grab a quick snack of peanuts, jerky or a candy bar. Reinforcements from other district crews – wildlife, timber and silviculture – were due to arrive but for now we were it. As the hours passed more people slowly wandered in, somewhat easing the burden. Then evening was upon us. But the line still wasn't finished. And because we don't ever stop unless the line is done we plodded on into dusk; onwards and upwards, swinging, chopping and sawing. Hot areas on our feet became blisters, our hands grew raw and our backs ached incessantly. With every step upward our legs screamed in exhaustion. But everyone kept up the effort through a constant deluge of friendly abuse and crass humor, all culminating in encouragement. Camaraderie was developing among us. Our diverse little group of mountain top ditch diggers.

The engine crew installed an inline pump below us and were now delivering water to the tail of the fire. The characteristic deep throbbing drone coming from the *Mark 3** reverberated around the surrounding rocky hills as the pump forced water through the two-inch canvas hose up the slope. We shouted abuse at the engine slugs below us for taking so long, but the water was, nevertheless, very welcome. Abuse was returned with equal enthusiasm over the noise of the pump with: "Aren't you done yet slackers?" We had been digging for eight solid hours; backs bent, swinging pulaskis, grinding upwards, still grinning – mostly. Or was that a grimace?

Finally, through the smoke we saw the crew from the opposite flank on the topside and knew we were close to tying in. It gave us the encouragement needed to persevere a little longer. The feeling of accomplishment after a such a hard slog is always immensely satisfying. When you can actually stop to appreciate it, it is even better. Although we were exhausted and wanted nothing more than to rest, we had to check the fireline to make sure it was holding. So after deciding which half of the crew would eat, and which would walk the line, I hobbled back down on raw feet to walk the line.

The loose dirt on the steep slope caused my feet to slide inside the new boots and I felt pus oozing from the blisters. On the way I met the new arrivals cutting a deep cup trench to catch any rolling embers. The more we walked the line the more it became secure. Then it was our turn to relax and after searching out a less smoky spot we tried to rest. But first we had to cut benches in the hillside so that we could sit comfortably without slipping down the slope.

While making coffee the engine crew arrived with boxes of rations, or rats, containing an assortment of canned meals; beans, chili, canned sausages, beef stew, corn and fruit cocktail. We broke

---

* An excellent portable high-pressure pump with a rugged 10 HP, one-cylinder, two-cycle, air-cooled engine, pushing out upwards of 98 gallons/min. Weighing under 60lbs easily enables one capable person to move and operate it. Once you acquire the knack to start a *Mark 3* it can run consistently all day with extra fuel.

into them like a pack of hyenas and devoured the contents without regard to any hygiene or lack of taste. The engine slugs had clearly high-graded – cherry picked or stolen – the better items leaving us the dregs. You couldn't live on the stuff for any length of time but we didn't care and ate it with relish, not even bothering to heat up some items while waiting for better ones to cook.

Being the newbie I was volunteered to venture down to the road to fetch a five-gallon plastic cube-container of water. After retrieving it from the engine I hauled myself back up the hill with the cubie on my back and arrived at our little camp half an hour later. By the time it arrived the water had a strange milky quality about it, thinking it was because I'd slipped and dropped it so many times on the way up, but was told the water was old and had been stored in plastic for too long. But no one cared, we mixed in powdered Gatorade and drank it by the quart.

We sat, sweaty and bruised, content in the knowledge that we had corralled a wildfire. Around the campfire conversation grew, revolving around the group according to wind direction. When the smoke engulfed the talker they would stop for a moment allowing another to pick up the conversation. Being an efficient method for stopping one person bullshitting for too long. I've often wished for something similar while out with a talkative date.

Long into the evening, the sun finally dipped behind distant hills, leaving only starlight, the temperature dropped considerably and the air became eerily stable. No wind, no breeze. Just stillness. Increased humidity starved the fire of warmth and flames began to dwindle, laying down as though tired. It was something we looked forward to on each and every fire; the arrival of the cold night air crew (CNA crew).

Chapter Four

— Ambition

Ambition has but one reward for all: A little power, a little transient fame; A grave to rest in, and a fading name!
– Walter Savage Landor

B EING ON A STEEP SLOPE that made standing upright quite difficult at the best of times was never going to be conducive to the most comfortable night's sleep. I was either sliding down the slope or trying to avoid the rock poking me in the back. I had dug a shallow shelf into the hillside, just wide enough to keep me level, but when I turned over I would run out of level and flop over the edge. I never rolled any distance down the hill but I continually dreamt that I was. And in this recurring dream I always found myself stuck in the alder brush while still inside my sleeping bag, unable to get out, whence I'd kick out my feet to free myself. This inevitably caused me to flop over the edge and restart the whole process over again.

Waking in the morning was in some ways wonderful and in others excruciatingly painful. This day was particularly beautiful. The sun was creeping up over the mountains in the distance and throwing a pleasant warming glow over the camp. In the higher elevations a growing opaque orange haze masked the surrounding craggy hills, while a thick smoky mist hid the lower valleys, creeks and rock-strewn riverbeds. After breathing smoke for most of the night the air was now fresh and clear. The cool katabatic* winds having rolled the smoke into the valley during the night, where, on the road below, the engine slugs were stuck in the middle of it. I thought it fitting for high-grading my dinner the previous night.

The pleasure of the moment soon passed, however, and reality set in as I struggled out of my sleeping bag to find that my hands were painfully raw. I thought I'd put them on a cactus, but they were blistered and torn from the previous day's work and the raw skin had dried curled and taut. When I stretched out my fingers the wounds cracked open. My back ached something fierce, mostly from the constant bending to dig the previous day, but also from the rock I'd slept on all night but hadn't noticed until the early hours when the dirt beneath me had settled and I was too tired to do anything about it. I sat up gingerly, trying not to trigger any new pains and tried to put my boots on. I discovered that either my feet had expanded or I had another's boots. But after persevering I managed to stand and force my sore feet into the rigid leather. Lacing them was then another painful story. Simply breathing was also a chore because my throat was scratchy as if I had contracted flu overnight, but it was nothing more than the result of inhaling so much dust and smoke. The flu would no doubt have been healthier.

I hobbled away behind a bush to relieve myself and enjoyed the warmth of the morning sun on my face, aware that others were beginning to stir. All tempted by Leon, our resolute squad leader, who already had a cooking fire going to boil water for his morning coffee and oatmeal. Leon lived on it morning, noon and night; with coffee, oatmeal and raisins; coffee, oatmeal and cinnamon; coffee, oatmeal and apple, and just plain coffee. I never discovered from where he got all his energy, but assumed it was an old Indian trick.

---

* From the Greek word katabatikos, meaning 'to go downhill.' Katabatic winds are the 'drainage winds' that carry high density (heavier) air downhill.

The crackling campfire attracted more blackened aluminum cans of bubbling water as people feverishly replenished calories lost during the previous day's exertion. Everyone had some sort of private pain and each moved gingerly. For the most part everyone was quiet within their own problems, except for the exception of course. There's always one bitching moaning exception.

And then there was resolute Leon. Leon had no pain. In fact I don't think Leon had any feelings at all. Everything he did was at full throttle, as though there was not enough time in his day. His bloodshot eyes would squint a subtle smile when someone burned their fingers on a hot cup, or inadvertently spilled boiling water on a pus filled blister. To Leon we were all amateurs. To him, for all their brilliant successes, the white man had learned nothing.

"What *is* your fucking problem?" Leon said, staring at the bitchin' culprit and spitting a wad of tobacco into the fire.

There was no response. And no more bitching either. Just a body trying to fuse itself into the terrain, disappearing for a while, sulking at the audacity of truth.

Leon had already walked the fireline and knew exactly where he wanted everyone to be after breakfast. As he sat on a log and explained his tactics he spat more tobacco into the fire between each sentence, causing it to flare and a sizzle on impact. It was a subconscious act but it instilled something in us, and had the effect of dispelling any doubts about his ability to command attention. If only for the fact that we didn't want to get covered with the putrid juices of chewed tobacco.

And so the second day on the fire started. We hauled up hose, installed another pump, dug out stumps, cut down snags, had lunch, re-arranged hose, dug out more stumps, cut down more snags, rearranged hose again, and then had dinner. By this time the fire was looking pretty good – meaning that it was almost out. After dinner we got down on our hands and knees and felt every inch of the fire with our fingers, trying to find hot spots that were, up to now, well hidden and playing hard-to-get. This really is the dirtiest part of firefighting and everyone, but everyone, absolutely hates it. But it's also one of the most important jobs in eliminating the risk of a re-burn.

No one in charge of a fire ever thinks the fire is completely out, not even if it's rained for days or snowed for a week. There's always that teeny-tiny chance that some puny little aspiring root hiding somewhere is still hot, and just waiting for a warm dry day to emerge, to become famous, and make someone's life a misery. It happens, and it happens to the best. It's wholly embarrassing and ruinous to reputations, promotions and credibility – both individual and organizational. Re-burns can be far more devastating than the original fire. Only now there's someone to blame other than God or a careless camper. And that is a lawyer's wet dream.

Even though most of us thought the fire was out Leon wanted to stay for one more afternoon, just to make sure. He released all the non-fire personnel, most of the engine crew, and kept four of us through the following day. We examined the fire microscopically, following a grid pattern inside and outside the fireline – gridding. As the heat increased in the afternoon sun we kept to the shade and just watched. But there was nothing. Not a scent. Not a whiff. Nada. Not even the telltale signs of gnats hovering over a hot spot. We were committed to leaving this dead, deceased, cold, chargrilled fire and get to the next. There'd been lightning during the night and we knew there were other fires out there, other adventures to go to.

At two o'clock we gathered beneath a tree and ate. Then a nose twitched and a head raised. Leon stopped sipping his coffee through a mouthful of tobacco and turned toward the fire. He raised a nose and stared intently into the powdery black dirt. All that was needed was a cheroot to finish the performance. Everyone instinctively knew what he was about and tried to smell it also. Somewhere in that expanse of cold black dirt there was a tiny smoke, and we would have to find it. Determined but sluggish after three days of backbreaking effort we left our food, got to our feet, picked up our tools, and saw that Leon was already pounding on a stump in the middle of the fire. With each violent swing his pulaski thumped into the stump, sending splinters flying in all directions. Wherever splinters landed small puffs of ash rose from the ground as if in spiritual approval. Clearly some unknown force drove Leon.

Finally, carefully removing a small splinter of wood, he smelled it with obvious satisfaction, plucked off the minutest piece of ember and buried it deep into the dirt. Then he looked up, spat out a drizzled piece of tobacco into the dust and said: "Pack your shit. We're done."

On the six-hour journey back to Canyon, Leon was the only topic of conversation. It was obvious that he already had quite the reputation and was damned good at his job, but on that trip home I also learned that he'd been badly screwed over by the FS, and was bitter – I learned this happened a lot, and for some inexplicable reason it happened, more often than not, to the most able and credible people I was ever fortunate enough to meet. The part I specifically remember about that jarring trip in the back of an old six-pack pick-up was that Leon had once been a smokejumper in Grangeville, Idaho. It all started to make sense.

This intrigued me. I had no idea what a smokejumper was and I listened carefully to what they were saying about these crazy jumpers. The more I listened the more I understood and the more I was fascinated. Apparently these adrenaline fueled junkies actually parachuted into fires. They didn't walk, drive, or get dropped off by helicopters, they leapt from airplanes, perfectly good airplanes.

I learned that smokejumpers, along with hotshots,[*] and maybe, if we're hard pushed, helitacks[†] and rapellers[‡] too, are considered to be the elite of the elite of wildland firefighting. Jumpers were self-sufficient, more experienced, independent of outside bureaucracy, and could get there quicker, dig fireline faster, and for longer, than anyone in the business. Which was all that mattered, because as far as I was concerned, that's how you stopped forest fires.

On another fire the following day – it was an unusually busy summer – I found myself with Leon once again. This time he had a chainsaw and was cutting swathes of wood like Leatherface in the *Texas Chainsaw Massacre*. It was suicidal to go near him. Even his pimp – sidekick who removed his debris – kept well clear. Then at one point, without hesitation, Leon put down the saw to clamber 50 feet up a Doug-fir because he thought he heard his old jump ship fly over. He climbed the tree as agile as a monkey, came down equally as swiftly, spat out a well chewed piece of tobacco, and immediately cranked up the saw to return to work. All without the slightest word to anyone.

Apart from when Leon had a chainsaw in his hand the only other time everyone stood well clear was when he had just placed another wad of tobacco in his lip, because the putrid juices would splatter everywhere when they got too much for him to swallow. It might look good in the movies but it wasn't particularly pleasant when it splattered all over our boots.

---

[*] An elite 20 person firefighting crew highly trained in wildfire suppression where crewmembers meet the strict fitness standards required of arduous mountain firefighting. Interagency Hotshots Crews can travel anywhere in the country with little notice to fight fires in all terrains.

[†] As the name suggests; experienced helicopter delivered firefighters well-versed in wildfire suppression, with the added, and immediate, support of a helicopter for water bucket drops, extra resources (manpower), etc..

[‡] Similar to helitacks except that they have the capability of rappelling (upwards of 250 feet) from the helicopter when no landing is possible.

It was at the end of this particular fire that I first met Bill. To my little Limey brain he appeared to be a typical Montanan: big, burly and totally sure of himself. But at the same time, polite, friendly, open to listening and willing to go out of his way to help anyone. And always wearing a crumpled old cowboy hat to further the impression. Bill had apparently been instrumental in getting me hired as a contractor – being the new Assistant Fire Management Officer (AFMO) – although at the time, and for a while afterwards, I never knew this. A group of us were resting on a log, like we always did when taking a break to grab a snack, and Bill arrived to introduce himself, immediately launching into an old jumper joke:

A bunch of rookies were off up for their first jump. Inside the aircraft the spotter told them: "Don't worry lads, all you have to do is jump, shout 'Geronimo!' and your chute will open."

The last two rookies had seen everyone before them jump and they were getting increasingly nervous. They checked and rechecked their gear and slowly made their way to the back of the plane, where the spotter was waiting.

They hooked up. At fifteen hundred feet the cattle in the fields below looked like ants on another world. These two rookies had never even been in a plane before. The first stood rigidly in the door trying to remember his procedure and the spotter slapped him out. The other left the plane a second later.

Happy it had all gone well, the spotter smiled, closed the door, and told the pilot all the jumpers were away. A minute later, as the plane banked away, there was a loud knocking at the door. With a confused look the spotter opened the door very slightly and saw the last rookie frantically flapping his arms. While looking at him in utter amazement the rookie said: "Quick sir. What's that f*^@#*g Indian's name again?"

As I listened, I noticed Bill's brass smokejumper belt buckle and I remember thinking, "these guys are so damned cool."

Bill told us about jumpers in his day – jumping from 1969 to 1980 – about the stuff they would get up to while traveling around the western states fighting fires. He admitted that he wouldn't have got away with half of it today. He said that once you landed in the woods everything was left behind, no wives, no girlfriends, no kids, no bosses and, moreover, no bureaucracy.* And nothing that couldn't be solved by basic hard work. Simply put: there was no bullshit out in the woods. It sounded terrific and a great job for a young single guy.

Despite being neither single or young I desperately wanted some of it. And for the first time since leaving Minnesota I had a distinct goal, the freedom to do it, and the unbridled passion to see it through.

---

* That was before the advent of cellphones, however, now all that follows you, if you let it.

Chapter Five

— Learning

If history repeats itself, and the unexpected always happens, how
incapable must Man be of learning from experience.

– George Bernard Shaw

I WAS DESPERATE TO FIND ANOTHER career because I couldn't now return to Minnesota after seeing what the West had to offer. Nothing could tempt me back to the land of ten thousand lakes and a zillion blood sucking mosquitoes. While life there had been good for a while, and it had, despite everything, it was now time to move on. The west provided us an opportunity to walk away and forget the misery. Forget the disastrous ending to what was but a chapter of life. I had made the initial break and was running with it, and, in the process, was having the time of my life on the fires in Idaho, somewhere that I had never dreamed of ever ending up. Much of it was due to the wonderful down-to-earth people that I was working with, but also because the job was exhilarating, and provided such a great sense of accomplishment and purpose. I hadn't seen it coming, but this job had grabbed me securely by the balls and I was hooked.

But it was a seasonal job, which meant, in those days at least, that few firefighters ever progressed into full-time employment by gaining what was called an appointment. At the time this made sense since fires aren't all that prolific in snow and the mountains were covered with the stuff during the long winter months. There were some opportunities, though, and I was determined to discover where they were and what they entailed. Though being a newbie, I was fully aware that there were countless others waiting for one of these exceedingly rare vacancies, and all of them with vastly more experience than I.

In the late '80s to early '90s the competition for appointments was fierce, and conflicts among longstanding seasonal workers were frequent, each inherently believing that they were better qualified than the other. In all likelihood everyone was equally qualified, some had just been doing it for longer. And although time served is an oft-expected criterion for advancement, especially in the public sector, it doesn't always provide for better competence or ability. A person can have the same recurring experience or multiple different experiences. The value, or ability, gained depends on one's inherent interest and inbred motivation.

Due to the lack of available appointments these conflicts sometimes became career-long feuds, and many continue to this day. Many others, realizing the futility, and becoming increasingly frustrated with waiting, simply moved on to something else. The great loss being that these were often the more ambitious and determined individuals. Tragically, in recent years, this has come to haunt the organization, although they will continue to deny it for a multitude of reasons – the paramount one, of course, based upon bureaucratic legality and never being able to accept blame. But an institution in denial is one in decline and hasty recruitment campaigns amid reactionary reorganizations in the late 1990s compounded the problem, and may well have led to catastrophe.

The appointments fiasco was instigated largely by upper management's innate inability to effectively promote strategic funding. Consequentially no one at district level ever had a clue how much their forest budget would be the following year, making it all but impossible to plan efficiently. In these situations people at the bottom, those at the sharp end, in the grafting role, are traditionally always the first to suffer. And they did, year after year, by prostituting themselves on the fires; wearing down their bodies in the hope of getting a real job, ignoring injuries because they'd be out of work, and yet staying fit in the off-season for a job that might not even be available when the time came. The amount of personal effort expended, and sacrifices made, by these temporary firefighters during this period was astounding, and would certainly be an anomaly in most occupations today. But this gift of effort was wholly ignored by the organization directly benefiting from it, namely the United States Forest Service. Some solutions to these issues eventually came about because of basic manpower needs, not by any conscience or hindsight from bloated swivel-chaired managers.

As summer on the North Fork continued we found ourselves increasingly used as a district helitack crew. We all assumed that this was not because anyone felt especially sorry for us walking to every fire, but because there were so many fires and it was the only effective way to staff them quickly and keep them adequately resourced. So instead of spending eight hours driving to a fire the size of a dustbin lid we could now fly to it, drink a quart or two of water, piss all over it, and find another fire all in the same day.

It was really quite efficient and most unlike anything I had seen so far. The fire would be located during a lightning storm by a lookout perched atop a mountain or someone in a spotter plane later in the evening or early the following morning. As soon as it was logged decisions were made at district level as to who to send. If we were available it would be us, if not, others would handle it. The others were frequently the jumpers from either Grangeville or Missoula. Although they were stealing our fires it didn't bother us, because there were plenty more to go around that summer.

Due to the swiftness in discovering fires, deciding what to do about them quickly, and then manning them if necessary, the fires were always young, small, and easy to control in a relatively safe environment. Speed was absolutely essential to the efficiency of our firefighting efforts and, moreover, to our safety. While the jumpers found that speed in their fleet of fixed-wing aircraft, we found it in helicopters and being geographically much closer.

I had been on a few helicopters before, old green army ones that would shake you to bits, but that had been during another lifetime. These were very different: here the pilots were friendly, the ships comfortable, powerful, and extremely agile. And the terrain we flew across was incredible; over baldly mountains nestled between taller snowcapped mountains, along rivers and valleys where we'd see the deer, moose and bear that inhabited this great expanse of land. Then we'd set down on some beautiful remote part of Idaho. Every flight was spectacular and we couldn't wait for the next. The drug had reached another level as we were inexorably drawn into needing more flights, more fires, more excitement. We could never go back to walking. It would have meant unthinkable withdrawals.

We were all learning so much so quickly and storing everything. Each time we went out we learnt something new, and after getting to know Leon better we even learned a few of his old Indian tricks. Only to find he had originally learnt many of them from a white man. We were all humbled and truly appreciative of Leon's help. He was a great teacher, whether he wanted to be or not. All we had to do was watch and emulate.

Pete was another great squad leader, but he was on a different rotation to me and stuck with engine slugs. He was a laid back, heavy smoking, hard working, constant presence and had been a major part of our successes during the burns earlier in the year. I have an indelible memory of Pete relaxing during a burn, smoking a cigarette without a care in the world while sitting on a jerrycan full of drip torch fuel.

Larry was also someone, by chance, that I seemed to end up with a lot on fires. I probably had four two-manners with him that summer. One of which took us eight hours to reach only to find a couple of early fall hunters having lunch. That was Fly Hill, an eternal lightning magnet and a somewhat eerie place where we often ended up. Firefighters have been fighting fires on Fly Hill for decades, and we always found discarded old food cans and old firefighting scars from previous visits. So lightning does, indeed, strike the same place twice, and often more. Anyone wishing to test the theory only needs stand on Fly Hill in August. Just don't stand too tall.

When we tried to figure out how old Larry was, according to his self-professed list of experiences, he would have to have been close to 80. But seeing as he still lived with his mum, who wasn't much over 50, we decided he was full of shit. Nevertheless, Larry was a character who was greatly missed when he was forced out of fire. I had a lot of good fires with him and although his ersatz life was sometimes annoying, he was generally really good company. Some individuals often embellish stories to show that they are better than their insecurity will let them believe. But stories, whether honest accounts, wild tales, or inflated experiences, are what make up the friendly banter and atmosphere on fires, and people who criticize one over another, through blinkered ignorance, insecurity or immaturity, are missing the point, and missing the greater value of camaraderie. If the situation necessitated, however, everyone would pull together, no matter what personalities were involved or issues that might otherwise be present. That was the selfless professionalism from a group of people barely averaging 22 years old.

We also had a wonderful girl with us. Sophie was half the weight of everyone else but put in twice the effort to make up for it. At some point she'd sustained some burns, yet she was always right in the middle of the action and was never fazed by anything. Another of the girls, Kat, was also a great worker who was interested in one of the guys on the crew, but they never once revealed any inappropriate behavior while working, showing that they were mature beyond their years, as were many of the teenagers on the fires (I've heard it's vastly different these days, though I sincerely hope not). They grew up fast. I never once thought anything of women being on fires. At the time I actually enjoyed their company. The ones I knew worked as well as anyone and as long as they didn't overtly change the dynamic of the group they were a pleasant change to have around.

Some of the older male firefighters, however, had serious reservations about women in the fire role. That was likely from an outdated discriminatory idea all too instinctive among the smaller insular towns. As far as I was concerned, if women could do the work equal to that of men I was fine with it. Later, though, I was to learn about quotas, an insidious ploy where a select group were given priority over appointments, simply because of their sex or color of their skin. That was a bitter pill for many to swallow and always caused bad feelings among firefighters. This brilliance was initiated by a wonderful theory of FS evolution, where a fire crew in Idaho was supposed to mirror the ethnic diversity of New York City or Chicago. The knucklehead who thought that one up was probably one of the dumb-nuts promoted out of a department instead of having their dumb-nuts fired. We all wished for them to take a stroll down the wrong street in New York City or Chicago to see exactly which bit of precious diversity they'd like to see in the mountains of Idaho. The whole idea was utterly ridiculous, and yet they tried, and still do.

Firefighters generally don't give a toss if other firefighters are women or men if they can do the job equally. But if they can't they should be gone. The problem arises, though, when the organization actively goes out to recruit a higher percentage of women solely to meet a preconceived agenda (quota), because requirements have to be lessened (as they were). Then if you lessen the requirements for women you've automatically lessened them for men too. And that is the absolute shits because you've just reduced the efficiency of the whole outfit. Of the strong jumper women we respected, all of them were equally aghast at some of the new female hires because it immediately put them in the same category by association, and somewhere they did not want to be because they had earned their credibility the hard way. In effect, then, the organization was soon split between an elite group and a mediocre one, with both men and women in the elite group and all women in the mediocre group – not all of whom were female, if you get my drift.

While we were going back and forth to the fires we sensed that Bill and Chuck were pleased with our work. They'd be at the helispot when we left, and be there when we returned, always with encouragement, gratitude and something to satisfy our thirst. We all knew they were good bosses and only ever had complimentary words for them, which was heartening but sadly uncommon among many other crews. We saw how good we had it in our little group when we mixed with other crews while on larger fires, seeing they were often so micro-managed as to be almost impotent. Whereas Chuck had confidence in us and left us alone to get on with it, with Leon and Pete providing the direction when needed. It was an efficient management style and it worked brilliantly for everyone.

The fires we fought were over a variety of terrain and fauna. Many, of course, were typical of the Clearwater forest; ugly great brush fields. These were always the worst, with us having to remove endless thick alder brush, debris, and iron-like roots. They were also often the wettest fires and when it rained we'd get thoroughly drenched, but even with water falling from the heavens there was still never enough to put out the fire. After a rain our boots would pick up large heavy clumps of mud, doubling the size of our feet. Our sleeping bags would remain damp for days and our clothes sodden, making life and household chores generally quite unpleasant. The only joy was the copious amounts of coffee and hot chocolate we drank throughout the day to keep us warm and awake. These miserable fires were the few that we often yearned to leave. But much of the Clearwater is made up of this and they were to remain a constant bear, especially later in the summer, when the greener, thicker, and more northern aspects had time to dry out, smolder and burn.

The Clearwater is also home to many magnificent old-growth Cedars. Sadly, these massive old trees burn all too easily, with the fires consuming the soft pulpy layers inside their hollow trunks. The sawyers earned every penny when cutting these monsters down. Being tall and hollow makes them incredibly dangerous. Sometimes they'd break off three quarters of the way up with little warning, sending the top 50 feet of tree plummeting to the ground. The only way to guarantee survival was to be nowhere near them. But that's not always on option. Decades of buildup had created several feet of deep litter around the base of these trees, and that takes a lot time to dig through, although once we were down to the mineral soil we found dampness, which aided in quickly cooling the fire. When we finished with these fires, which often took many days, we'd leave behind huge hollow stumps that could swallow up a Volkswagen. The devastation to this old growth timber was complete and very ugly, but undoubtedly necessary in stopping the fire from further spreading into these magnificent woods.

My favorite fires were always in the high alpine firs. The trees were small, being almost at the tip of the mountains and starved of nutrition, and the views from atop the bear-grass meadows were staggering. On the lower fires there was never much of a view to speak of, the tree canopy usually being too thick, or from being too low in the valley, meaning that we'd just be looking at the same slope on the other side. These high alpine fires, however, were far above everything and we could see for miles in beautiful, fresh, smokeless sky. Being miles away from any habitation in this vast uncluttered landscape, with the stars seemingly within touching distance, and with just one other person and a few critters for company, was absolutely fantastic. It further drew me into this job. We would get dropped off by Jet Ranger a few feet from a smoldering fire, spend a few hours digging line around it in the tough bear grass, have lunch, work on the interior, have dinner, work a little more as the air cooled, have supper, and then relax to monitor the fire while the CNA crew went to work. The following day, after declaring the fire toast, we'd call a helicopter for the ride out and be hopeful of getting on another. Everything about these high alpine fires was fun. And we were getting paid for it!

Chapter Six

— Season's End

Now this is not the end. It is not even the beginning of the end. But it is, perhaps, the end of the beginning.

– Winston Churchill

SINCE STARTING ON THE CREW we'd all spent a good 70 percent of our time actively involved with fire in some way. Either doing prep work for future burns, on the burns in the form of igniting or holding, or on a variety of actual wildfires. The remaining 30 percent was taken up with either travel to and from the various burning units and fires or equipment maintenance: sharpening pulaskis, shovels, chainsaws and anything else with an edge; refurbishing pumps and washing mile upon mile of charcoaled, mud-encrusted hose. It was tedious work but only done during the slow times, when there were no fires. Nevertheless, despite the monotony, it was vital work. Without well-maintained, sharpened, and dependable tools, we could have been in serious trouble. A sharp pulaski can mean the difference between energy and fatigue. In the extreme, a sharp saw can be the difference of putting the fire out, or not, and between life and death of those fighting it.

If the equipment was too damaged or too old it was replaced. This was more frequently the hose, but also pulaskis, sleeping bags and pumps, and the cargo nets used by helicopters to bring us supplies and sling out our gear. The hose needed replacing more often because it was always left laying in the wet dirt and would get punctured on rocks or the sharp punji sticks that the saws left behind. That, or it would simply get burned up, leaving only couplings and melted rubber behind. Adequate water pressure was dependent on the hose having no leaks so replacing it was a prerequisite. Replacing it was also a good way to get the more modern synthetic stuff, which wasn't as stiff and awkward to handle as the older woven canvas hose that we had been using. For this we would drive to Missoula, to the Region One Fire Cache, where everything you could ever imagine being used on a fire, and a whole lot more, is stored. Missoula is also the home to the Missoula Smokejumpers.

We would often argue over who got the driving detail, up over Hoodoo Pass into Montana and lasting the whole day. It was a good trip. The road was great to drive when you weren't using your own vehicle: three hours of washboard gravel, blind curves and steep cliffs, all surrounded by a continuous, unblemished, carpet of forest. Thousands of small rocks slammed against the underside of the vehicle as we slid around the bends and bounced over the bumps while throwing a long dust cloud behind us, further adding to the dirty, sandy-grey covering of the small trees lining either side of the road. In its own distinct way this was some of the nicest countryside I had yet seen. I'd driven the road on my first trip to Canyon and enjoyed every minute of it, except for the fact that my old Subaru was never quite the same afterwards. It forever rattled after going over the corrugations, which rather took the fun out of it at the time. But in a green FS pick-up designed for such terrain it was a brilliant experience.

On one of these trips in June, after exchanging our equipment at the cache, I went next door to visit the jump base. After learning the name of the teacher from Frazee, Minnesota, from one of the ex-jumpers working at the North Fork District office at Orofino, Idaho, I called Chuck before leaving Canyon, and he told me to just show up at the visitor center and ask for him.

I walked in and an amenable ex-jumper, Tim, immediately escorted me to the canteen where everyone was watching video footage of that morning's training jumps. The room was in semi-darkness with a large television in the front showing some grainy, jerky videos. Every now and again raucous laughter would erupt, followed by a series of collective groans before someone could be heard making excuses, which inevitably led to more laughter, this time with added ridicule. At the front of the room was a balding bull of a man who was obviously in charge because everyone went quiet when he spoke. There seemed to be no order in the room, with people spread out in a variety of lazy postures. Some on the floor, some on the edge of tables and others scattered about on chairs. A few even looked as though they were sleeping. Those wearing sunglasses in the darkened room certainly were.

Chuck emerged from the darkness looking rather relieved. He didn't strike me as being a teacher and neither did he look much like any smokejumper I'd envisaged.

"Thanks, that was getting rough," Chuck said immediately, even before I'd had a chance to introduce myself.

Apparently, as he explained to me, Chuck had managed to leave the room a few seconds before his morning's performance was shown on the screen, because I immediately heard another much louder groan before everyone erupted in laughter, followed by, "Where the fuck is Chuck?!"

Chuck was already ushering me out the door. From where he showed me around the base while talking about people we both knew in Frazee. The rest of the base was empty since everyone was in the canteen, but I remember seeing the tower and the loft where they hung and packed the hundreds of parachutes that were stacked tidily on scores of wooden shelves. The tower itself was full of dozens of red, white and blue nylon chutes hanging from hooks hoisted 40 feet up to the ceiling.

Steering the conversation to jumping, Chuck told me he knew the ex-jumpers at Canyon and suggested that I just continue to work hard to get noticed for a good recommendation. Apart from that there was little else I could do. He also warned me that there were always many hundreds of people applying for only a few positions each year, and many of those accepted never made it through rookie training anyway. Chuck didn't hold out much hope for me, but he didn't put me off either, he just told it like it was. It was my first direct contact with the jump base and, despite being not overly optimistic, it gave me great encouragement. I thanked Chuck and he disappeared quietly back into the darkness of the canteen, only to sustain a barrage of stored insults.

On the drive back to Canyon I thought more about the jump base and visualized being there, wondering what it would be like, which, considering my experience so far and the large number of potential recruits, was highly presumptuous. Despite this, though, I was driven, and decided to work even harder, train more and learn faster. I thought that if fire had grabbed me by the balls I should do something about it.

Twenty years previous my grandfather had always told me that if I ever joined the army not to volunteer for anything. I did join the army and, like a dummy, I did tend to volunteer. I only hope that my grandfather had excused that previous error in his eyes, and now understood that the FS was not like the army he knew and forgave me. Because, once again, I started to volunteer for absolutely anything and everything. And it was all fun to me. If someone wanted a pump carried up the mountain, I carried it. If someone wanted hose, I brought it. If the crew needed more water,

I fetched it. If they wanted a fire building for coffee, I built it. But only once did they ever ask the Limey to make coffee.

It was on a particularly steep and nasty burn during the last few weeks of the season that I accelerated the effort to prove my worth. Because the burn was so steep we knew we would never stop it from slopping over the top despite prepping the area heavily with sprinklers and foam. Also, the holders had to be held back until the fire had been drawn well into the center, or they'd be fried to a crisp. One of the sawyers carved a chair from a stump and placed it at the slop over point, from where Bill could, if he wished, sit and oversee the proceedings in comfort. As usual, Bill took the well intentioned humor in his stride but declined the invitation to be a chargrilled spectator.

Igniting the burn was especially exciting because we found ourselves in the path of a couple of logs that broke loose and thundered their way to the base of the hill before smashing onto the rocks below, all while we were scrambling like spiders through three feet of slash on the hillside. To complete the ignition we just needed one more quick strip at the base, and Bill's voice came over the radio: "Tell the Limey to put his running shoes on." So with three others watching for rollers I scrambled across with the drip torch and laid the last trail of fire. It was a blast. I was full of adrenaline and behaving like a child with a new toy. Initially, I took the request as a compliment, and only later realized that the Limey might simply have been the more easily expendable – and, hence, not liable under USFS worker compensation.[*]

By this time we were so deep into the draw that we had to clamber out using the hoses as climbing ropes in places. It was the best burn yet. We were all drenched in sweat, thirsty, but eager for more. Which was just as well because we still had two more units to burn. It was due to turn to rain the next day and Chuck was in a

---

[*] If hurt, I would have been seriously damaged, both physically and financially.

hurry to get his acreage finished. It was Chuck's most ambitious night so far. Proving once again that he was the man to work for.

When we finally crawled our way out of the draw we discovered the holding crew had experienced quite the time of it. The slop over stretched a good 50 yards into the trees. Bill's chair was rather the worse for wear, but it had been somewhat expected given the steepness of the slope and loaded to the gills with slash. It was later decided not to log the remainder of those slopes because of the problems associated with replanting. This was only too obvious at the time. If it had rained any substantial amount a few days after our burn there wouldn't have been a grain of soil left on the mountain.

This sort of slop over was the only form of collateral damage that anyone could reasonably justify. Having some scorched trees a few feet outside a burn boundary was always to be expected with flame lengths exceeding a 100 feet leaping into the night sky. The term 'collateral damage' was to have a different connotation later, however, when a self-centered, pseudo-scientist made an inane comment about homes lost to fire being an inevitable part of collateral damage during management fires. This bland, somewhat callous, and completely idiotic comment was jumped upon by anyone with slightly more common sense than a deranged monkey, only to be immediately defended by the culprit's spouse – an equally brainless wonder. This level of insanity was thankfully rare among most I met. Nevertheless, it remains a worrying perspective within some areas of the Forest Service. God protect us, and our property, from the likes of such lunatics.

The days began to draw in as summer ended. Temperatures dropped considerably and the mornings started to deliver a frosty reception, giving the wildlife-grazed grass along the river tints of sparkling grey. An early morning haze now hung over the quietly meandering river, enveloping the occasional wandering mule deer within an opaque cloak, leaving only their legs visible against the shade of the forest on the far bank. Clouds pushed by changing winds cascaded down over the ridge tops and wafted gently into the trees. Soon there would be days without sunlight in this tight little valley, turning it into a frigid winter icebox. With the onset of this lasting seasonal change in the weather the lightning season was officially over. The only fires we had after that were a couple of small hunter fires, where a campfire wasn't fully extinguished or because some idiot had set light to their toilet paper. All of them stayed small, often just went out on their own or were never even noticed, being unable to prosper in the cold damp air that was now upon us.

The upside of the cooler temperatures was that my runs were easier and more enjoyable. No longer did I have the constant sting of sweat in my eyes from 90-degree heat, or swarms of bugs chasing me back down the mountain trails. It was pleasant and my mileage increased dramatically. My legs were so much stronger after a summer of clambering up and down the slopes; they'd completely lost their flatlander memory and expected every run to involve a hill. I'd also been steadily increasing my pack weight by adding another rock every now and again. In Minnesota I had weighed it at a little over 50lbs, always trying to average about a third of my body weight. But with these trails I'd removed some rocks earlier in the summer so as not to exhaust myself and make me useless for work. It's not only humbling but very embarrassing to be seen struggling to exhaustion with a pack full of rocks, especially when it's by choice. Everybody already thought I was quite mad, and it wasn't until I weighed my pack a few weeks later, to discover that I really had 62lbs in it, that I realized I might indeed be mad. No wonder I had been having difficulty jogging up the mountain. But the effort was worthwhile: it provided a solid base from which to start my jumper fitness training. Although no one ever admitted to putting those extra rocks in my pack.

Canyon Work Center sits in a hole alongside the North Fork of the Clearwater, on the only piece of discernible flat ground for miles. A hundred feet on either side are two steep hillsides that block the sun from the valley for most of the winter. And although we hadn't yet reached that point, the daily frosts were starting to make driving around the district's roads quite treacherous. Many roads never saw enough sunlight to melt the frost and black ice built up easily. I saw several nasty accidents where the occupants of the vehicles were fortunate not to have crashed into the river or gone over the side of a precipice.

One accident in particular was very sad. A group of hunters pulling a horse trailer clearly had no idea of the roads and had taken a blind bend much too fast. Fortunately for them the trailer had become separated from the truck. But the horses plummeted to their death, rattling around the inside a large disintegrating tin can as it tumbled 300 feet down a rocky incline. Explosives had to be used later on the rotting carcasses to stop them attracting bears.

On one of these nice crisp days, while the camp was in an unusually relaxed state after having had dinner, a series of pistol shots reverberated off the valley walls. As I walked onto the porch outside I could see rounds whipping through the leaves of a tree down by the river, about 50 feet from where I was standing. The shots were being fired from about 60 yards down the river. My neighbor also came out and immediately suggested drunk hunters. Don was the local law enforcement officer (LEO) and the majority of his time was currently being taken up with monitoring the dozens of hunters now in the woods, and trying not to let them kill each other in large enough numbers that would attract attention. Only a few days before we had been monitoring an old fire and a rifle bullet had struck a rock a few feet from us. When we looked to see where it had come from all we could see was a trail of dust on a road in the distance.

On this occasion, though, Don and I jumped into a pick-up and headed down the road. And sure enough, there was a big burly individual trying to balance himself on a couple of rocks with a Bud in one hand and a .44 in the other. His friend, meanwhile, was pitching empty cans into the river for target practice, totally oblivious to the buildings on the other side of the trees, with the rounds ricocheting off the rocks and going straight through the work center barely inches above head height. It was pure fortune that only trees were being hit because we had all been playing volleyball there an hour before.

Getting out of the FS rig, Don politely suggested they move to a more suitable range a few miles up the road. He was probably used to it, but it had to be a little worrying telling a large, drunk, Idahoan with a .44 where to go.

With the season almost over most of the crew had disappeared off to college, which meant we now only had a handful left on the crew. And with most of them being squad leaders, it left me and one other as the only grunts. And who does the work? You got it!

It was nice not to have such a large crowd around anymore. We got away with doing things that we could never have done before. Like taking the Honda 250cc trials bike that we'd found hidden in the store shed up onto the burns so that we could patrol on wheels. On the steep slopes it was all we could do to keep the bike upright. Not just a few times did we end up ass-over-tit and covered in mud. On one occasion we were trick riding around the camp when the camp manager popped his head out to see what the commotion was. All he saw was a bike with what looked like no rider as we took it in turns to ride by hanging off the other side of the bike. Although he usually didn't care much for those antics, and would normally have come down hard on any such foolery, his self esteem had been heavily blunted a few days earlier when he had almost set himself on fire.

He'd been trying to light a large bonfire containing the whole season's waste. It was quite the large pile. Carrying a jerrycan full of fuel – unaware of it leaking from the bottom – he'd walked up to the pile and doused a decent helping of drip torch fuel on the wood to give it a good start before lighting it with a long stick and walking casually away, still carrying the jerrycan. As expected, the fire spread quickly and immediately followed the narrow stream coming from the base of his can. Realizing what was happening he walked faster, though not fast enough, until finally, after stumbling a few more paces, he flung the jerrycan away just as the trailing flame was lapping at his heels. The vapor in the jerrycan then ignited, sending it flying several feet in the air with a whoof. To do that in private is one thing. To have a score of witnesses that you've been berating all summer long is just plain embarrassing.

When we accomplished a few small burns later in the season we got some help from the jump base. It was common practice to farm out jumpers later in the year to the districts. It worked well because just as the district crews dwindled the jumpers became more available. The burns were easier compared to what we had done in the spring and were generally on more sedate slopes, which was pleasant after a long busy summer.

One of the jumpers had been through Canyon earlier that year after coming off a fire near the work center. I remembered hearing about the fire because one of the jumpers had been injured and they'd had to call for a medevac. One of the girls had broken her ankle on falling from a tree after parachuting into it. However, this group didn't hold much sympathy for her, so we initially thought they were a tough callous bunch. But what did we know? We were just enjoying their company because they had more energy than most of the people that we'd been working with all summer long and it was refreshing. They were happy to show us some other methods of firefighting that not even Leon had shown us. But we simply put that down to them being from a different tribe.

Time finally came to leave. It wasn't in any way by choice but a simple subtle directive from the government. They removed everyone's funding. They did it at this time every year, as regular as clockwork. The summer had literally flown by. It seemed like only yesterday that I was driving into Canyon for the first time and scrounging for work. Personally, it was probably the most intense, consistent period of enjoyment that I'd ever had in my life and I had learned something new and valuable every single exhausting day. We had been continually busy, barely stopping for anything and only taking a few mandatory days off. But now it was over.

After thanking everyone who had helped us, Anne and I said our goodbyes and headed off to Missoula. We now had to find work that would see us through the winter. It was my first real experience of seasonal work and inevitably became something that haunted me for the rest of my time with the Forest Service. Once the work was done, you were done. It was just a different logic to what most people are used to. But although being laid-off was disappointing, there was something more pressing that we needed to take care of rather quickly once reaching Missoula; we had to find somewhere to live.

Chapter Seven

— Winter Training

With all the limits now placed upon speed, skiing is one of the few enjoyments where you can go as exhilaratingly fast as you like, completely out of control, and hurt only yourself.

– Author

RRIVING IN MISSOULA WE CHECKED into a cheap motel on the outskirts of town and immediately began sifting through the local rentals. Most of them were easily eliminated after a quick phone call because we needed enough room for a small herd of farmyard pets that we had yet to retrieve from Minnesota. Anne's father had been looking after them at his small ranch on Buffalo Lake. We had naturally missed them over the summer and wanted them with us, but finding somewhere suitable was proving difficult.

Nevertheless, as luck would have it, we found a small trout farm 60 miles north of Missoula that had a couple of acres and the owner needed someone to manage it for a reduction in rent. We jumped on it and immediately set up a meeting with the dental surgeon who owned it. The following day we drove north to look at it and agreed to the lease on the spot. Although an hour away from Missoula it was ideal. The house wasn't up to much, just a basic un-insulated, old wooden bungalow with a tiny wood stove in the living room that looked like it would have trouble boiling a kettle. But being the only heat source we hoped it managed better. Outside there were a series of long feeder ponds where the trout were raised until large enough to migrate into the main fishing pond, with a splendid assortment of tall trees around the property that provided shelter and privacy. With four cats, a dog, and an ornery quarter horse it would be a little cramped, but we had long managed with less.

Anne found a job at the local ranch store, Quality Supply, in Missoula within a few days. It seemed to be so easy for a good-looking girl to waltz into a business, hand over a resume, and get called back for a job even before returning home. Her veterinary qualification had clearly proved useful again and she was hired in the equine section of the store. After scanning the classifieds for a couple of weeks I eventually found work on a local dairy farm, doing relief milking four days a week on a four hundred cow herd. Everything seemed to be falling into place and all we had to do was return to Minnesota to bring out the animals and everything else we owned.

We had a few days before either of us started our new jobs and set off immediately, arriving at the lake-side ranch twenty-two hours later. We quickly bought a 16-foot horse trailer that we intended to sell once we'd moved everything, and managed to fit everything into it, including the horse. However, after a less than successful test drive we thought it best to leave the horse behind to lessen the weight. So when we left, Anne had her two house cats in the Subaru, and I pulled the trailer with the Bronco, with Sheila, our fat black lab for company. Since we had to leave the horse for another time we also left the two farm cats. They seemed to be happy enough where they were and a few weeks of Minnesota fall wouldn't hurt them anymore than the frigid winters that they had endured so far.

The Bronco's petrol gauge dropped visibly as I coaxed it over the passes at barely 25mph. We made the journey in two long days and were relieved to have our few belongings with us in Montana. The little cottage started to look like home with the cats huddled together next to the little fireplace and Sheila chasing critters in the deep snow outside.

We soon settled into a familiar winter schedule, with Anne travelling to work in Missoula while I went off to milk the cows, did the chores around the fishponds, and chopped wood into teeny-little pieces for the tiny wood stove. Since losing my chainsaw in our barn fire I was reduced to using an old Swede Saw, which provided a good daily workout. We bought a cord of firewood for emergencies but apart from that I cut all the standing dead wood around the property. By the time I had cut, hauled and split the wood small enough to fit into the stove, I was often warm enough that I no longer needed it.

On one of the more pleasant late fall mornings I was surprised to receive a treasury check from the Forest Service for $600. Apparently someone at North Fork had decided I was due a cash award to make up for not getting any overtime. I felt honored, and grateful that someone should have thought of me. While we weren't totally poor it certainly helped us get by for a while.

The cottage was only a mile or two from the foothills of the Mission Mountains and the views from the east side windows were breathtaking. No one believed me when I took a photograph and sent it home. The pond in the foreground reflected the orange and reds of the autumn foliage on the surrounding hardwoods. Behind them, taller firs provided a thick, green windbreak. In the near distance the pine and fir-laden foothills rose steeply before turning into rugged rocky peaks that reached up toward the heavens. The snow-capped tops finished the perfection and every once in a while a bald eagle soared high on the winds overhead. Even our animals seemed to be in awe. They would sit quietly on the back stoop and just stare, as if mesmerized by their new surroundings. They had never seen a hill before let alone the cathedral-like mountains that now stood before them.

One afternoon I found Sheila barking fiercely at something in the yard. She rarely made a noise that was not playful but this time she sounded desperate. When I turned the corner of the house I saw her hackles up, she was clearly in protection mode. Going a little further I gingerly peered around the corner and came face to face with a young cocklebur covered grizzly, standing tall and nonchalantly plucking old fruit from the plum tree. He was totally unperturbed at anything around him and continued unabated to enjoy his dessert. I left him be and immediately beckoned Sheila into the house. I did not want to be surprised by its mum.

This inquisitive youngster became a frequent visitor over the next few weeks. Apart from leaving us huge piles of plum scat on the back lawn he was never a bother or a worry, and was probably only claiming back his territory on emerging from the Missions, which is renowned for grizzlies. I half expected to see him up to his waist in the fish pond chasing trout one day, but never did.

Since leaving Canyon I had thought of smokejumping every day. I knew the chances of getting in were remote, but it was worth the try. You don't get anywhere without trying. So I studied the requirements and found that, on paper at least, I met them all. My agricultural background made up for a lack of FS work, I had a little city fire experience and had had much more than a normal fire season on the North Fork. And I was sure that if anyone contacted the North Fork they'd put in a good word for me. But I still wasn't confident. There were many more experienced people interested. Nevertheless, I redid and redid my application until I was satisfied it was perfect, sent it in, crossed my fingers and hoped for the best. But all the while wondering if I had missed something, that one reference, that one vital fact.

#   #   #

WHETHER OR NOT IT COUNTED for anything, my squadron had been trained as firemen while in the Royal Engineers thirteen years earlier in 1977, when the real firemen had gone on strike. For a couple of months a few of us sappers were based at RAF Abingdon in Oxfordshire, and worked 24 hours on, 24 standby, and 24 hours off. It was a great schedule for eager new sappers. We drove around the lanes in old 1950s Bedford *Green Goddesses* that had only recently been taken out of mothballs. When we got a fire call the police would meet us at the gate to guide us and then high-tail it off down the road. After a minute or two all we could see was a little blue flashing light above the hedgerows in the distance. The police never got used to the fact that the top speed on a *Goddess* in 1977 seemed to be little more than an excruciating 45mph (in 1953 their top speed was a hair-raising 65mph). A further problem we soon realized was they were exceedingly top heavy when full of water – 'sensitive' the instruction book said. I'll say! Steering them around the narrow winding country roads at the unenviable speed of 45mph was often quite an education in elementary physics. Sixty-five was suicidal!

We were intensively (hurriedly) trained over a two-day period and consistently told by the Brigade Commander, "Don't worry, it's not rocket science. Just hang on and point it over there." To which we wondered why, then, if it were so easy, were the firemen on strike? Seemed like a good gig to me, more money than I was making, better hours, and fighting fires was exciting, right?

But that was before we tried hanging onto those massive four-inch hoses pushing out so much pressure that they would lift two of us completely off the ground with unbridled ease if we weren't properly braced. One of us would point the nozzle while the other two would lean into the force of the water and use every ounce of our strength to stop the hose from behaving like a deranged snake, and whipping us about in the air. It was quite the experience, and provided us all a good example of living in someone else's shoes before deciding if something was easy.

One particular incident involved us returning to the airfield after a call to a burning kitchen, that we were able to put out with a fire blanket, very boring. During the past several weeks we had grown accustomed (complacent) to the roads around camp and knew where all the cars and aircraft were usually parked. One day, as we turned a blind corner going full tilt (a whopping 25mph!), we saw an RAF Jaguar aircraft sitting directly in front of us. There was little time to stop, barely room to squeak by and we instantly saw our wages going to the government for the next few hundred years. As we skated by, holding our breath, with a loud screeching of tires, I looked back and thought I saw the plane rock.

This particular aircraft hadn't managed to take off for weeks. Each morning we would watch it tear down the runway with an almighty roar, only to wimp out at the penultimate moment. But a day after our near miss it soared into the air as though grateful to be relieved from the burdens of mother earth, and far away from crazy army sappers.

#   #   #

JOHN, AN OLD FRIEND IN MINNESOTA, was coming to Montana's Whitefish to ski and offered to bring anything we'd left behind. We couldn't expect him to bring the horse, but I traveled back on a Greyhound and collected our two chunky farm cats and a some last possessions. The cats were remarkably content for the whole journey, lolling about in the back of the pick-up with their inquisitive eyes intrigued at the world now passing them by. Being a fuel-efficient diesel we stopped only twice for fuel. While filling up next to a huge tractor-trailer, its massive driver strolled menacingly towards me. We thought maybe we had parked in his spot. His arms were the size of a man's thighs and he had to have been six-four. He walked up, peered into the back of the pick-up and said: "Hey! You got cats in there?"

"Uh huh," I said, a little worried about the next bit.

"Could I see? I haven't seen mine for a week. I kinda miss the little beggars."

I was speechless, but opened the side window so he could see them. As his huge hand reached through the window I hoped Arthur wouldn't let rip with his claws at the intrusion. But the orange tabby just sauntered over and rubbed his cheek against the man's hand like they were the best of friends.

"Thanks man," he said as he shook my hand. "I thought I saw them when you went by me at the pass. Take care now, you hear." And walked off to haul his massive frame back up into his cab.

At Bozeman the temperature dropped considerably, which was unusual since the west side of the divide was usually warmer. And once we reached St. Ignatius it was snowing heavily and bitterly cold. Anne had the furnace almost glowing red but the windows still had frost on the inside. The two sets of cats initially seemed happy to see each other, but soon returned to their more characteristic behavior, vying for territorial control of the sofa.

The following month reminded us of Minnesota. The weather was frigid for weeks, with temperatures continually only rising to minus 20 during the day. Trying to keep enough wood in the house was a full time job and the Swede saw became both a curse and a savior. Despite the frigid conditions John still went skiing, but on his return each evening he looked as though he'd been on a trek across Antarctica.

The furnace's iron casing was almost glowing red but was failing miserably in keeping the house warm. So we put plastic over the windows, blankets over the doors, and even left the oven on to give an expensive boost of heat every now and again. The cats slept close to us on the waterbed and Sheila, our fat lab, nudged me awake each night to remind me to put more wood in the stove. Getting up in the mornings and leaving the comfort of the warm bed demanded some major incentive.

Despite the frigid weather we managed to go cross-country skiing almost every day in the foothills after getting a pass to access the tribal lands below Saint Mary's Peak. Sheila quickly lost weight as she accompanied me on each ski and was always a good gauge of my fitness; if she was ahead of me, I was unfit, if she lagged far behind either I was fit or she was fat. Although a couple of times she deliberately lagged behind to gorge herself on a decaying carcass. Going through the woods she would always take the easiest route; directly behind and right in my ski tracks. I tried to teach her out of the habit because the return journey was so much more fun in unspoiled tracks. And being a smart puppy she understood perfectly. So that every time I turned to reprimand her she hopped out, only to hop straight back in the moment I wasn't looking. It was a great game for her.

The foothills were wonderfully secluded and an excellent place to ski. The skis were so quiet gliding across the new snow that the wildlife never spooked. When they finally did see us they'd prick up their ears, raise their snouts to the air and bound off though the deep snow with graceful nonchalant ease. Every time we went out I would try to get a little further up until finally there was nowhere else to go but down. At the top we would rest and appreciate the view over the smoky valley far below us.

There was little resting for Sheila. Once at the top she would soon get bored and take off back down the mountain, galloping down through the deep powder to get a head start. Occasionally she'd smell something, stop in mid-track, and then go bounding off after it, her tail rotating like a propeller as she buried her head deep into a drift looking for some elusive critter that she stood no chance of catching in a million years.

Getting bored of our usual route one day I thought I'd try a different way down and decided on a trail that was steeper and narrower but went roughly in the right direction. As I was picking up speed on a straight shot, feeling the satisfying sting of cold wind on my face, I noticed Sheila off to my right chasing another snowy critter, and failed to see the sheer drop. I sailed through the air with the greatest of ease, arms flailing. One of those 'oh shit' moments where you hope you're not in a James Bond movie falling off the edge of a precipice without a parachute. It wasn't a great drop, maybe fifteen feet or so, but I wouldn't have won any style points as I pancaked into the thankfully fresh powdery snow. Brushing snow off my face I looked up to see Sheila wagging her tail on the ledge above, as if to say, "That was fun. Do it again."

With all the exercise my stamina was building and the legs were getting stronger. During years of farming I'd never had to work out that much because everyday activity took care of it. But now I wasn't doing any great physical work, apart from cutting wood, and had to concentrate on improving my upper body strength. So in the mornings Sheila and I would go off skiing and in the afternoons I would work out, doing push-ups, countless sit-ups and pull-ups, anything but going to the gym that I couldn't afford. To get more exercise I carried logs up to the house instead of splitting them where they fell. If I could make exercise out of stuff I would.

Having a rigid routine is paramount to getting fit and once the weather improved there was more time to train since we needed less wood to stay warm. There were various routes to choose from depending on whether it was to be a fast, long, or easy run. Most of them took me into the foothills, however, and away from the hard roads and stroppy reservation dogs that were all too keen to take a chunk out of my calf.

The smokejumper application packet contained a rookie video about what we could expect and what they expected from us. There was an understandably high demand placed on physical fitness, specifically manual worker fitness rather than gym fitness. I couldn't foresee myself having problems because I could already easily pass the PT (physical fitness) test, and probably could have on any day of my life. It was a standard test consisting of a basic 25 push-ups, 45 sit-ups, and seven pull-ups, finished with a mile and a half run in under eleven minutes. Pretty basic. Although it was constantly stressed that these were basic minimums and a lot more effort was required to get through a month of rookie training. As an example, they suggested that each exercise be doubled and the run done in nine and a half minutes, with everything repeated in regular intervals.

Nothing about it really worried me apart from the run in nine and a half minutes. I had always run, but for years I had trained to carry weight over long distances, not being particularly fast over short ones. So I stepped up my speed work and, despite being initially disappointed, I managed to gain some decent times for an older guy with worn out knees.

My running so far had been on slippery hard-packed snow or icy roads, so I knew once the roads were dry I would fare better. In the meantime I inserted hex screws into the soles of my shoes so that they didn't slip on the compacted snow and ice, something I'd done for years in Minnesota, and with Montana being warmer my feet didn't freeze as much from the screws conducting the cold. However, I did get a few strange looks when people heard me running up a metaled road on what sounded like hob-nailed boots.

By January I was running and working out every day, skiing alternate days and getting fitter than I'd been in years. Sheila was looking pretty trim too. But then I caught the flu. At first I tried to ignore it, which wasn't the best thing to do since it got worse and ended up as bronchitis, putting a stop to everything immediately.

After going to the doctor for antibiotics I learned I might have damaged my lungs a little during the previous year, breathing too much smoke and making them more susceptible to infection. This wasn't particularly good news for someone looking for a career in firefighting. But apart from feeling down at losing fitness, I knew it wouldn't stop me from trying. So after a few weeks of incessant hacking, and many nights of no sleep, I slowly got back into some mild exercise. By then it was warmer which allowed me to do more running and less cross-country skiing.

I'd been told that everyone would hear whether we'd been accepted in March, and as February passed I started to get anxious. I stepped up my training regime, unsure of whether I was really fit enough. But that was paranoia. A week later the letter arrived.

"Due to an unusually high number of qualified applicants... "

There was no point in reading further, it was a tremendous disappointment. I felt like ditching the run and getting drunk. But knew that would only make me more morose so I took off for one of the longest runs ever. I returned hours later so exhausted I couldn't think about anything but a hot shower and an ice pack for my knees. Then I read the rest of the letter. It was the "please try again next year," that particularly hurt because it was getting to the point where I wouldn't be able to do it next year. Not because of any physical problem, but for the need to make some money in a real job. I'd goofed around long enough since leaving the farm and was feeling the pressure of conformity on my shoulders.

That day was a double disappointment. Leaving for work we saw Arthur, our favorite orange cat, lying dead in the road. We went over hoping to see some sign of life, but there was nothing. We had lost a good many animals over the years but losing Arthur really got to me. We had known the road was a problem, even though it wasn't that busy, but it was right next to the house. We also knew that we couldn't have kept that curious cat cooped up inside, he would have been utterly miserable. He was a curious outdoor adventurist and needed his freedom. So we had let him have it and he died while hopefully doing what he loved. Dying happier than if we'd kept him inside for our pleasure rather than his. We buried him under his favorite spot by a tree overlooking the pond. Where he would spend hours watching the water, being intrigued by the trout teasing him just beneath the surface. I still miss that big dumb orange cat.

Back on the farm we frequently had kittens dumped on us, invariably finding them at five o'clock as we trudged through the morning snow to start milking, a tiny bundle of fur huddling miserably against the wind by the barn door. An uncle's farm in the north of England had been inundated with cats, but we didn't want to get to that point so we took care of them until they were old enough to be spayed and then found homes for them.

One pair dumped on us during a minus 20 snowstorm were so tiny we had to rear them in the house. Once inside, comfortable, and safe, they turned into little terrors. Climbing the curtains and making life generally miserable for everything else in the house. One afternoon, after putting on an old record I fell fast asleep, and woke up to find it skipping, with one of the kittens going around in circles on top of Jethro Tull. We found them homes the next day.

Arthur and his sister I had picked up from a neighboring farmer back in Minnesota. He had two female tabbies and a two ginger toms that I had noticed during milk testing a month earlier. Two were particularly mischievous and on my next visit I asked if I could take them. Arthur had us both clambering over hay bales and crawling along rafters to try and catch him. After unsuccessful attempts the farmer suggested I take the other one instead, which was obviously much tamer. But I wanted this one. He was ornery and special. We finally caught him and I took him home with his sister. They remained as farm cats and wouldn't have had it any different, they mellowed and got to be good company around the farm. And for whatever reason, with them around, we never got abandoned kittens again. They got on well with the farm animals and loved rummaging around the buildings. During the winter they would snuggle up in the thick straw next to the newborn calves. Our home seemed empty without old Arthur.

With not being able to start jumping, the next few weeks were spent looking for real work, this time on a district fire crew closer to Missoula. I relaxed my running schedule to every other day and took Sheila for more lazy walks instead, which she seemed to prefer. There was also extra work around the cottage because the fishponds needed cleaning and adult fish needed to be migrated to the bigger pond. And there was always plenty of yard work to do.

As nice as the place was we had to look for another rental in Missoula because Anne was getting tired of traveling an hour to and from work every day on Montana's most dangerous highway. I was happy on the trout farm, it was secluded, peaceful and an altogether nice place to live, but we also needed to move closer to town to find better work, and got lucky finding a house outside of the city, close to one of the expansive forested recreation areas. It was ideal; with a large yard and two bedrooms, and for not much more than we had been paying. The landlords lived next door and their daughter mowed the lawn, so good all round.

Just before moving a letter arrived from the Forest Service explaining that due to severity funding I had now been accepted to attend the preliminary PT test prior to rookie training at the Missoula Smokejumper base starting June 4th. I couldn't believe it. It was great news! The best news! There was now real incentive to improve my fitness, and used the nearby Blue Mountain recreation area every single day until the 2nd of June. All we had to provide were a suitable pair of worn in fire boots, a knife, watch, socks and t-shirts for a week. Everything else was provided. The boots had to be at least eight inches high with a Vibram sole. Most firefighters at the time wore White's, with a high heel to ease walking on steep terrain. I didn't much like the idea of parachuting with a boot with a high heel but in those days we didn't have a choice.

From that moment I put in five, eight and twelve mile runs on the hills and followed them up with short fast runs on the flats. The pull-up bar in the garage became an absolute necessity. To practice for the packouts I filled my rucksack with a 120lbs of rocks and climbed the north-facing vistas overlooking Missoula. I must have looked quite the sight struggling up those rock-strewn slopes off the main paths, and even more so when I tripped over a tuft of unforgiving grass on the way back down, and turning turtle. Trying to right myself while exhausted with 120lbs on my back even had me laughing.

Chapter Eight

— Rookie Week

It takes very little talent, just raw effort and a will to succeed. And yet even that is too great a demand for some.

– Author

ETTING TO THE BASE EARLY Monday morning along with 34 other nervous hopefuls I saw that many recruits already knew each other from fire crews across the northwest. Some even knew the smokejumper base quite well and a few preferential candidates had even been mentored through their pre-rookie training by jumpers assigned to training.

The nervous, or more appropriately, apprehensive atmosphere wasn't limited to rookies, however. Tragically, the base had just had a parachuting fatality that previous Friday. There's obviously never a good time for tragedy but the timing of this was especially unfortunate being just before an influx of new recruits. The base had been evaluating and testing a new square canopy to match that of the Bureau of Land Management (BLM). The transition from a basic round, static line parachute to a drogue deployed square was a contentious issue, and would remain so for over a decade. Right or wrong, Gary, the base manager, was instrumental in pushing the Forest Service, and Missoula in particular, towards this system.

The accident investigation team had yet to be assembled let alone had time evaluating the evidence, but preliminary indications learned from video footage showed the jumper had failed to deploy either of his chutes. The base was naturally despondent and there were accusations flying around about what, or who, was to blame. The trainers, however, were extremely professional and adamant to keep all new hires removed from this unfortunate event. Apart from a brief meeting to discuss and explain the process behind using the squares, it never once affected our training. For our part, we were in no position to discuss anything since we knew so little. Sadly, the residual trauma of this event haunted the base for years; friendships were lost, some firefighters quit or were fired, and it removed the likelihood that the Missoula would transition over to square chutes in the near future.* Some were determined to keep it that way, others wished to push forward regardless. But the organization was but a small part of a bigger bureaucracy and the square process came grinding to a halt after the accident. We were just thankful that our training had not been equally curtailed, as it very easily could have been.

The accident, however, was rumored to have removed one of the more traditional events of the day; where veteran jumpers put on an exhibition jump for the new recruits. Having never seen it myself, but later being told of the proceedings, it seems someone thought it a good idea, at some stage of the jump, to throw out an iron test dummy attached to an equally dumbed-down useless parachute, with obvious results. This would naturally create some concern among the rookies while providing a little hazing humor for the veterans. Typical for the era but almost unheard of now.

Years later a few attempted to bring back the tradition, but the morale-sucking, non-jumping administrative management quashed it immediately. A twist was to be added by having someone pop up

---

* As of writing, recent developments have changed all that, with mixed loads now common in Missoula after sending small groups of round jumpers to Alaska to transition over to squares.

from the dusty ground immediately after the dummy had crashed, then brushing themselves off and continuing on as though nothing had happened. If nothing else it would instill how tough jumpers expected new recruits to be, and would complement the collection of 'no whining' signs on the base (that have since been removed). It actually wasn't too exaggerated an idea because one old jumper, Floyd, escaped a major parachute malfunction by bouncing down the side of a steep mountain after plummeting to earth at 60mph with little more than a bog-roll of silk streaming behind him. When they found him he was leaning against a tree smoking a cigarette. A similar episode happened to Everrett years later when jumping a test canopy. His main chute emerged looking like a pile of garbage and when he pulled his reserve it fell limp between his legs. His main then half opened and trees saved him from serious injury.

As with anything government there was plenty of paperwork before we could continue. This didn't seem to make much sense since there would have been a lot less once the initial PT failures had left. Nevertheless, the base manager, Gary, and the training foreman, Walt, welcomed us and informed us about what we could expect over the next month and what they expected from us. Which was effort and more effort, and anything less would not be acceptable. I recognized Walt immediately as the man I'd seen the previous summer with Chuck. Seeing him now I understood why everyone gave him a great deal of deserved respect. His marine-like physique and exaggerated gestures held everyone's attention, exuding both confidence and ability.

After formalities we went to the loft and were split into three groups to perform the various PT requirements. At each station the test was demonstrated and described in detail. Cheating in any way was not condoned; repetitions were only counted once the full motion of that particular exercise had been done properly and to the trainer's satisfaction. If an arm was not outstretched or a sit-up not rigid there was no count. It was much like many see countless times in the army so I knew the drill. But there were some that couldn't grasp the concept and quickly learned that a correct pull-up actually requires a lot more effort than those done in front of an impressionable girlfriend.

Our group started with push-ups and everyone managed the required 25 quite easily. Moving to sit-ups we took turns holding each other's feet down. After doing mine I held my partner's feet so that he could do the same. Practice in front of a television each evening would make this a pretty easy exercise for anyone and yet we lost one already. I couldn't believe how anyone could show up, knowing full-well the requirements, and still not pass such an basic test. But we were to lose even more.

Being somewhat lighter than most I never had a problem with pull-ups and seven seemed a doddle. But being watched intently by Jim, who looked as though he'd been doing pull-ups since the day he was born, was somewhat disconcerting and only added to the pressure. The veins on Jim's arms protruded like railroad tracks as he demonstrated the proper, and only acceptable, technique to the group. Some began to get a little nervous after several struggled to accomplish the final two, and by those who should otherwise have had no problem. In the end all but three managed to pass. One other squeaked through by a hair. We were now down to 30 and the run was yet to come.

We were allowed a few minutes to warm up before stepping to the start line on the aircraft ramp, where we were told to do five laps in under eleven minutes. Before we lined up, however, there was a last minute request from the ladies in the warehouse that the rookies remove their baggy shorts from over their tight running pants. And they obliged. I shit you not! Traffic cones marked the oval track and when we started the greyhounds powered on ahead as the main pack bumped and jostled for position around the first lap. A few stragglers were soon struggling. On the second lap a few of us broke lose from the pack and began reeling in some of the exuberant greyhounds as they lost wind. The fifth lap was the puker as everyone sprinted to the finish to get a good time and impress the trainers. I passed in a little over eight and a half minutes which I didn't think too shabby for a 34 year old, while a couple of gazelles did it in an amazing seven and a half. Two misjudged the race entirely and never met the eleven minutes. One just kept running, ran straight out the gate and took off in his car. Neither was ever seen again.

The easy part over we were all visibly relieved. The pressure of the event had proved far worse than the activity itself, to those of us remaining anyway. Afterwards we were herded down into the basement and issued with equipment; personal gear bags (PG bags), packout bags, Nomex fire shirts and trousers, jump suits, helmets and parachute harnesses. Humping that stuff up the stairs we started to feel like we were really on our way and barely two hours later we were putting up tents and building camp somewhere in the Bitterroot Mountains; our home for Rookie 'Hell' Week.

Rookie Week, as the name implies, is considered the hardest part of training and is respected by the successful, resented by the failed, and generally dreaded by everyone. Like all such tests it is designed to train, weed out under-performers, and introduce the organizational ethos to new recruits through basic hard work and endurance. That same afternoon we were shown the preferred method of digging line, where each jumper constructs finished line instead of each firefighter steadily improving the line. When a jumper finishes his section he bumps forward and everyone along the line moves forward to a fresh location. It's a more efficient method if everyone pulls equal weight, which is what this week was designed to instill. During this exhaustive and repetitive work everyone carried at least an 18lb PG bag, which is designed to sit a little lower on the back than a normal rucksack, and with a variety of adjustable straps that hold it firmly against the lower back while digging. Inside are the mandatory fire shelter, food, water, and spare clothes. We all carried at least a gallon and a half of water, if not more, and it disappeared quickly after a few hours work.

By mid-afternoon we were building fireline and getting a start on the blisters that would become a burden for the rest of the week. Twenty-eight motivated people can dig a lot of line and the local district was to acquire some nice new trails on their forest. Every hour we stopped briefly for water. As we bent, dug and swung the squad leaders roamed around and critiqued our productivity. It was thought to be a bad sign to see a squad leader writing something in a notebook after studying recruit's output. There was no chance to ease off even a little because one or two squad leaders would hide in the brush and when they caught someone slacking they would appear as if from nowhere, then either quietly stare from behind dark glasses or yell abuse. Good squaddie, bad squaddie.

After six hours of continuous line digging we headed back to camp. It had just been a preliminary easy dig to gauge our abilities and show us what was really expected. More was to come. A lot more. But even though preliminary, the exuberance of the first day was wearing off and we were becoming tired and our new blisters already needed care. We ate brown packets of MREs for supper and washed the sticky mass down with large mugs of hot chocolate before gratefully turning in to bed, where a cacophony of snoring quickly replaced any lingering conversation.

At five o'clock the next morning we woke and washed in the stream, and were told to wear running shoes, shorts and T-shirts to be ready for the first organized PT of the week. We started doing the usual push-ups, sit-ups and calisthenics. Then more push-ups and a run. During the run we sprinted from the back to the front in turn, jogged up and down the embankments, and carried each other around using fireman's lifts. Everything was designed to wear us down before building us back up again. After an hour of non-stop intensity it was, at the very least, wearing us down.

Afterwards we returned for a quick breakfast of oatmeal and coffee before grabbing our tools and heading off to dig more line. It was no surprise that line digging was going be relentless during the week, and rightly so. Jumpers are renowned for their ability to dig line efficiently across all terrain and in all conditions, and they didn't want individuals in their team who couldn't meet the high standards developed and respected over the years. We dug for ten hours, with everyone rotating between lead digger and tail-end-Charlie. The squad leaders watched us every step, and occasionally someone was picked out and told in no uncertain terms to either increase the pace or get out. Once in a while two diggers would be removed from the line to do a timed competitive speed dig, which were especially exhausting and left us struggling for breath. But our ever-present, ever-watchful training foreman gave us incentive to persevere as he encouraged us on, all the while clenching his teeth and rubbing his arms raw in apparent frustration. For most, the fear of failure overrode any feeling of pain, no matter how much the body wanted to stop and rest.

The body would get no rest anytime soon, though. The walk back to camp ended up being a speed march, which further etched burning blisters into our already torn feet. I would have preferred to jog but it wasn't allowed. Anything that made life easier wasn't allowed, just like military basic training. Back at camp there was no rest either and we did more push-ups and an assortment of other awkward physical exercises dreamed up sadists. Our backs ached, we were tired, starving, thirsty and stinking. All we wanted was food first and then rest. A cold beer would have been nice as well.

But it was not to be. We were gathered together and shown how to put our jump suits and harnesses on and told that we would be expected to do it in a minute and a half. This didn't sound too difficult until we tried it. First we had to tip the clothing out of the floppy packout bag, place the empty bag on our backs, and put the heavy woven Kevlar jacket on top. Then get into the trousers with the legs straps under the heels, providing the groin protection, and finally placing the harness, gloves, and helmet on, with the wire cage snapped closed. The plastic zippers on the jacket and trousers caused most of the problems. We were also taught how to coil our let down rope; a 100-foot taped rope that we use to rappel from trees, and always kept in the right hand leg pocket of the jump suit.

Once that particular training was completed to satisfaction we had an hour to ourselves before eating, and everyone thought that was it for the day. But that was a pipe-dream soon forgotten as we were told to haul our tools down the trail again. It was the dreaded night dig. Our muscles had stiffened and they ached continuously. We had to constantly stretch just to maintain movement. Our hands were bloody and blistered and our feet raw from traversing across the slopes. But we dug and dug and dug some more. The endless clinking of steel on stone was audible proof of our relentless effort and the long caterpillar of twinkling headlamps visible evidence to our existence. Good separation between diggers was vital in the dark to avoid accidents such as a sharp tool against a fragile head.

Barely two hours into the dig we went through a copse and had to chop down a series of small trees. As I was digging away in the middle of the group one of these trees came crashing down on the back of my neck like a karate chop, thrusting me into the dirt. The person who cut it was clearly oblivious and only my digging partner noticed it. After discarding the tree I shrugged off the initial pain and continued digging. But I knew I had been hurt. Stopping was impossible, though, and would have been the worst thing to do. I started popping Ibuprofen to numb the pain because it felt like a migraine starting up, the nerve in my neck screaming every time the pulaski met the dirt.

The effort to continue working for hours on end when every muscle fiber stresses the need for rest demands huge motivation. Halfway into the shift everyone was suffering in some form: aches, pains, blisters, and excessive lactic acid were all common. Regular stops for hydration and calorie intake were critical in enabling our bodies to continue exerting so much effort while fatigued. Minor body stance adjustments allowed periods of slight rest for isolated muscles. First one would dig from the right, then from the left, with the right foot forward, then the left. Every time we found a fraction of rest it was a brief relief from the pain. Concentrating on eliminating a specific pain is an old tactic in any endurance activity and here was no different.

We had now been out for fourteen hours. When finished the sun was just appearing over the horizon and we rested our weary backs against stumps in the early morning drizzle. Uncaring about the weather we were comfortable in the brief relaxation afforded to us as daylight slowly appeared over the mountains to the east. To end the episode we did another speed march back to camp where, unknown to us at the time, hot food was waiting. There is no substitute for fresh hot food during a spell of exhaustive work. It not only replenishes energy but does wonders for morale. As we neared the camp the smell of cooking raised our spirits and we quickened the pace, knowing the end was in sight. For a while.

Later that morning, after yet another run, we practiced tree climbing with spurs and rope. We were expected to go a minimum of 50 feet up and do a limb over, which involves disconnecting the rope from the harness briefly and wrapping it over a limb so we could continue up the tree by passing over the limbs. It's a simple confidence booster but a necessary task to master. However, in reality, once among the limbs the rope is usually discarded and jumpers generally just free climb the remainder. The rope can be used for safety again when jumpers need to work in the tree. But for practice we had to do it by the book. Some were nervous about going up the large pines and they got plenty of encouragement yelled at them from the trainers on the ground. It was fun relief from digging miles of fireline and gave our aching backs some temporary respite from the repetitive bending and swinging motion of using a pulaski.

Bob, a rookie I'd been teamed up with, was practicing a limb over when a torrent of encouragement erupted a few feet away. I watched as Bob looked down, clearly wondering who the hell this guy was, since he wasn't any of our regular trainers and actually looked more like the janitor. Nevertheless, Bob took the advice in his stride and completed his task. We later discovered the janitor was actually the operations foreman. This wasn't the only time rookies made such a mistake. So far we had met only a few of the jumpers, the rest would slowly emerge over the next few weeks, cloaked in a variety of disguises. Jumpers come in all shapes, sizes and genders, and from all sorts of wonderful backgrounds. There is no way to recognize one in the street, except for maybe a slightly bowed stance and a subtle limp from carrying huge weights around the mountains for years.

In the afternoon we practiced with crosscut saws, which was murderous on already fatigued backs and arms. These saws were double handled, six feet long and razor sharp, all sharpened and maintained by a series of meticulous jumpers. With a good sawyer at each end they cut through wood like butter. But we were tired, not yet very proficient, and made the work harder than necessary. Being much lighter than chainsaws they are the preferred tool if there was ever to be a long packout from a fire, and are mandatory within designated wilderness areas where chainsaws are only used by special permission, which is rarely forthcoming. Although requiring a heap more effort than a chainsaw, crosscuts are always a pleasure to use so long as there's a proficient partner at the other end, and they instill a terrific sense of tradition. Especially after the job is done.

The start of the fourth day brought the inevitable morning PT and another required test: the 85lb packout. We were driven to a suitably muddy hill and handed rock-filled packs by our smiling trainers. They were going to enjoy this bit. Once the requirements had been explained we proceeded to stumble and slip across the wet course in a stretching line of hunched over yellow shirts. It was soon clear who had not practiced. We had an hour and a half to complete the three-mile course, which should have been plenty even with the mud and the hills, yet there were a couple who only just finished in the time allowed. The end of the course involved a particularly muddy embankment, chosen again by sadists designed to induce further humility, because it had us all literally crawling up through the mud on our hands and knees. It was really quite unnecessary for we were all humbled already. The squad leaders did seem to get an inordinate amount of pleasure out of it.

Crawling out of our sleeping bags the following morning was a slow, painful and laborious process for most since everybody had some nagging pain. The nerve in my neck in particular provided me with a well maintained annoying headache, leaving me feeling as though I had a perpetual hangover, and my weary muscles were as stiff as they had ever been, fighting against even the slightest movement. I looked around to see if anyone noticed my difficulty but was selfishly heartened to see others also suffering, and some far worse. So it was not just my age! A few rookies were in an awful state with blisters literally covering half their feet. Cuts and bruises, strains and abrasions were commonplace. The aches the price for unrelenting effort. Yet once we dragged ourselves from our slumber most of us were ready, willing and eager to do it all over again. With grim determination to fulfill the challenge and by using sarcastic humor to shun the pain.

The last day involved another dig followed by the dreaded 120lb packout test. The last mandatory requirement that had to be done before continuing on to jump training. Most who had trained for it knew exactly what to expect, and knew that it would hurt no matter what. But those who hadn't were tormented more by the mere thought than the effort itself. The packs were lifted onto our shoulders from the back of a truck by two trainers and the straps immediately tore into our shoulders. We made the most of the time by finding somewhere to rest before the start, but standing up was a comedic struggle under so much weight.

As usual, the long-legged gazelles hurtled off up the dirt road with the shorter ones trying desperately to keep up. Walking on the hard packed road jarred every joint and care was needed to avoid hyper-extending a knee, which would have been an instant career ending injury before a career had begun. Some were constantly re-arranging their packs to try and make them more comfortable, but it was best just to forget it, get on with it, and grunt it out. There was no way that much weight was going to be comfortable. When some of us passed the halfway mark one of the trainers commented that it looked as though we were "walking in the park." We didn't know if it was a criticism or compliment so we picked up the pace regardless. I was content to finish behind a couple of the gazelles, and after ditching our packs, and feeling instantly lighter than air, we floated back up the road to give the others encouragement. The effort some people were putting in was outstanding. While my pack weighed 30lbs less than my body weight, and felt immense, there were a couple of women who only weighed ten pounds more than their pack! But they were not the last to finish, which proved the different levels of effort people were willing to expend.

With that last massive effort Hell Week was over. We were completely exhausted, sore, and yet exhilarated at completing it. We clambered into the vans with all our gear and headed back to Missoula. That's when we first noticed we hadn't showered for a week. We literally stank. The van quickly became infested with the stench of ten reeking rookies and the driver was forced to open every window available. We had no idea who he was. We thought that he was maybe another one of the janitors. But Miguel was a seasoned veteran and no stranger to the stench of firefighters. What was affecting him more was the incessant farting coming from Rick, an American Indian from the southwest, who clearly had an issue with the MREs over the previous week.

Stopping at the traffic lights as we entered Missoula we pulled alongside a Suburban full of chubby kids, each chomping down on a supersized hamburger as if it was their last meal. It looked a bit like an episode of The Simpsons. Miguel looked over and saw my amazed expression as I watched this feeding frenzy. Then laughter erupted. It was impossible not to. One vehicle contained a group that had spent the previous week undergoing an excessive amount of exercise to get fit on little food. The other was undergoing an exercise in eating itself to oblivion – and near to success.

We were still in one piece and glad to have finished the first week, but we lost two more rookies in the process. One for not pulling his weight during the line digs and another who simply said, "Fuck this for a game of soldiers," and quit.

While some term it hell week, it was, in fact, nothing like a military hell week, even if some like to think so, and anyone going through the military version would quickly realize the difference. The past rookie week was not particularly easy, but it was also not that difficult given preparation. All that was required was effort in spades for brief periods of time. Screaming drill instructors were absent and there was no forcing people past a level of exhaustion to where they would collapse, and no hazing in the middle of the night to obstruct sleep. Nor were there any insults or ridicule, and no one was ever singled out to be made an example. Apart from the night dig there was never a time when the end was not known. We never heard the old "just around the next bend" only to discover it wasn't. The week was simply to gauge if recruits were willing and able to put out a little more effort than is normally required, do so as a cohesive unit for the betterment of the whole group and, moreover, uphold the respect and credibility earned by others over the previous 50 years.

The first week was over and the next three weeks promised to be more fun. Before the new week started, however, I desperately needed to find a chiropractor to sort out my neck. Regular popping of Ibuprofen had numbed the pain a little but the seizing up of the muscles was severely hampering any movement and the constant headache was becoming tiresome. Scot, one of the squad leaders, recommended Chris, a local chiropractor who had dealt with a few jumpers before, knew of their desire to get back to work as soon as possible, and was willing to keep quiet about it. But over the past week I had been doing too much and the surrounding muscles had completely seized in an effort to protect the area. It needed time to relax over the weekend so he could have another go on Monday. Meanwhile I pondered buying shares in Advil.

All that was par for the course, however, and we all knew, just like the trainers, that we would each just have to gut it out and work through our individual aches and pains. We had two days to recover. Jump training started on Monday.

Chapter Nine

— Jump Training

When you feel you're going through hell, keep going.
– Winston Churchill

O VER THE YEARS I HAD FOUND running was a great way to sort through problems, both physical and mental. It provided time to think and was good at alleviating the occasional ache and pain, especially those nagging headaches that I was susceptible to every once in a while. But the trapped nerve was hindering everything I did, including sleep, and I couldn't rely on popping Ibuprofen or drinking pints of Guinness to conceal the pain, no matter how enjoyable the latter. So, because the previous week hadn't quite been as strenuous as some of us had expected a couple of us went for a run in the hills to expend some pent up energy, and for me to try and release the muscles in my neck. Bob and I got together on Saturday and went for a six-mile run up the narrow trails of Blue Mountain with 40lb day packs just for fun. Bob had never run with a pack before but you would never have known. The trails were uneven and rocky but we managed to keep up a steady pace, and on the flats even talked about the previous weeks activities, while looking forward to new adventures in the coming weeks. Bob later got his own back by dragging me up the long switchback trail behind Mount Sentinel, leaving me in the dust. The run did nothing for my neck, however, although drinking a few pints of Guinness later in the evening did take the edge off.

But I still longed for a more permanent fix, which would have to wait until Chris could perform his chiropractor magic.

It's amazing what a couple of days of rest can do for a group of fit young people exposed to days of rigorous exercise. First thing on Monday morning everyone appeared completely refreshed and keen to get on with training again. We were a stark difference from the blistered, dirty, exhausted group that had left the previous Friday. And it was just as well, because we all had to concentrate and absorb the various aspects of jump training. Our first jump was in two weeks. And yet, between jump training and the classroom, there was still plenty of organized PT to keep us heading towards that elusive point of peak fitness that was expected of us.

We had a full day of classwork before going to the units, which constituted the different specific elements of smokejumper parachuting, such as; emergency aircraft procedures, aircraft exits, parachute manipulation, parachute landing rolls (or PLFs[*]) and let-downs (rappelling from trees). Then, should we get to enjoy these too much there was an obstacle course designed to remove any remaining energy and lingering hubris.

Theory consisted of numerous hours of fire, fuels, weather, equipment training, parachute handling and emergency procedure classes. Getting through these, which were always in the afternoon right after lunch, and without falling asleep, was in itself a test, and one that many failed miserably. But even in the darkened room there was never any escape from observation and reprimands were quick, constant and severe. Push-ups continued to be instantaneous punishment for anything, everything and, indeed, nothing at all.

Over the previous weekend everyone had dutifully practiced getting into their jump gear. Now we had to do it while in the units for real. It was practice, practice, and more practice. And to provide incentive for improvement every time someone failed to

---

[*] Military version is called the 'Parachute Landing Fall,' hence PLF, not PLR

accomplish anything in the required time everyone in the group did push-ups. It really didn't matter what was wrong, push-ups were always there to instill memory, and had to be done while suited up in 30lbs of hot, sweaty, bulky gear, bouncing our face cages off the dirt below us. We once did push-ups because a rookie got dressed faster than anyone but then failed to help the others.

There were now just 28 left and we were split into four groups each rotating between six main jump units and the obstacle course. Our group's first unit was landings and I quickly discovered the nerve in my neck would be a major hindrance unless it was sorted soon. The landing simulator, better known as the 'slamulator,' for obvious reasons, was where we practiced dozens of PLFs time and time again, and always a major part of jump training. If you can't do this right there's little point in moving to where you'll need it.

The PLF is designed to spread landing impact over the whole length of the body instead of just pummeling the feet and ankles. Standup landings might look really cool, and be acceptable under a square canopy, but with the greater vertical descent inherent to a round canopy it's not altogether recommended. If a jumper breaks something on landing he's of no use to anyone but a physician.

After getting warmed up and practicing PLFs off three and six-foot ramps we were harnessed to the simulator, which hoisted us 20 feet into the air before hurling us to the ground forwards, backwards and sideways. The rate of descent was regulated by the unit trainers, but few seemed to be fully proficient in the technique. So that now and again we'd hear an audible "oh shit" as an unfortunate rookie ended up in a cloud of dust after creaming into the ground a little faster than expected.

Clearly it was not going too well for me because my neck pain was excruciating. On each landing the heavy helmet snapped my neck sideways as I rolled, leaving me quietly wincing in pain. Although the trainers seemed pleased enough, and Steve made a comment at one point that I was "grinning like a Cheshire cat," unaware that my grin of pleasure was actually clenched teeth in a grimace of pain.

One trick after standing up from the PLF was to twist around and straighten the risers before the trainer hoisted us up again. If the risers were twisted there was a good chance of being strangled and, with some of the trainers not overly proficient in the quirks of the machine, such an eventuality did not seem entirely implausible. But everyone soon got used to it and the whole procedure took on the appearance of being a well-choreographed exercise. Even if it was clearly not.

We rotated units and went to emergency aircraft procedures, learning what to do if the plane decided to plummet towards earth. Having parachutes meant that we would be perfectly safe once we got out of the plane, but if it was spiraling downwards getting out would prove difficult. The G-forces would hold everyone prisoner and those few able to escape would have to be very near the door. For a lesser emergency an organized mass exit could be done, and time determined whether a jumper hooked up or simply hopped out using nothing but his reserve. No word was mentioned on what was the pilot's intention, being no longer in control of a perfectly good airplane.

Letdowns followed and is often where rookies encounter most problems, being done under pressure of time with a series of steps to memorize – not a lot, but for some one more step seemed to be a problem. The unit simulates hanging from a tree and rappelling safely down to the ground. We carried a 100-foot coiled letdown rope in our leg pockets and the only reason for it not being there was because either we or a JP was already using it. Finding oneself hanging, literally, by a few spindly threads of nylon, 100 feet up a tree, would not be much fun without a rope. And it would take more than a case of beer to bribe a JP to bring one, especially with the archaic tree climbing equipment we had at the time. (In reality, few jumpers ever enjoyed climbing trees until we got comfortable and reliable harnesses, and then everyone wanted to do it.) It's no easy graft being stuck up a tree for hours on end getting shredded by branches and covered in sap. Walt once reputedly spent over six hours in a monster pine delicately removing his prized customized parachute. I can well imagine the exotic language used during that lengthy procedure.

In order to rappel we had a couple of steel rings sewn into our jump suit, called D-rings. When the end of the letdown rope was removed from the leg pocket, after first moving aside the PG bag and reserve, it was threaded through these rings in order to create friction – yes, some have forgotten this initial, easy, but crucial step, resulting in a rude awakening during an accelerated descent. The rope is then tied off to one of the tight risers of the parachute, just above the Capewell – the connector that joins the parachute webbing to the harness. Once tied off the remainder of the rope is removed from the leg pocket and dropped – forever hoping that it's long enough to reach the ground.[*]

After doing a four-point check to make sure the rope is tied off, through the rings, under the legs and in the hand, and after feeling to make sure there are no parachute cords dangling around the neck, the jumper then has to do a complete one-arm pull-up to release the loose Capewell. The second Capewell is released in the same fashion, making sure it's done in one rapid but fluid motion. The jumper then simply rappels down to safety. The idea is to do it as quickly and smoothly as possible so as not to dislodge the delicately hung canopy, and at the units the process is done under pressure of time. It needs to be a smooth procedure because there is no guarantee the canopy is stable, and any unnecessary jostling

---

[*] It was often not long enough, which is why a 150-foot rope is now provided. And in some parts of the country even that is not long enough.

may loosen its fragile hold or even break off the branches that hold it. In this instance the remainder of the journey is accomplished in exciting freefall, with the added jollies of bouncing off numerous, steadily thickening, branches on the way down. If the canopy is not stable, however, the jumper can also tie off to both a riser and the tree if they're lucky enough to be close enough to the trunk or any major branch. The whole procedure is practiced repeatedly until it becomes second nature, because thoughtful logic sometimes gets lost when people are swaying high above the ground, held only by a gossamer-thin piece of nylon and a stick. So practice, practice, practice, attempts to make such life-saving actions second nature.

Once the single rope letdown was mastered a double rope letdown was explained. This is for those really amusing trees over 150 feet tall grown just for our pleasure. Despite heavy logging for most the last century there are still a surprising number of them left around the forests of the northwest United States, tending to grow especially well around our jump spots. This very necessary second rope, then, is hopefully being provided by an amenable JP, who has to be already on the ground and willing and able to climb the tree to hand it over. Quite simply, the two ropes are then tied together using a basic reef, or square, knot. The trick on reaching this knot is to feed it cleanly through the rings on the jump suit. Not just a few rookies have managed to get well and truly stuck on this knot and been left hanging, which immediately brings home the fact that if things are to go wrong, as they most assuredly will, it's better they go wrong during training. No matter how much we trained, though, the cluster and the brain fart were an unfortunate, though thankfully infrequent, occurrence in our lives.

The next unit was parachute emergency procedures, covering both major and partial malfunctions. For these we were coupled to an overhead steel cable 20 feet long strung between two 10-foot stanchions. We would leap off the decking and, hopefully, do the correct emergency procedure for the specific malfunction being yelled into our ears. For the mass exit everyone slammed into each other as if skittles and our helmets smashed together like in a Newton's Cradle, leaving us dangling helplessly on the cable as though a bunch of Michelin Men. It created some amusement in an otherwise extremely serious unit. The trainers seemed to especially enjoy the mass exit procedure.

Exit training started with everyone learning the correct door position on the ground. Limited room around the aircraft door and strict safety procedures meant that everyone had to know exactly where to be at any given moment, and this process makes it easier for the spotters to monitor everything going on. Once everyone understood the basic procedure we were led 40 feet up the clanging steel steps of the jump tower. The tower, resembling a section of an aircraft fuselage, has doors on either side that can be modified to simulate the different exits for a variety of aircraft. There were four main types of exit: standup, step, sitting and a fuck-up. Before leaping for the first time each jumper was hooked to one of two cables that ran from above the tower to a dirt ramp 50 yards away.

If something went wrong, falling from 40 feet wasn't enough to kill us but it would probably hurt, and just about everyone was mildly apprehensive about this first tower exit, but mostly because we had to be seen to do it right. It's also the unit that everyone watches because it's the most exciting and consistently the most fun. Up high we were now in full view of everyone in the units, which inevitably added to the pressure. After two jumpers were hooked up the spotter went through the procedure as though it was a real jump run, further building the apprehension and excitement. Looking down from the stationary open door to the trainers 40 feet below was slightly disconcerting for the first time and it demanded a leap of confidence to get out the door, for what is basically an unnatural act. As I leapt out I kept falling for what seemed forever before the straps suddenly tightened and halted my fall, sending me spinning and sliding sideways along the cable towards the ground 50 yards away. Once this initial jump was out of the way the remainder were a piece of cake, and training quickly became a lot of fun – even with those incessant push-ups.

We practiced three different exits, doing two of each type, while getting videotaped and critiqued for correct position, or form, each time – they should have held up score-cards. The most disconcerting was the sitting position simulating an exit from a small Cessna, where we simply slipped off the side of the door and literally just fell. Leaping vigorously in a stand-up position from a large door seemed to be the much preferred method.

Correct exits, without question, are *the* most important part of the jump sequence. A bad exit can mean the difference between making the jump spot or not and, therefore, between pain or pleasure and, literally, between life and death Peer ridicule can be painful enough but smashing a knee into a rock permanently more so. A poor exit is also not very pretty, and every exit we did for the next three weeks was videotaped for all to see, creating some great conversational material and a continual torrent of reprimands from Walt, who wanted nothing less than perfection.

Jumping through a 105-knot slipstream in the correct position is vital to a good exit so we consistently tried to leap with more and more vigor. A rigid, bent forward, body position is required to remain stable while falling before the static line pulls the lines and canopy from the parachute container. Having an unstable position opens the chance of getting twisted, or coming down inverted with feet caught in the parachute cords, which isn't nice either. Nor is getting a static line wrapped around the neck – although with the plane traveling at 105-knots the snappy end is probably pretty darn quick. Such accidents do still happen.

After an exit, and once on the ground, we'd disconnect our harness from the cable and run the risers back to the tower using a letdown rope. As with everything else we did, there was never any walking, so running while dressed in thickly padded jumpsuits and helmets, with a bulky PG bag swaying between our legs like an old cow's udder was quite comical. Then waddling up the steps of the tower to practice again drained us further. Whenever we finished this unit we were always drenched with sweat, but exhilarated.

When we had mastered the basic procedure the spotter started to put mental obstacles in front of us. So instead of slapping us out he would shout: "GO," which was an incorrect command but one that tricked a few into exiting anyway. The great laugh was when the second jumper also left, because he would have just screwed himself royally. Such things, while being fun, were designed to get us to listen, watch, and understand the correct commands, and not react incorrectly to obscure movements or shouts. The worst thing that could happen if a jumper chose not to leave the aircraft, for whatever reason, would be to fly another pattern, whereas leaving the aircraft prematurely might have dire consequences. Not only would the jump spot be missed but the jumper might also be at the wrong altitude, which is easy in mountainous terrain. Finding you were only 300 feet above the ground instead of 1,500 would be an unpleasant surprise – though not for long.

Red ribbons were also covertly attached to a jumper's harness to denote a series of malfunctions for which the proper corrective procedure would have to be performed. The trainers had particular fun doing this, always screwing with us in a variety of ways. If a rookie failed to perform correctly he would be asked to "explain why you are now a deceased rookie?" And be rewarded with 20 push-ups as a reminder to stay alive next time. The spotter in the tower often tricked rookies out the door too early. Other times he would pretend to miss the spot entirely, placing his outstretched arm across the door to stop anyone from leaving, only to see, on more than one occasion, a rookie actually fight his way past his arm to exit the door anyway. Needless to say, anyone who did got quite the bollocking.

The units are located in the corner of a field a few yards from Missoula's main airport runway, and I can only imagine what the taxiing airplane passengers thought as they looked from their little windows to see dozens of strangely padded creatures waddling around in the field. It was almost impossible to walk normally no matter how much we got used to all the gear. The motorcycle helmet, with its wire-caged mask, completed the image of an alien invasion in this quiet corner of Montana.

From exits we went straight to the obstacle course. While it was pleasant getting out of our sweaty jumpsuits for a while, we were about to be exerting more energy than we had on any unit so far. The course wasn't exceptionally long but doing it at a sprint was exhausting. First there was an eight-foot wall to vault over, a trampoline to somersault onto, overhead bars to traverse, numerous ramps for PLFs, a rope over a rank, stinking pond, more PLFs and a sprint on wood chips to the finish. The requirement was to finish under a minute and a half by the end of the week, so we had to give it everything on each attempt, doing it twice on each visit to the units. After the obstacle course we did the ever-present push-ups followed by pull-ups and sit-ups to exhaustion, then climbed ropes before finishing with sprinted laps around the field. At times it felt as though my lungs would explode, and if we were doing it as a Northwest flight was leaving we would inhale a lungful of lovely Avgas to boot.

When a couple of us managed 22 pull-ups, twice that of most, we felt quite pleased with ourselves. Then Gary, the base manager, casually walked over and eased out a quick 26 just to remind us of where we were and who we were dealing with. We could do little to impress and our muscles were almost done for.

The trainers, while being professional, constantly behaved as though they didn't really care if we succeeded or not, seeming to almost relish failure. We assumed it was due to a tough course requiring a certain level of failure to justify its toughness.

Finishing the obstacle course with nothing but sweat dripping from us was a relief, because a couple of unlucky rookies fell from the overhand rope into what looked, and smelled, like sewage. It must have been embarrassing scrambling out of the putrid looking sludge in full view of every other rookie and trainer on the field. Such things weren't easily forgotten and everyone knew that an unfortunate nickname gained here might last forever.

The final unit was parachute manipulation in the basement of the loft, where toggles hung from the ceiling were connected to a computer with a video monitor, and as we pulled on the toggles to simulate turns the monitor showed the simulation of our descent. The video game was a good training tool that taught us the basics of parachute manipulation and the value of staying inside the wind cone – the airspace we had to stay within in order to land in the designated jump spot. The main difference between smokejumping and sport jumping is obviously the terrain, the jump spots are always different, always smaller, invariably surrounded by trees, rocks and snags, and all waiting to make mincemeat of a mistake.

Throughout the week we continued the routine of morning units and afternoon classes, so that by Friday we were so stiff that some of us had trouble hopping up onto a barstool. Everyone had a stiff neck from the slamulator and sore arms from doing dozens of one-armed pull-ups on the letdown tower. Joints ached from pounding around the obstacle course, a few untidy landings and the daily exhaustive PT.

By the end of the week, for the most part, we were starting to 'get it.' But to progress to jumping we needed a satisfactory score on each unit and it was expected that if we were failing in one we improved in our own time. So during the weekend rookies could be seen practicing exits in all sorts of places; tables replaced the landing ramps and tower, and equipment was sprawled everywhere as people practiced getting suited up. For some a doorway was a suitable place to practice and they could be seen practicing exits all over town; bars and coffee shops being no exception. Missoulians seemed somewhat bemused by this strange behavior and largely ignored it. Tourists probably thought Montanans a weird bunch.

I was doing okay on everything but exits. The tower was fun but exiting created a severe jarring pain in my neck. Having my neck cracked every other evening by the chiropractor still left me swallowing more and more Ibuprofen to numb the pain and lessen the stiffness. Walt saw that I was having problems and asked if I needed to see a doctor. But that was quick ticket out. No doctor would allow anyone to continue with an injury, and we'd already lost one of the girls because she had a shoulder injury and couldn't manage the monkey bars on the obstacle course. After seeing her ousted so easily it was well understood by all that there was no leeway for injuries. It was basically; get injured, admit it, and say "bye-bye." I wasn't going to admit it and hoped that Chris could alleviate the pain at some point. Despite the nagging discomfort I was still having more fun than I'd had in years.

That second weekend saw us in totally different spirits. We had progressed through the exhausting grunt stage to half-way through jump training. All that was left was some fine-tuning at the units before having our first jump on Wednesday. Everyone was naturally getting anxious about the jumps, but were excited to still be there, and Friday night gave us a chance to get to know each other better, while relaxing and telling tall tales in the bars around Missoula.

Missoula is a liberal college town in western Montana. Many say it's not part of Montana at all, and in recent years they're right. In the early '90s, though, it was a mostly eclectic town, devoid of politics, full of jocks, cheerleaders, doctors, students, academics, loggers, mill workers, forest workers, nurses, tourists and anyone else stopping by, all enjoying the atmosphere of a friendly western town. Missoula's fortunate location, built because of the railroad, makes it a mecca for outdoor activities from skiing to mountain biking, parasailing to hiking, and climbing to kayaking. Fleece was always the spoilt man's clothing of choice while Carhart's were the blue collar worker's clothing of practicality. Both could be seen on the steep slopes of Snowbowl.

I was surprised to see that most of the more youthful rookies were not yet picking up the arrogant 'para' attitude common to many in the military fraternity, with: 'tennis balls under the armpits and Y-fronts too small.' They remained confident, though, and were still trying to pick up every piece of skirt in town. But hadn't yet realized that most of the girls had seen it all before and weren't that impressed. However, one rookie who had a tendency to brag a little too much about his limited ability was told by a few veteran jumpers, in no uncertain terms, to remove his "fucking" smokejumper T-shirt – because he wasn't yet a "fucking" jumper, and "fucking" wouldn't be if he continued this way. He seemed to be more interested in acting the part and everyone had picked up on it Such things don't go down well with any jumper and it made the rest of us look bad by association. He didn't last long.

Chapter Ten

— Jump Week

If you close your eyes trooper, every jump is a night jump.

— Unknown Para

B Y MONDAY MORNING EVERYONE had recovered from their celebratory hangovers and were anxious to continue with training. This was the big week and Walt spelt out the plans for the next few days and told us individually which units needed work before our first jump on Wednesday. After a couple of days to relax, the units on Monday and Tuesday went extremely well. No one had any great problems although some needed a few minor tweaks to lift them up to Walt's high standard. We ran the obstacle course for last time on Monday and were expected to put out maximum effort to achieve our individual fastest time. Not surprisingly, just about everyone did.

On Tuesday a long run up in the hills saw us as a real team. As with everything else, those who had prepared found it easy, while those who hadn't rightly suffered. But everyone managed to do it in their own way. Keith, short, and built like the proverbial brick shit house, earned the temporary nickname Hershall for his efforts. He wasn't a distance runner but he certainly inspired the look of a sprinter as he closed toward the finish, urged on by Gary. The run was a team effort with everyone encouraging everyone. We had each encountered bad days and knew we would again. But those days would be easier with the support of others; camaraderie.

Tuesday afternoon saw everyone getting a little edgy and that nervous energy was spent constantly checking and rechecking our equipment, making it ready for the following day; that leg straps on kevlar pants were tightened and knotted, bunched up shoulder pads were flattened and re-sown into jackets, PG bags were readied and snaps checked for cracks, and fresh chin padding was sewn into face cages. The next day wasn't the time for equipment failure. Everything was arranged and rearranged in a nervous ritual until it became a subconscious act.

We had a couple of hours of down time in the afternoon to wander around the base and explore what was going on outside of rookie training. So far we had only met our trainers, but there were many other jumpers around. Some were in the loft repairing and packing parachutes, more were in the manufacturing room building PG and packout bags, others were constructing cargo boxes in the loadmaster area ready for the upcoming fire season, and another dozen were on assignment in New Mexico. Everyone was active and doing something. There was a distinct vibrant energy in the air and the fire news from New Mexico made us aware of what this job was all about.

Later in the afternoon the anticipated jump list was pinned to the message board. We were assigned single man sticks to start with and everyone studied the board repeatedly as if it would mysteriously change before our eyes. The list brought closer the realization of what we were doing and our nerves peaked again, sending us back to reorganize equipment for the umpteenth time.

That evening there were few rookies in the bars and those that were decided to make an early night of it, despite the attempts of some determined veterans to keep them out until the early hours to test their mettle – or foolhardiness. This was one time we ignored their goading. No one wanted to throw up on the aircraft the next day and earn the infamous nickname 'Puker.'

As soon as I woke up the following morning I looked out to check the weather. It was a little cloudy but otherwise fine, there would be no rain. We were due to jump at Blue Mountain, on the flats below the trails where I had done all my pre-rookie training, in a large open meadow well away from large trees and fences. When I arrived at the base each rookie was already going though his personal kit again and laying it out in readiness for suiting up. After roll call Walt called everyone to the canteen to go over the final briefing and his expectations for the jump. The pilots also gave their input, explained their procedures, and wished us well. The Shorts Sherpa was parked on the ramp in front of the ready room where everyone's kit was ready to go The plane was fueled and the pilots were doing a pre-flight, and grinning at the nervous group of onlookers as they removed the rear door.

The Sherpa is often referred to as the 'Flying Winnebago.' Its fuselage is boxy and on first glance one would think that it could never fly. But its shape provides a false impression because the fuselage actually enhances its flight characteristics and the high wing design makes for a more than suitable jump aircraft, albeit an ugly one. The Forest Service's fleet of Short Sherpa aircraft were originally U.S. light military aircraft, designated C-23s.

Looking over to the south we could see that the sky over Blue Mountain was clear and blue, and the spot crew soon radioed back saying that the wind was a mere three miles an hour from the west. Everything was ready, everyone was ready, we were eager to go.

The moment we had anticipated arrived when the loudspeaker clicked and erupted with the words, "First load. SUIT UP!"

Eyes got wide, hearts pounded, stomachs sunk a little and bladders rushed off to be emptied. The remainder jogged to their bins and began getting into their jump gear. There were plenty of folks milling around, some there to help and some just watching; admin people, warehouse workers, pilots and janitors, and even a lucky group of tourists on a guided tour. Once all zipped up and harnessed, parachutes were put on the rookies' backs, Capewells were snapped and reserves clipped to chests. Spotters carried out pre-jump checks on everyone, making sure leg straps were under the heels of their boots and tight, PG bag straps visible and ready. They checked pins on the reserve, that the main chute's Capewells were encased and snapped close, and that the static line was routed correctly. Finally making sure each jumper had their letdown rope, gloves, helmet, and PG bag. Once in a while they would check someone for a puke bag.

It had taken less than five minutes to get the twelve rookies ready to board the aircraft. The rest of us watched in anticipation, knowing it would be our turn next. In their jump gear they walked, or waddled, the few feet across the ramp, up the steps and into the aircraft, each sitting on the floor facing the rear door between the legs of the person behind. The props spurted to life and a sickly cloud of jet-A vapor filled the air. The engines growing to a steady crescendo as the plane rocked as it was held on its brakes, like a racehorse in the start gate. The ramp manager, face hidden behind the dark-visor of his air force helmet, looked around, saw it was clear and motioned the plane forward in one fluid, overly-dramatic gesture as though he was directing a Tomcat off a carrier deck.

A few minutes later we watched as the Sherpa raced down the runway, its whining Pratt and Whitney turboprops heaving it gently into the Montana sky. Once in the air it banked right to head straight toward Blue Mountain a couple of miles away. After a few passes over the spot the first parachute was seen to pop open, one of the trainers was testing the air and showing the way down. As if there was another way.

The rest of us were getting a head start on the next suit up command and already had our yellow fire shirts on with the empty packout bags sitting limp on our backs. Anxious but determined to get this done the bathroom seemed to be the most popular place as rookies relieved themselves after numerous cups of coffee. Then we heard the now familiar sound of the Sherpa and looked out to see it just touching down, a quick wisp of burned rubber as the wheels hit the tarmac. We instantly wondered if everyone had jumped. Was it carrying an embarrassed rookie back home?

"Second load. SUIT UP!"

There it was. Finally. The moment we had been waiting for. I jogged to my bin where all my gear was laid out in order and ready to go, grabbed my jacket and placed it over my packout bag, pulling it tight over my shoulders in order to close the zip. I then took my jump pants, swung the straps over each shoulder, stepped into the heel straps, and bent stiffly in the thick Kevlar to zip up both legs, taking care not to rush and compromise the finicky plastic zippers. Lifting the webbing harness off a hook I swung it over my shoulders, making sure not to slap one of the many bystanders in the face with its heavy hardware. Now I was ready to receive my main chute and Geno arrived to place it on my back as I bent forward. I reached behind, straightened a little and held it in place as he snapped the chute's hardware into the Capewells on my harness. He then picked up the reserve and clipped it to my chest, checking that the pins holding the drogue spring were solidly in place. Then, loosening the yellow static line from my pack, he passed it over my left shoulder and slid the clip into the elastic on my reserve. Finished, he gave me a good hard slap on the back.

"Good to go," Geno said, smiling. "Have a good one."

I picked up my helmet, gloves and PG bag and waited in line for a pre-jump check from the spotter. While waiting, I watched one of the other rookies walk past, oblivious to a trail of blue nylon dragging behind him. Some of the veterans were joking with each other as he sauntered out toward the ramp.

"Hey! ROOKIE! Need a check?!" Someone yelled.

He turned, embarrassed, and walked back to the ready room where one of the veterans spun him around and pulled out a large wad of material from his parachute.

"You won't need this," the vet said. Then looking around: "Hey John, did you pack this chute? Except for this poor sucker everyone knows not to grab your packs."

The rookie looked a little concerned as a wad of parachute material was pulled away from his back and casually discarded onto the floor. He looked at John who had a sheepish grin on his face. Was it a knowing grin, or a guilty grin, he wondered?

"Don't worry. You won't need all of it," John said.

By this time the rookie didn't quite know what to believe, but in an attempt not to look stupid he got in line for his check, placing a surreptitious hand behind him to feel for more loose material.

We were wearing about 65lbs of gear. The suits were hot and sweaty and reeked from years of stale perspiration. The bulk made moving difficult so we lay in the morning sun on the tarmac while the Sherpa taxied back to the ramp and shut down its left engine. Jim, the spotter, hopped out and grabbed the pile of deployment bags from the previous load. Walking into the ready room he dumped them on a trolley and grabbed the next jump list. Once outside again he read the list aloud in reverse order to let us know our loading sequence. I was number eight.

The ramp manager had already dragged the steel steps to the Sherpa door and we clambered up and found our spots on the floor inside the aircraft. It was hot and stuffy inside with a faint sickly smell of jumper sweat and jet-A, making a few rooks immediately nauseous. Some were already looking for puke bags while holding their Nomex gloves over their faces. Sitting with our legs apart on the floor was cramped and uncomfortable and we couldn't see anything but sky out of the little square windows higher up on the fuselage, and not being able to see out the windows wasn't helping those with airsickness.

With us all finally settled, and sweating profusely, the steps were hauled away. Then as soon as the spotter climbed aboard the left engine restarted, sending another fresh plume of jet-A into the cabin. The engines roared briefly and we started to move.

We bounced along the taxiway for what seemed like miles before reaching the runway, inviting the obvious remark, "We're going to have to go faster than this to take off." But no one was listening. We were all visualizing everything we had to do; from snapping our cages shut to keeping our feet and knees together.

"Helmets and gloves," Jim motioned above the engine noise.

We put on our helmets and gloves and waited as the engines reached a crescendo. Then we all slid in unison as the acceleration jerked us toward the back of the plane. After a few hundred feet the plane lifted off and we watched as the ground dropped away from the open doorway. At 800 feet we removed our helmets and gloves and jostled around to get more comfortable, vying for window space to get an early view of the jump spot.

In a few minutes we were circling the spot and could see parachutes littering the ground below. In the center of the spot was a large orange square and nearby a windsock on a pole. The plane lined up with the orange square and Jim threw a couple of colored streamers out the door, one red, one yellow. We never saw either of them. We were supposed to watch them to the ground but couldn't see them against the multi-colored backdrop below us. Then someone thought they saw something off the tip of the wing and we all strained to look. But there was nothing.

The assistant spotter timing the streamer's descent shouted, "SIXTY-NINE!"

Jim unwrapped another set of streamers and talked the pilot onto the wind line. Tapping off the seconds with his hand he then threw another set out the door. These we saw. They were falling a little to the east of the spot and visible just under the left wing of the aircraft as it circled around the spot, eventually landing a few yards from the main trail that snaked its way up to the top of Blue Mountain.

"First one. HOOK UP!" Jim shouted, beckoning a rookie.

The first rookie walked forward. He already had his helmet, gloves and PG bag strapped on. Since being first he had never removed them for fear of not being able to get them back on in time. He clipped his static line onto the upright cable opposite the door and stepped forward, his left foot a few inches from the door. From our position further forward in the aircraft we heard a few muffled commands, watched him shuffle into the door, recoil, and leap. The air pressure in the cabin changed for a fleeting second, creating a momentary sucking sound, then he was gone.

As the plane circled allowing the next rookie to get ready we watched as the first floated gently to the ground. Then before we knew it another was sucked out into the wide blue. The cable rattling as the static line reached the end of its tether, becoming taut as it dragged out the flimsy nylon that would keep the jumper alive. The rest of us realized that this was going to be quick work and started getting our gear together. I shoved on my helmet and snapped the cage shut. Put on my Nomex flight gloves and zipped up my jump jacket under my chin. I then tightened my leg straps so that I could hardly walk and snapped my PG bag to the plastic clips on my harness. Soon there was no longer anyone in front of me and I was motioned toward to the back of the plane.

I have the all-important static line clip in my hand and snap it cleanly onto the vertical cable, inserting the pin before turning to let the assistant spotter see that I'm clear of obstructions. The assistant spotter watches my every move and removes a little more static line from the rubber bands and shouts: "YOU'RE CLEAR!"

Jim briefs me to the conditions of the jump: "We're at fifteen hundred and flying into the wind. Only three miles an hour on the ground and everyone is making it in. Keep tight. Any questions?"

I look at him through my cage and shake my head. As the plane banks onto final I can see the spot looming up ahead, just below the tilted wing. The ground is a long way down and I try to concentrate on the horizon and remember the procedure. Jim grabs my left foot and places it into the door, signaling we are on final. A few seconds later:

"GET READY!"

I slide my hands down to grip both sides of the door, palms inwards, shuffle my right foot to get a better stance, and recoil.

SLAP!

I heaved myself out the door and immediately got smacked by the slipstream, sending me spinning uncontrollably. In fact, I think I felt the fuselage scrape by my helmet, but with my eyes clasped firmly shut I never saw it, I had dizzying white spots in front of my eyes from the sudden excruciating pain in my neck. Nevertheless, after shouting off the seconds my chute opened on four and gave me a comforting jerk. Still a little dizzy I looked up to make sure the material was where it was supposed to be and immediately noticed the twisted lines above my head. I kicked to reverse the spin, pried open the risers as wide as I could and managed to stop the spin reversing in the opposite direction. Now able to steer my chute I concentrated on the little yellow square below me. I didn't have much opportunity to look at the surroundings because I was concentrating on everything that I had to do, but I'm sure the view was quite spectacular as I floated down in complete silence. This first jump, however, was not spectacular.

At two hundred feet I turned into the wind, kept my knees and feet together, and descended neatly about thirty feet away from the orange panel for my PLF, right among a group of earlier rookies.

Ground rush was something I was already familiar with and I was determined to do the roll right even if the preceding bit had been dreadful. I did, and hopped up onto my feet before the canopy had deflated, along with a piercing headache. My joy was short-lived.

"HUBBLE! The landing was okay Hubble. But what the hell was that?" Walt bellowed, looking up to the plane overhead.

Clearly it wasn't good or I wouldn't have had the red paint on my helmet. Kind of gave the game away I suppose.

Walt stared at me intently and said, "The next had better be a good one," before lifting his cap to scratch his balding head and clenching his teeth as he strode away to scold someone else.

I removed my sweaty gear, collected my parachute and stuffed it all into my packout bag. After hauling it to the center of the jump spot I waited in mild trepidation for my next bollocking, which I knew would be in front of everyone else during the post-jump debriefing. However, I soon realized I wasn't the only one who had messed up royally, even if mine was probably the most spectacular screw up of the day for that portion if it. Although, thankfully, it wasn't the balls-up that received the most sustained ridicule because only a couple of people had witnessed it. Problem was, those who did notice it were the only two that mattered. The two with the loudest bark, the two who governed our destiny, and neither were likely to forget it.

The rookies never ridiculed each other, however. That would have been blatantly hypocritical, for at this early stage all of us were making mistakes and we were each due to make many more before the week and, indeed, the month was over. Although our misfortunes were often given due appreciation at the bar later, causing raucous laughter to erupt after countless excuses and even more outrageous denials. One who received most attention that day was Mark, who hadn't done anything wrong except for almost landing astride one of the free-grazing cows. Knowing Mark, the cow would probably have come off worst. He was one tough mother. For a little while Walt affectionately called him Butterball, possibly being the only one who could. But even Walt left it alone after a while.

Back at the base and in the canteen[*] we sat in embarrassed terror as we watched video footage of our landings. I was greatly relieved that there was no permanent proof of my exit, if indeed that's what it was, apart, of course, from the subtle scrape down the side of the plane. No one had been hurt today but Walt was adamant, and made it quite clear, that we all needed to do better.

My exit problem stemmed mainly from that damned nerve in my neck. Every sudden movement pinched it and my body would rebel by instantly seizing up. It was a completely involuntary response. So that evening I arranged yet another chiropractor visit and after some heat treatment and electrical stimulation Chris managed to relieve the pain a little, but it was still far from being perfect. These visits were costing me dearly and since I hadn't been paid the bank balance was dwindling fast. I sincerely hoped it wasn't going to be an ongoing problem, with me paying a portion of my wages to Chris each week just to maintain my job.

---

[*] Yes, Missoula SMJ base had a canteen in the early '90s, but it was closed down after a 'manager' virtually bankrupted it. Then, in typical reactionary FS splendor, instead of firing the manager and getting someone to run it properly, they gave her another job and closed the canteen. In effect, punishing the jumpers, because the canteen was brilliant, serving breakfast, lunch and dinner to everyone, not just those living in the barracks.

Chapter Eleven

— Classroom

War is the province of uncertainty, three-fourths of those things upon which action in war must be calculated, are hidden more or less in the clouds of great uncertainty.

– Carl von Clausewitz

U P TO NOW WE'D BEEN CONCENTRATING on the exciting and more enjoyable aspects of smokejumping; namely parachuting. But in all reality this romanticized piece of silk just provides smokejumpers with a glorified means of transport for their primary role as wildland firefighters. True, the learning curve and initial expense to train individuals with no prior parachuting experience might be higher than driving or walking, but the unarguable advantage of getting manpower and resources to fires more quickly has never failed to justify this investment. Although jump training, and its requirement for a higher level of fitness, to offset injuries, is a major portion of rookie training, understanding fire behavior is still by far the most important aspect of training. So to meet this requirement, intermingled with running hills, circuit training, obstacle courses and parachute training, we spent a great deal of our time in the classroom learning, or being refreshed on, the many ways of fighting fire.

Every single USFS wildland firefighter is mandated to take a very basic fire training class before heading out onto the fireline. New jumpers are expected to already possess that knowledge from working on previous crews, and so rookie fire training progresses deeper into the realm of fire behavior; learning more about how weather, topography and fuels directly and indirectly affect fire, and how a variety of different fires can best be fought, or not, by examining and critiquing a myriad different examples. To most of us this was common sense, but this was a government job, with an inherent cover your ass (CYA) policy, and accordingly we were expected to pass adolescent multiple choice tests at the end of each session in order to satisfy a paperwork trail. So that our esteemed overseers would be completely absolved in the event that anyone of us ever did anything exceptionally stupid.

Most of these common sense classes were extremely boring, tediously monotonous, and based on little more than rote learning thanks to the inane popularity of Microsoft PowerPoint, a largely misused tool that directly inhibits actual learning – the learning of the reason why – in favor of overt repetition to ingrain specific answers to simple questions using the accepted, and only the accepted, syntax. Remembering rote-learned answers will never guarantee or provide a basis for intelligence, and yet these classes, and the plethora of credentials they provide, by definition, state that those who answer correctly are entitled to control people and fire in preference over longstanding firefighters with many many more years of valued experience. It is knowing and understanding the procedures necessary to reach those answers that is important. The basic purpose of learning is completely lost with modern lazy teaching aids that do little more that drill how to pass exams.

It had been years since I had taken any test whatsoever and the system now in use reminded me of the question and answer sessions in the comics when I was a child. Each question had only three or four possible answers and with a little basic common sense one could usually fathom the answers even with no foreknowledge of the subject. The tests seemed to be designed so that one had to be a complete idiot to fail them. And while, through life, I have mostly fallen into that category, I nevertheless always passed with the exact same scores as everyone else.

Fire behavior has evolved to become a highly studied science, a direct response to the tragedy at Mann Gulch in 1949. So there is a lot we now understand that previously we did not, thanks to decades of information gathering through fire-science experiments, first-hand experience and, most of all, from tragedy. However, if we are honest, for all that we do know there's still an awful lot that we don't. Nothing is guaranteed. To acknowledge and understand that fact is paramount to firefighter survival. While we might be smarter than we were a decade or two ago, we are still incalculably dumber compared to where we should be a decade to two hence, so long as we do not get complacent and think ourselves brilliant. For now, though, there is a specific list of known variables associated with fire, the trick being to recognize them, but more importantly, to thoroughly understand them. And at the same time be aware of those unforeseen variables that will inevitably always pop-up out of the blue to throw a wrench into even the best laid plans, and create a good old-fashioned clusterfuck. Mix fire and people and you have a perfect environment for this, a Petri dish almost, for Murphy's Law.

People have always died in fires and always will for as long as we fight them. Every time someone does, another scientist steps forward wearing an 'I told you so' t-shirt and carrying a briefcase full of data that prophesied that specific event, but of course only now mentions it in hindsight. 'Specific' being important, of course, because two events, or incidents, are rarely identical, and therein lies the problem. However, most events don't need a scientist to evaluate the variables, anyone who has fought fire for any length of time can explain the errors, miscalculations and misjudgments for the tragedy that has just taken place. But being in a CYA-driven bureaucracy we are forced to take heed of all these numbers and act accordingly. And God help us if we don't.

We didn't know yet, but we had just scratched the surface of what was about to happen a few years later after a few more people died. It's a strange concept that those surviving a tragedy, even, on occasion, those completely detached from it, ultimately get blamed for it and suffer the consequences, whereas those who die rarely collect any blame for their actions. Humans have an innate ability to be quite stupid at times and, in extreme stressful situations, that stupidity can often be compounded with disastrous consequences. To instigate a concept that ignores inherent human stupidity in favor of data induced protectionism is flawed. Relying solely on figures does nothing to help the situation. Especially, God forbid, if the data has been willfully manipulated to support a hypothesis, or is simply flawed. The more data firefighters are forced to collect and analyze before fighting a fire the less fires will ever be fought. Whether that is good or bad obviously depends on the fire, and the perception of each might well change in hindsight. But practical situations demand, by their very nature, practical common sense training, designed primarily from experience and while supported by accurate science. Not training instigated by bureaucrats waging a protectionist campaign designed to do little but cover their ass. Otherwise firefighters will inevitably become fixated on collecting, logging and communicating data to the detriment of action and common sense.

Around the turn of the century smokejumpers jumped a few fires where more firefighters were involved in collecting and transmitting data than were involved in actually fighting the fire, and little was thought of this imbalance by an academic-minded IC until it was brought to his attention that the reason why the fire was still active was because only three out of eight people were doing any productive work. Two of the pseudo-scientists collecting data were even oblivious to the dangers of wandering about without any lookouts on a steep, heavily fuel-laden hillside directly above a fire that had not yet been contained.

Ultimately most firefighters do the job because they enjoy it, with the added thrill for many being the inherent risk, as much as there is risk these days, and which, in itself, is largely subjective. This subjective regard to risk inevitably also alters with maturity and it is no coincidence that fighter pilots and front-line troops are always recruited from the immortally-minded young. Removing known risk is obviously important to everyone, and should be paramount in any activity, but removing all risk is impossible and would, anyway, remove the fundamental enjoyment that most people associate with the job and the life that revolves around it. Some people like to work in banks, some like to ride bulls, others like to join an elite, gung-ho, testosterone-charged groups and fight an enemy. Many people over the preceding years have accused smokejumpers of being adrenaline junkie'd lunatics, but they are nothing of the kind. Nothing would scare me more than to work in a bank, and to know that I would spend the rest of my working life caged up in a cubicle. To this day I cannot work in an office. In necessity I have tried and hated every single moment of it. Others do it with a passion. People are different.

So, all the rookies now being in the classroom, and to mitigate all past transgressions, we were learning about fuel loading, aspect ratios, heat transfer, complex weather systems, ignition points, topographical idiosyncrasies, and, of course, the ten standard fire orders and eighteen watch out situations, which were repeatedly repeated in rote fashion at every opportunity. The problem of remembering facts and figures: kings, queens, dates, fire orders and such, is that, in reality, it provides little, and rarely serves any practical purpose in real situations. If firefighters followed each rule and guideline to the letter, basically working to rule, the forests would be ablaze every summer and the valleys thick with smoke for months on end. Even within this group of experienced firefighters we could only hope to recite half of the list, and indeed the only one that meant anything to anyone was the final order to "fight fire aggressively!"

According to the National Interagency Fire Center the "Ten Standard Fire Orders were developed in 1957 by a task force studying ways to prevent firefighter injuries and fatalities. Shortly after the Standard Fire Orders were incorporated into firefighter training, the 18 Situations That Shout Watch Out were developed. These 18 situations are more specific and cautionary than the Standard Fire Orders and described situations that expand the 10 points of the Fire Orders. If firefighters follow the 10 Standard Fire Orders and are alerted to the 18 Watch Out Situations, much of the risk of firefighting can be reduced."

Trying to remember that little lot, even when not being chased up a hill by a fire, was impossible for many of our obviously feeble brains. So little cards were produced with the ten rigid rules and eighteen flexible guidelines neatly printed out, so that before we were forced to gallop up a hill, getting licked by a wall of fast gaining orange flames, we could pull out the card and realize that we hadn't done the right thing, and now needed to cover our asses.

As if to prove the fallibility of these lists, or at least the mistaken value placed on them, by analysts, administrators, and a few anal-retentive firefighters with heaps of paper credentials, the order of the list has changed twice, and is now, ironically, though not surprisingly, back to exactly where it was at its inception in 1957. That's not to say it's all been a complete waste, or that the preceding years of experience from 1957 have been forgotten, for it most certainly is not and they haven't, something is obviously needed, but as a guide, not a command. And certainly not as a tool to be used in later lawsuits spouting blame, which inevitably they always are.

Analysts, pseudo fire experts and administrators will forever search for utopia in fire orders, witness the fact that they constantly change. However, those on the ground well know that that's impossible. But that won't stop administrators from implementing CYA reactionary rules after every incident that results in an injury, often after misinterpreting the recommendations of the fact-finding team, at the expense of causing more of the very incidents they are intent on stopping. Sometimes, when on the line, firefighters now feel as though they are little more than guinea pigs in a grand experiment, having to ask permission, and explain the reasoning, behind every move they intend to make to some condescending faceless personality on the radio. When that happens crew morale slides and personal responsibility tends to migrate away from the immediate task because peoples' ability is being questioned. To longstanding, experienced firefighters such a thing is demeaning, indeed insulting, and results in many of them removing themselves from the decision making process.

The main fear for many old-school veterans is that firefighters will soon be too overly reliant on an ever-increasing set of figures. Forgetting that keeping one's eyes open, seeing something, and, more importantly, recognizing what one is seeing, provides the wherewithal and common sense that is far more valuable than constantly waiting for a specific set of variables to announce themselves by reaching a pre-determined trigger point. Because when that happens we are likely to discover a previously unknown variable that has already bitten us in the ass. Or find ourselves unable to ever pass the trigger point to be effective, whereupon the fire then becomes larger, more costly, and much more dangerous.

Much of the problem resides with having to maintain one fire fighting discipline among many fire crews with vastly differing levels of experience spread across a wide-ranging, nationwide landscape full of diverse challenges. One would never recommend the tactic of fighting fire downhill to an inexperienced crew. And yet well trained crews with experienced supervisors, aware of the enhanced requirements for such an action, often do exactly that, and do it safely.

So while there is obvious value to having a set of rules, there has to be some flexibility to allow for experience, otherwise the more difficult fires will never be fought. Strict rules would never allow for it. Some, however, would say this is correct, others would not. While no home, swath of timber or possession is ever worth a person's life there has to be a well-judged balance, not at all based upon rigidity.

Basic instinct is largely ignored in firefighting, and a topic that is rarely discussed in any great detail in the classroom. But after any major incident people always talk about it 'feeling like it was always going to go wrong' but everyone either chose to ignore it or didn't recognize it for what it was – a human being's inherent early warning system.

Being pounded by science for hours on end it was no wonder people inevitably fell asleep in the classroom, especially after lunch. Sitting at the back of the room, watching heads bobbing up and down uncontrollably was quite amusing, though probably not to the person delivering the PowerPoint presentation.

While some of the more elementary fire classes were boring, they didn't hold a candle to the excruciatingly mundane ethics and conduct classes that became mandatory year after year. In these we were supposed to understand why we couldn't have a tree planting business in the off-season – even while no longer in the employ of the USFS – because it contravened a conflict of interest guideline. The whole thing was bland hypocrisy because high government officials have been flouting far more serious examples for years. I guess that's why they weren't specified as rules, but 'guidelines,' for only the poor destitute suckers like us to abide. The situation was laughable and everyone knew it. But as years progressed the propaganda began to have an effect; new hires actually started to believe it. That, or a few brown-nosing suck-ups wanted to make it look like they believed it so as to get ahead. And it quickly became the only way to get ahead, because if someone made a disparaging remark about administrative procedure, or questioned management style, they were forever ostracized from that moment on, and the childish grudges often lasted whole careers.

Some examples of this stupidity included not being allowed to jumpstart a citizen's stalled vehicle when it was miles away from anywhere along a deserted forest road; not being allowed to drive them to safety; and not being allowed to give them a gallon of fuel to get them to a gas station. The rules were probably made up by some bored, under-worked, desk-jockey who had never set foot in the woods and who was determined to circumvent every single disaster that an administrative brain could possibly conceive. We rarely heeded these ridiculous rules, however, but God help us if we ever got caught. All they did was create a 'don't ask, don't tell' policy, where we never asked if we could and never told them that we had. The great irony was when we did help someone it actually put the FS in a good light, rather than the public thinking that we were just a organization full of self-serving government jackasses.

All these mandatory classes were doing was compounding the belief that we never wanted to work for the FS, which was why we were all trying to be smokejumpers. Smokejumping was generally seen to be independent and somewhat removed from the Law of Administrative and Managerial Bullshit that was endemic to the rest of the organization. This was also the reason why some others in the organization hated us. And did so with a passion.

Many of those who hated smokejumpers had previously failed to pass rookie selection and were jealous. Others ignorantly saw the camaraderie as elitism and translated it to be a problem rather than an advantage. Ignorance always played a large part in the problems associated with other crews and jumpers, whether it was ignorance to our abilities, our methods or our structure. So, as another lecture started, we were supposed to learn how to get along with people who made up the other aspects of firefighting: the helitacks, hotshots, and other interagency crews. This was another ridiculous exercise, however, because we had all originated from these types of crews. The problems weren't so much associated with the actual working members of other crews, as with the management's perception of there being a problem. Call it a problem and a problem will no doubt arise.

In hindsight, it's obvious that the fire lectures, while being dry and sleep inducing, were the most valuable and interesting of all the classes we took. It's one thing to have lots of experience, but when that experience is simple duplication then nothing is gained. The greatest value of the fire classes was that once diverted away from the regimented approach, valuable discussion was initiated. We learned far more by listening to others' experiences than we ever did in the rote subject being taught.

The trainers were especially fervent for us to do well in these classes because other crews often looked up to smokejumpers for experience and guidance, whether their managers liked it or not. So it was important to lay the groundwork for that expectation to perpetuate, and give potential recruits something to strive for.

Chapter Twelve

— Small Spots and Timber

Everybody had been talking romantically about the 'silence of
parachuting.' They must have had too much time on their hands,
because I was too busy wondering how I was going to steer
32 feet of silk into a dime surrounded by 90-foot Douglas-firs.

– Author

J UST BECAUSE WE HAD MANAGED to fall, one way or
another, into a very large meadow at Blue Mountain did not
mean that we were in any way proficient. But that didn't
stop us from celebrating. It was a great relief to get the first jump
over with, and knowing that we could get out the door voluntarily
made the thought of all future jumps that much easier.

However, we weren't fully appreciative of exactly how small
the jump spots would become, even though we'd heard countless
stories of spots being so small that a parachute couldn't be laid out
in them. The next jump spot wasn't as big as Blue Mountain but it
still provided plenty of room for error. It was more the thought of
the surrounding trees that created the worry. We soon learned that
the more we worried about trees the more we focused on them, and
subsequently, subconsciously, the more we steered towards them.
It was quite strange. We quickly learned to ignore the trees and
focus on the exact spot we wanted to land on. Most of the time it
worked. But as the jump spots became increasingly smaller it was
equally increasingly more difficult to ignore the trees, because

from 1,500 feet it always looked like there was nothing but trees all over the landscape, like a giant green carpet.

It was only a matter of time before the first rookie got hung up like a tree frog. The odds were against us, the margin of error was dwindling and the fringe bush gobblers were already at work. Taking Keith as their first victim.

The wind had shifted a little since the first half of the load had jumped. Rookies were now starting to get drawn to the northern end of the jump spot near the road. Someone had already almost landed on the roof of one of our fourteen passenger vans. Keith initially looked as though he was destined for the same fate but managed to steer away at the last moment. Only to fall prey to the bush gobbler. The mass of tangled brush seemed to open up the instant before he hit it, swallowing him whole and then closing around him, engulfing him completely. Keith's chute then floated gently down and covered the bush like a table cloth, from which it took a good five minutes to extricate himself and another half-hour to retrieve his parachute. The whole episode was caught on video, to great amusement later during our debriefing.

The next spot was smaller still, and although there was no brush there were, instead, many spindly 60-foot lodgepole pines encircling it. And right in the middle a big ugly fir. From the air it didn't look like there was much room for us and once we left the aircraft, 400 yards away due to the wind, it was difficult to even see the spot. But as we got nearer it opened up, though the threat of that big central fir was real and everyone was landing well away from it. Mark steered too far away from it and didn't land at all. When he shouted he was found dangling 40 feet up the side of one of the tallest, most spindly, lodgepoles around. He wasn't at all worried, however. Although this was the first time it had happened to anyone of us we had all been trained for it, with the practice, practice, practice, on the letdown unit. Mark's chute had capped three trees perfectly so he was in no danger of falling, unless the tip of the trees broke free under 260lbs of him and gear.

A couple of squad leaders rushed to make sure Mark didn't start his letdown without supervision and forget something vital, like tying off. After that, Mark managed to get to the ground with relative ease, albeit maybe a little embarrassed at being the first rookie in a tree. But worse was to come.

Once Mark was on the ground we watched as the second load arrived overhead. Each of their red, white and blue chutes making it cleanly into the spot. Then a very pretty white customized chute appeared. It was Walt. He was always instantly recognizable under his personal white lo-po (low porosity chute), which had a reduced rate of descent. Everyone watched the training foreman make his approach and line himself up perfectly for final approach, right in the middle of the spot. We wondered if Walt was about to do some marvelous maneuver that we hadn't yet seen to go around the tree, and then watched in stunned silence as he didn't. He slammed into the tree like a cannonball, swearing up a storm of expletives as he crashed through the branches. A moment later a white helmet came flying out of the tree, followed by a further torrent of abuse.

All rookies looked on in amazement. We couldn't believe it. Walt was our leader. This shouldn't happen. Then, as he emerged down his letdown rope, everyone turned away and pretended not to have noticed. But it was false hope. He knew we knew, and we knew he knew we knew. It didn't bode well for our debriefing. At this point in our training we thought that if ever we got on a fire with Walt we would probably be more afraid of Walt than the fire.

Clearly he wasn't going to be in the best of moods for the rest of the day and we prepared ourselves for the worst. Not least the task of getting Mark's chute out of that lodgepole. But Walt was better than that. Once he'd retrieved his own chute, which was only draped on the outside and easily pulled down, he was in better spirits and joked about his brainless act.

Mark, meanwhile, was sweating profusely as he climbed up the thin trunk of his tree using an old set of climbing spurs. Once in the branches he managed to free climb and began sawing off the branches that held his chute, with some of us tugging on the rope, and bending the tree to an uncomfortable angle with Mark still in it. The chute finally broke free and fell to the earth covered in sap and splintered debris, leaving Mark hanging on for his life as the tree swung back and forth in recoil. His parachute was torn to shreds – winter work for Eric in the loft.

Mark's encounter had shown us first-hand how to deal with a tree landing and how to best extract our parachute. While Walt had shown us that shit can happen to anyone. Walt's tree landing and wonderful use of profanity was caught on video but somebody, no telling who, must have since erased all copies of it.

The one jump we'd all been quietly dreading was the tree jump. It was to be our sixth. The day before, we watched a video of special forces parachutists doing exactly the same jump that we were about to do. The Missoula Smokejumper base also doubles as the Rough Terrain Parachute School, and as such trains small specialist military teams the art of rough terrain mountain jumping. The video we saw wasn't very encouraging for our upcoming jump or the safety of the country. We watched as two very experienced parachutists collided in mid-air a hundred feet off the ground and fell to earth in a heap, making everyone at the time think they were either badly broken or dead. Thankfully it was neither. Another clip involved canopy walking, where a jumper steered himself right over his JP's parachute, in effect cutting off his own air so he literally fell onto the canopy below. Not a good situation for either of them. These two were also lucky. The higher jumper managed to walk off his JP's chute allowing his own to re-inflate. A process always drilled into military jumpers because they exit so close together in mass jumps under canopies with little or no steering.

Video footage of their CO in a tree was also worrying because it was obvious that he was panicking; actually frozen in fear, and Walt had to climb another tree in an attempt to talk him down. The CO seemed to be more concerned over a torn flight glove than extracting himself from his predicament, for which he had received exactly the same training as we had.

These dismal performances were blamed on arrogance and an inflated appreciation of their abilities. These actions soon brought them crashing down to earth, however, though thankfully not literally. Although one would be correct to wonder if they actually learned anything from the experience. It was made perfectly clear to us that no one was going to allow this to happen to our group.

Long before suiting up we usually went to the loft to pick our favorite parachute off the rack. If it wasn't available we generally chose one close to the same number. Supposedly by doing this we were using chutes from the same batch which, therefore, should all have the same flight characteristics. Even though all the chutes looked identical each would vary ever so slightly causing them to fly differently. Being rookies, though, we really had no clue as to which chutes were better, we just listened to the veterans who told us this – probably because they were attempting to stop us from damaging their own precious parachutes.

But on tree jump day we didn't get to choose our own. There was a pile of old chutes assigned to us in the knowledge that this might be the last jump they ever made, depending on the damage they sustained. Our choice, then, was between some of the oldest chutes on the shelves, those which sell by dates were long passed.

All parachute materials degrade over time, silk more than nylon, after sustaining a lot of sunlight, creating a risk that panels might burst under the pressure of descent thereby enabling gravity to be efficient with obvious consequences. With an abundance of sunlight in Montana, especially during the summer fire season, and while I can't say we were overly worried about using these older chutes, there was certain apprehensiveness. On this jump we were reminded to be especially careful when looking for damaged gores while doing our canopy check, and to decide if the damage and the increased rate of descent warranted pulling our reserve.

As we flew over the spot (what spot?) we could see that, this time, there really was nothing down there but trees. There wasn't the slightest opening in the tree canopy for miles and a little grey smoke wafting through the lodgepole blanket pointed us toward our destination. Walt was also on the ground with a megaphone, yelling directions should we not be going in the right direction.

The technique had been drummed into us; on nearing the ground, brake to come down vertically, cap the tree and keep tight. Pretty simple really, but to do it for real for the first time took a leap of confidence, or Walt screaming encouragement in our ears below us. From the aircraft it looked as though everyone was doing okay and parachutes soon littered the velvety green tops of the trees. A couple had broken through to the ground but that was to be expected. One rookie landed right on top of the little camp fire and people had to scramble to stop the chute from melting.

It was soon my turn and as I stood in the door and looked down there was nothing but a landscape of spiky green trees. An occasional wisp of smoke rose between the dozen or so parachutes that draped the trees. The actual jump was quite easy. There was very little wind and after the jarring pain in my head subsided I floated down quite content with the notion that I would soon be crashing through the limbs of a 60-foot lodgepole.

Nearer the ground I heard Walt giving me directions, steering me away from the smoke and into an area of trees as yet without any parachutes. I pulled gently on one toggle, turned into the wind and pulled a little brakes, enabling me to descend vertically. Then, picking out my tree I clamped my feet and knees tight together, as to be dart. As soon as my feet hit the top of the tree I pulled my arms in tightly to my body, making myself as thin as possible. The first few branches were tiny and they either snapped off or bent as I went through them. The further down I went the harder they became until one just about tore my foot off. I thought I might have broken my ankle but soon had other things to worry about as I hit another solid branch and immediately flipped upside down, now crashing through the branches backwards. I prayed the tree was tall enough to catch my canopy before my head drove into the ground. The padding around my shoulders took most of the punishment and then just as suddenly I was flipped back upright again as the chute capped the tree. I bounced a few times on the end of the cords and finally came to a standstill, 30 feet in the air.

Looking up I saw a channel of broken branches and my chute securely draped over a couple of trees. Looking down, Miguel, my designated tutor for the day, was waiting patiently. His job being to make sure I didn't do anything irretrievably stupid.

"Hey Miguel. How's it going?" I asked.

"Oh, it's the bloody Englishman is it? How are you old chap?" Miguel said, in a terrible English accent.

"Not bad mate. Thanks."

"Mate? I'll have you know that I have a girlfriend."

Americans hate being called 'mate'. Some get quite offended.

"Why do you Limeys always call each other mate? Are you all tap dancers or something?" Miguel asked.

"Old navy term," I said, knowing Miguel was proud of his Spanish heritage. "Something that started around the time of the Armada I think. You remember the Armada don't you Miguel?"

"Oh, I remember a little. But right now I'm wondering how you're going to get down out of that tree with two broken legs." Miguel said quietly.

I knew he wouldn't. Or at least I think I knew. But also knew that he could. He was a big bugger.

As I continued the letdown I noticed Miguel was paying no attention at all. He was sitting down leaning against a tree reading a book like he was on a picnic. Nevertheless, I did my four-point check, checked for lines around my neck and released the first Capewell, swinging me to one side. Then again checked for loose lines around my neck before releasing the other Capewell and rappelling down to the ground in front of Miguel.

"Took you long enough," he said.

"Thanks for taking time away from your book to care," I said.

"You're welcome. Spurs are over there somewhere. You're not going to need any help are you? This is a good bit," he said.

"Nah, no worries. You just sit. I don't want to spoil the day."

With that I wandered over to the campfire to retrieve a set of spurs. Where a group was congregating and laughing, and drinking remnants of the coffee Keith had just spilt after landing in the fire, and who was now trying to sort out his melted parachute. In doing so he spilt the can of water boiling more coffee, which was enough to put the little signal fire out, leaving everyone without coffee and no directional smoke for next round of jumpers. Although with parachutes littering the tops of trees it was no longer really needed. And Walt could always yell louder. Keith couldn't be faulted. He had landed closer than anybody. Even if that was not the point.

After putting on the spurs and harness and wrapping the rope around the tree I started to climb. The equipment was old and uncomfortable and no one wanted to spend too long in it, but it was the only way to get back up the tree. The lodgepole was much like climbing a telegraph pole, except for the spindly branches every few feet or so. It wasn't worth doing limb-overs with these small branches so the ones I could break by hand I snapped off. Then as I passed above them I kicked the remains with my boot so the trunk would be free from anything snagging my rope on the way down. At about 30 feet I tried free climbing but the branches were still too weak and kept breaking off, so I continued with what was working.

"That tree will be little more than a telegraph pole by the time you're done with it," Miguel yelled up.

I was now using my little saw to cut off the branches cleanly and one fell close to where he was yelling. My aim was a little off.

Miguel looked up, put on his hard hat, and continued reading.

I smirked a little and continued up, sending the odd branch in his direction just to remind him that I was still in the tree, and not crumpled in a heap on the ground. By now I was in the green limbs and able to free climb the remainder so I released myself from the rope and weaved in and out between the sappy little branches. At this height the trunk was only about four inches wide and swaying backwards and forwards in the breeze. We had been warned not to go up too far up because the trees had suffered through a few years of drought and were getting brittle, meaning that they might break off at any moment. I tested some of the branches and they seemed okay so I leaned out and started to untangle the lines.

In situations like this the jumper on the ground pulls hard on the letdown rope that is still attached to the risers of the parachute. Then as soon as enough of the lines have been removed from the tree it should, in theory, come out. The problem arises when there are as many lines on the other side of the tree from which the chute is being pulled, in which case the workload increases dramatically. Further options involve either cutting the tree down completely or removing the parachute lines from the risers so the ends are free. If there are only a few lines over the tree it's sometimes possible to gather them together and move them as a group, although it's a time consuming process in a sticky tree. If there are multiple lines all over the place the tree is usually topped. So that when the chute comes out so does the top of the tree. This is what I was going to have to do since there was no way I was able to move all the lines to one side. We had been told to only remove lines from risers if absolutely necessary, and never to cut them unless we wished the same to happen to our nuts.

"Let me know when you want some help," Miguel shouted.

"Let me get this last one and then try to yank it out," I said.

"Who you calling a Yank?

With that Miguel started pulling. The top of the tree bent over at what seemed to me, being at the tip of it, an alarming angle. He then tied the end of the rope to another tree, keeping the tension on the chute while I plucked off pieces of material from the branches. The tree curved like a longbow and I could imagine getting shot out of it like an arrow if Miguel's Spanish navy knot came undone. He was now climbing up the angled rope to add more tension, but it wasn't moving. I'd have to top it.

I took out my little saw and started cutting through the three-inch trunk six feet from the top. It was sappy and tough to get through with the blunt little blade but I was soon finished with the back-cut. Then before I could say anything Miguel tugged hard on the rope again, breaking the top off and pulling it to the ground, carrying the torn chute with it. I was left holding on for dear life as the top of the tree swayed back and forth. Looking down now I thought that maybe I should have tied off to something.

When I got to the ground Miguel was picking out the debris from the material and gathering together the tangled lines.

"Good job Bob," he said.

"Bob now is it?" I said.

"Well, it didn't look like you needed much help. You seemed to know what you were doing," he said. "But that tree is nothing but a telegraph pole now."

We both looked up and I saw he was right. I'd removed all the branches for the first 40 feet, then there were a few straggly green branches before its flat top. It would have made a good pole.

"Not much more you could have done though. On a fire we'd have just cut it down, especially if you'd capped a few of them."

With that we heard a chainsaw crank up and a few moments later the sound of trees crashing down. One chute had capped five different trees and there was no way anyone was going to remove it before next week. Dropping a couple was the only option.

It took me half an hour to separate the lines and material from sap covered branches and other debris before I could pack it away. The whole episode had taken a little over an hour, half of it in the tree. It had been a pretty easy extraction. We had all heard horror stories of six-hour extractions that we hoped never to experience. Not using the same archaic equipment anyway.

Chapter Thirteen

— Rookie Wings

*I am impelled, not to squeak like a grateful and apologetic mouse, but
to roar like a lion out of pride in my profession.*

– John Steinbeck

WHILE THE TIMBER JUMP had initiated the most trepidation among the rookies it was also a stressful time for Walt. Getting twenty-five people crashing into trees under canopy is not in itself very difficult, just throw them out of an aircraft over the forest and the rest is obvious. But getting it accomplished without an injury would seem to warrant a miracle. If anyone has witnessed the sound of humans crashing though scores of branches at eighteen feet per second – ignoring the associated profanity – they could be forgiven for suspecting some type of divine intervention if not a single person gets hurt.

Such is testament to the professionalism of our training that, indeed, no one was hurt, apart from the unavoidable scrapes and bruises from hitting large immovable objects. With a single jump before completion of rookie training one cannot praise enough the quality of the training we had undergone in the weeks leading to this point. Now that the timber jump was over we naturally fell to the belief that the most physically demanding, and possibly the mentally hardest, part was over. But the last jump in the sequence would prove equally difficult in another way; precision.

Throughout the previous three weeks we had heard a lot about Little Stoney on the rumor mill. By all accounts this tiny patch of lush meadow near Ninemile, in the Lolo National Forest, contained barely enough room to spread two or three canopies on the ground. Which meant getting two jumpers into it at the same time required constant verbal communication and proficient parachute handling. While we'd been steadily getting into smaller and smaller spots as the week progressed this one still tweaked a concern, especially to those who had become used to a more comfortable margin of error. Without that margin for error the reality of our upcoming situation became very real. Although we had also learned that necessity was often the catalyst for success, and looked forward to this latest and last challenge with our usual apprehensive excitement.

As fate would have it, it rained the morning of our seventh and last rookie jump. And because the cloud ceiling was expected to be too low for the remainder of the day the jump was postponed until Friday. Instead, we hauled ourselves off to the canteen for what we hoped was the last mandatory class, and tuition in per diem, which would later prove invaluable in determining the return for travel expenses. To one veteran jumper in particular this was his only source of ready cash during the entire summer because the per diem check could be sent to a different address, where it could be cashed without the cash-strapped missus ever finding out.

The end of training Rookie Party is not just expected, it is mandated by years of tradition. All successful rookies are required to arrange a celebratory and appropriately boozy dinner for the entire jump base. The organization of which is sometimes no easy feat after previous groups of rowdy jumpers have been routinely banned from some of the more obvious venues over the years. But once a suitable, and amenable, location has been found, getting enough barrels of beer to satiate such a group is easy. Charlie, of *Charlie B's*, is always willing to help, providing us an assortment of beers to satisfy everyone's taste. Food is also easy. After several weeks of hard graft rookies will eat just about anything.

For some reason those organizing this years party had selected *The Lumberjack*. It sounded fine and was somewhere that we hadn't been banned from, yet, but it was twenty-odd miles from Missoula. So if spouses weren't into using the communal bus they would be forced into being designated drivers, which led to various levels of vocal disappointment among some couples. Nevertheless, the veteran jumpers were constantly asking where, when, and how much beer there was going to be, trying to make sure there would be enough. And with some asking whether more girls might show up. Collectively the rookies coughed up enough money to pay for half the costs while the base welfare fund kicked in the remainder. A few rookies still had to borrow the money, however, because we were yet to receive a paycheck.

Before the party we still had one last jump and Friday was the last chance to do it. Otherwise we would be having a party without any graduated rookies. Unthinkable.

Friday morning was beautiful. The previous day's wind and rain had freshened the air, removing the pulp mill's stale stench, and the sun was slowly burning off a light mist covering the hills to the south. We arrived in good spirits to find the jump list already pinned to the board. I was partnered with Steve again, with whom I had had most of my jumps so far. We made good jump partners because Steve was a good thirty pounds heavier and when jumping first he was always far below me by the time my chute opened, so we never had to worry too much about vertical separation. After checking the list one more time and getting our gear together we went to the loft and picked our favorite chutes. Mine was FS-12 #75, it had served me well so far. It might well have had a mind of its own – one smarter than mine – because it always found its way and always delivered me to the spot in one piece.

An hour later we were circling over Ninemile in the DC-3 and searching around for a clearing in the forest below. The only place resembling a jump spot was a good half a mile away and we were heading nowhere near it. Then the spotter dropped a couple of streamers and we watched as they disappeared into the vast expanse of velvety green below us. Initially we thought the spotter was joking. Until he called the first two forward to hook up.

"Did you see it?" I asked Steve.

"Didn't see anything."

"Well, when you get out the door, you find it. Because I'm following you," I said, smiling.

The first two rookies hadn't been expecting it either and they frantically fastened their cages, clipped on their PG-bags, and tightened their leg straps as they waddled back toward the open door. They were ready in the door on base leg, just as the plane turned onto final. From this angle there was not a spot to be seen anywhere, but a few seconds later there was a rush of wind and a clatter of cables and both were away and gone, floating down to the great unending forest below. From the aircraft it looked like another timber jump, until at the last moment the forest seemed to open and swallow both parachutes, one after the other. Then they were nowhere to be seen.

"They made it in okay," the spotter said.

"D'you believe him?" Someone asked.

"Dunno. But I'm going to follow him," I said, smiling and pointing toward Steve.

With our heads pressed against the windows, waiting for the wing to get out of the way, we could just make out a patch of blue and white nylon sitting on the ground as the plane turned. There wasn't much grass around it and it would have made a wonderful hide for a solitary Harrier jump jet.

I noticed a cold bead of sweat trickling down my back as I put my helmet on and felt my stomach sink as the plane bucked a little in the turbulence. Steve walked ahead and hooked himself to the overhead cable. I followed and did the same, double checking that the clip was properly fastened and the pin in correctly. The spotter watching our every move.

The morning air was decidedly chilly and the spotter's cold face was being distorted by the wind as he stuck his head out to guide the pilot on line. Now and again ducking his head back in to speak into his microphone and give directions, before going back out into the slipstream as he concentrated on the spot coming into view. With the turn finished and the plane flying straight and level he manhandled Steve's left foot into the door.

Being second I had no real view from the door but I assumed Steve could now see where we needed to go. I planned to follow along behind him so I sure hoped that he did!

"YOU'RE CLEAR!" The assistant spotter yelled into my ear.

I placed my right foot directly behind Steve's twitching right foot and when he heaved himself out the door I placed my left foot on the doorframe and followed him a second and a half later. I kept tight, counted to three thousand, and felt the comforting tug of the lines as the canopy popped open above me. Reaching up to grab my toggles I watched the plane fly away and start to bank to the left, which meant that my exit this time had been perfect. Steve was a hundred feet below and already steering away from the plane toward where I hoped the spot would be because I still couldn't see it. But the spot had to be down there somewhere and as long as we followed the wind line, and stayed aloft long enough, we would have to bump into it eventually. With his heavier bodyweight able to generate more forward speed from the parachute Steve was well ahead of me by now, hopefully providing him a better view than I had, because I could still see nothing but trees.

Then I saw it. It was tiny. My toggles had been up all the way to gain maximum forward speed to get over the spot, but now I started quartering the canopy because I didn't want to fly past it with no chance of getting back into the wind. I had already made that mistake once and didn't want to repeat it, so I made a series of turns to keep the wind gauge in my favor. Steve was far below me by now and turning onto final, pulling on both toggles to brake the canopy and fly it perfectly between two 70-foot pines on the far side of the spot. I did a couple more quartering turns to slow my approach and remain on the wind line. At about 200 feet I did a one-eighty to turn into the wind and descended slowly above the trees without any forward speed. The wind had picked up and I briefly worried about being blown backwards out of the spot. With the toggles up I hoped the canopy would gain some more forward speed and fly. Slowly making progress I passed just a few feet over the larger trees on the edge of the spot. Then there were a few smaller trees to navigate around before the spot opened up for me.

At this height it seemed much bigger than the legend claimed and I glided in easily, my feet landing near the edge of the meadow as I rolled onto the soft ground. My chute continuing to waft over my head and flutter gracefully to the ground in front of me. Steve looked over to check that I was okay. He had a big wide grin on his face. I think everyone in the meadow did at this point. Rookie training was over, to the great relief of everyone present.

On the ground a journalist from Japanese Playboy magazine had been photographing the landings and was already talking with Sarah, who had landed a few minutes earlier. Being female in a predominantly male occupation the journalist had paid special attention to Sarah's progress over the past weeks. Once published the article was quite complimentary. She was a tough cookie, as were most of the female jumpers in those days. We hadn't yet got to the point of relaxing training requirements that were to make some rookies a laughing stock, and result in an erroneous hire that almost met the ultimate fate.

Little Stoney has been a great success. Mostly everyone had made it into the spot and no one was hung in a tree. Those who didn't manage to land in the main spot found tiny roll your own openings elsewhere. Everyone was elated. This had been our last rookie jump and barring unforeseen circumstances all of us had qualified to become rookie smokejumpers. There was a communal sense of pride at having completed something worthwhile. All that was left was the final initiation.

Back at base we were called into the canteen to be presented with our wings. There were more than a few lumps in throats as we were each called forward in turn to receive a small treasured set of Forest Service Smokejumper wings. I'm not sure if it was a sense of pride that instilled that feeling or relief that the group effort over the previous weeks, and all the individual effort over the preceding months, was finally over. Probably both.

Growing up in a family with roots in London during the Blitz had always instilled a different perspective on life. Where most need to directly experience life's difficulties to gain perspective, those fortunate to grow up in families such as mine have had that perspective drilled into us from an early age. Although we didn't always appreciate it at the time, being kids, sooner or later it makes a distinct impression – whether from an inherent appreciation or from constant repetition. The impression ingrained in me was what we initially perceive as the hardest times in our lives are often the most memorable and, in retrospect, the happiest. The challenge in getting through them, whatever it is, makes this so.

I have since consciously remembered and forced myself to live by that philosophy throughout my life. So that when things appear to be completely covered in crap, I know that this is what I shall remember and endeavor to try and enjoy it. So, God forbid, when in that end-of-life-wheelchair I shall have few regrets.

After our little wings ceremony we were herded to have our group picture taken, first by the pride of the FS fleet, the wonderful tail-dragging DC-3, and then in front of the ready-room. As more and more amateur photographers gathered in front of us we could sense something was afoot...*

We were now jumpers. Or rather we were rookie jumpers. We had stepped into a family with a great history and a longstanding tradition. Being accepted, however, would depend on our work over the coming fire season, because as the new crop of rookies we were expected to put out maximum effort all the time. During the summer we would be forever watched to make sure we upheld the smokejumper ethos and work ethic. For now, though, we had given everything our best effort and emerged stronger. Pride was visible on everyone's face. Not just rookies but trainers as well. Although in their case it was probably more a sense of utter relief, which, for their efforts, they deserved special appreciation.

They had done an outstanding job in making jumpers out of men and women, students, teachers, soldiers, ranchers, carpenters and contractors, as well as the unemployed, the self-employed and literally, one burned out dairy farmer. For the first time we thought we saw Walt crack a smile. But it might well have been a clenched teeth grimace, in expectation of the inevitable list of future rookie induced cockups.

Returning to the loft we saw the summer's jump list had been drawn already. Each rookie had been interspersed between veteran jumpers – to their annual disgust. At the top, número uno, was Ed. At the bottom was Steve, right next to me. The two of us wouldn't be going anywhere anytime soon.

---

* Tradition dictates that we cannot say more for fear of upsetting *Big Ernie*.

Chapter Fourteen

— Yellowstone

*The Mountains south east of our Camp and on the road to the
lake looking toward the Yellowstone Country [are] glorious, and I do
not expect to see any finer general view of the Rocky Mountains.*
– Thomas Moran, Artist on the 1871 Yellowstone Hayden Exhibition

ANNE WAS FORCED TO STOP and pull over several times on the way home from the rookie party because Jeff needed to puke. He had been celebrating well and spent most of the evening being enamored with a squad leader's wife. The rest of us spent most of the evening trying to ignore him. Until we thought it better to explain the facts of life: in that having a heavy crush on someone's wife can get awfully messy in the best of circumstances, but here especially it would not be taken lightly and could become a career-ending maneuver at the very least.

When we saw Jeff on Monday he couldn't remember a thing.

During the evening Missoula had received a booster call from Alaska. There are a number of Forest Service and Bureau of Land Management (BLM) bases in the Lower 48 and one BLM base in Alaska. Anytime a base is exceptionally busy or jumped out they call for reinforcements to boost their numbers. The BLM base in Fairbanks had called for twenty FS smokejumpers from Missoula, Grangeville and West Yellowstone, and looking at the list it was easy to see who was going and who didn't stand a chance in hell. Steve and I didn't stand a chance in hell. Lucky Ed was definitely going. He was number one and would be on his way to Alaska the following day.

But next day Ed was not to be seen and missed his flight. An inauspicious start to say the least. In such cases a reserve jumper is usually ready to go at a moment's notice, but in this instance, with Ed a rookie, someone must have been in a forgiving mood because they allowed him go up the following day. No doubt to a taunting reception because Alaska jumpers are not shy about showing their disappointment – especially to rookies.

For those staying behind it was base work and all new rookies were assigned to loadmasters, where all the food, water, tools and equipment are stored and then organized, packed and transformed into paracargo. We began with the basics, constructing the cargo boxes themselves. And like everything we did, there was one way to do it and one way only, and so James was assigned to show us how to do it, how to bundle and tie them so that they survived the drop intact and didn't get strewn across the landscape like a yard sale. We soon learned the myriad jumper uses for 100mph tape. Without which the boxes wouldn't have stood a chance and the jump door on the DC-3 would have been flapping in the breeze; proving the significance of the tape's name.

The individual cargo boxes contained everything one jumper needed for three unsupported days, including sleeping bag, pulaski, two and a half gallons of water, assorted dried food, chocolate and candy, a first-aid pouch and a file for sharpening the pulaski. Five-gallon containers of water were also boxed up, as were chainsaws and fuel. Crosscut saws are strapped to the outside of jumper cargo boxes in the aircraft as and when needed.

Missoula was fortunate in that it had a series of longstanding veterans who were experienced crosscut saw sharpeners. Their job to ensure that each saw cuts through wood like butter. Sharpening these old saws, with dozens of razor sharp teeth, is almost a lost art outside of the world of fire. So is finding replacements for those bent, broken and plain worn out – saws that is, not jumpers.

There was a knack to getting everything inside the boxes and placing it exactly so nothing exploded on impact. That was also James's job. He was excellent at demonstrating and explaining what to do. Not only would he work as hard, if not harder, than the rookies, but he would keep a constant eye on us to make sure we did everything right, always providing advice on better methods. In fact, all the veterans were only too willing to help. Initially we had thought we might be invading their territory but that was not the case at all, and quickly felt part of the team. The true test, however, as we all knew, would be our effort on the fires.

A week later there was another booster call and ten jumpers left for Oregon, leaving the base feeling empty and the number of people packing boxes dwindling fast. Country music echoed from the deserted loft and only an occasional revving sewing machine meant there was anyone still working in manufacturing.

With more gone, Steve and I had moved up to five and six on the rotating list. Surely the next call would mean us, we hoped. Otherwise everyone else would be back with a fire jump under their belt before we had gone anywhere. But the days rolled by; more boxes and more boxes. The warehouse was getting full to the rafters with boxes, literally. It wasn't even as if we could get to know everyone else while we were stuck building boxes, because there was no one else around. It was like being in limbo.

Every day took the normal course; after morning roll call we would do an hour of PT, either running the track or the hills or lifting weights in the tiny one-room gym. After showering and getting fire ready – Nomex trousers and boots – we'd all meet in loadmasters and work until lunch. In the afternoon we just do more of the same; more boxes.

Up until the early '90s Missoula had a functioning canteen serving breakfast, lunch and dinner – unheard of today – and all the exercise we had done before and during rookie training seemed to be getting wasted as we waited and ate and waited some more.

Then it came, completely unexpected. The siren went off and our hearts missed a beat. We looked around briefly, wondering if this was for real, before running to the ready room to suit up. The operations foreman came out and informed us we were boosting West Yellowstone. Most of their jumpers being in Alaska, Oregon or out on local fires, and the park was expecting lightning to roll though later that afternoon.

The Sherpa was already warming up and the loadmaster was throwing in extra food boxes and our red bags – overnight bags with clean fire clothes and a few basic civvies. Only six of us were going which meant there were six vacant spots that could be filled with cargo. Within five minutes of the siren we had our helmets and gloves on and were rolling down the runway, taking to the air. In a single moment life had changed for us. This was more like it!

With the tarmac rushing by beneath us we looked over to see the now deserted aircraft ramp. The base was briefly empty except for a few overhead in operations and loadmasters, although the Oregon crew was returning later in the day. We banked over Blue Mountain and made our way to the southeast. On the ground it was hot enough but in the cabin of the aircraft, in all our gear, it was stifling. We moved around in search of cool wind coming through the door and tried to relax and enjoy the ride. The plane bucked a little as we hit turbulence going over the peaks: hot air being forced against the mountains and rising, taking us with it. The vast carpeted landscape beneath us was spectacular.

This was the first time we had really seen it. Behind us were the rugged Bitterroot Mountains with just a smattering of snow left on Lolo Peak. Below were the Pintlers and the scenic Big Hole. In front, the Beaverhead Mountains of Jeremiah Johnson. Wonderful majestic places steeped in history. We were soon over the winding Madison River and then the Gallatin before arriving over the flats of the Yellowstone Plateau.

West Yellowstone's airport sits a few miles outside town. The town itself is a flat square on the edge of the Caldera right on the border of the park, just inside Montana, and is predominantly filled with tourist motels. We were going to the Interagency Jump Base, sitting by itself at one end of the runway and consisting of a small loft, a dorm and a couple of trailer homes. It has since grown considerably in recent years thanks to the efforts of some talented jumpers who have pretty much built everything themselves.

We banked over the river and descended onto final. West Yellowstone is 3,400 feet higher than Missoula at 6,600 feet. After landing we half stepped and half stumbled out of the Sherpa and waddled to the loft carrying our PG bags and helmets. A couple of Westies unloaded the cargo while we unsuited. Our shirts were sodden and we laid out our jump suits and fire shirts on the ramp in the sun to dry them. The sun was fierce at this altitude and there wasn't a breeze to be felt anywhere. It was the middle of July.

While the plane was being unloaded we were given a standard briefing in the loft as we sat aside two long packing tables. The loft was small, with only about 40 chutes neatly stacked on the shelves compared to Missoula's almost 400. It felt comfortable and more relaxed than Missoula and we felt at home immediately. Outside the Sherpa cranked up, preparing to return to Missoula, while we went into the town for lunch and fought over space with literally hundreds of tourists. There were RVs of all shapes and sizes and campers everywhere. Countless overfed families strolled in and out of the various knick-knack shops all wearing the same new t-shirts. Maybe so they could spot each other in a crowd, who knows? It looked pretty stupid.

Back at the airport, Jiggs, the retardant manager and part-time smokejumper, had us working right away on cleaning up the ramp. Providing us with wire brushes and scrapers to remove old yellow paint from the helipad. Jiggs was old ex-bodybuilder and no one was going to argue. His logic was to keep us busy to keep us out of trouble. Logic he had probably picked up in Korea. We had a lot of fun with Jiggs, even if he always worked us to the bone.

Most SMJ bases have a siren, a bell, or a megaphone for fire calls. West Yellowstone has the William Tell Overture. As we bent on hands and knees, brushing off the yellow paint, we heard that brilliant tune blaring over the ramp and saw a few Westies run towards the loft. We immediately dropped our tools and did the same. Greg, the base manager, was waiting and told us not to hurry as we were only going out on a patrol flight. While a fire hadn't yet been reported it didn't mean that we wouldn't find one. So we got dressed casually, put on our chutes, had a spotter check, and sat down on the ramp facing the late afternoon sun while the King Air was readied.

The King Air carried six jumpers, and it was tight with six. We sat where we could on boxes, sideways, three on each side with the spotter initially up front next to the pilot. Once we were above 800 feet we removed our helmets and gloves and positioned ourselves as comfortably as possible to enjoy the ride. The two by the back door had it good. Not only was it much cooler there but they could stretch out their legs and watch the scenery unfold beneath them. The rest of us fought for leg space with each other and the cargo and twisted around to look out of the windows at the breathtaking scenery.

We crossed the park, headed over the Beartooth Mountains and circled around the Gallatin National Forest and Livingston, then to Spanish Peaks and Big Sky before completing the circle at West. Again, the scenery was spectacular. Everywhere we looked there was something new. Bighorn sheep clung to vertical cliffs on the Beartooths. The last snow draping over the peaks was dirty and melting away into the valleys where moose grazed the lush edges of streams. Beef cows sporadically grazed mile upon mile of open range. Irrigated fields had been cut and great long swathes of hay were drying in the evening sun. It brought back earlier wonderful memories of farming and I could imagine the sweet dusty aroma of the freshly cut grass.

Without the hurly-burly rushing about and surge of adrenaline of going to a fire it was a relaxing flight. Yet, even though we were in awe of the scenery and absorbing every square mile, we kept our eyes peeled for that telltale whiff of smoke that would signal a fire, a better paycheck, and the sole reason for us being there.

The early evening air was still, the flight pleasantly smooth, and the King Air the only aircraft in an expanse of blue. Its shadow followed us fleetingly on the sides of the mountains as the orange sun occasionally glinted off the wings while we weaved our way in and out of the tall peaks. In the distance the mountains of the West were starting to silhouette against the approaching dusk as the sun dipped slowly behind them to end another day. We headed home.

We soon realized that West Yellowstone really was the place to be. It was a hard working base, everyone had something to do and did it without ever being asked. It was also a close-knit base with most jumpers living in the dorm, two to a room, and eating and drinking together. After closing the loft and getting out of our fire clothes we showered and drove into town to meet everyone for dinner.

There was little for excitement in West Yellowstone in those days. Most bars and restaurants closed around ten o'clock simply because the tourists had gone to bed by then. There were only one or two open later so we generally ended up at one of those. One being the Stage Coach, where its downstairs bar was frequently our meeting point, initiating endless jump stories from the older guys. People seemed to pop out of the woodwork from nowhere. There were far more folks around the table than we had seen at the base. Dispatchers and some local district people also showed up, all ex-jumpers. I hadn't seen such a group since leaving the army and I'd always missed that sort of camaraderie. Although here it seemed as though I had found it again, and it felt good.

The standard trick for Westie veterans in particular was to get the new rookies drunk enough so that they would buy all the beer, see their condition in the morning, and test if they'd even show up. Despite being too old for such trickery I made a customary attempt and woke up much the worse for wear the following day, as I was supposed to. However that self-induced lethargy soon disappeared during a dusty five mile run at 6,600 feet with fleet-footed Miguel, who seemed to have lungs of steel. Then, after exhaustive PT and a briefing, to give us the bad news that there had been no lightning after all, we were released to go into town for breakfast. We knew we could get used to this.

But Jiggs was there to bring us back down to earth, giving us our duties for the morning, a choice of scraping paint, painting the retardant tanks, or rolling crepe paper streamers. So we baked and burned as a searing sun rose steadily overhead, acclimatizing us to the local conditions.

Returning to base after a greasy lunch, Missoula's Sherpa was sitting on the ramp and the Westies' personal fire boxes were being transferred from the King Air. Four Westies were already getting into their gear and no sooner had we stopped the van than we heard

William Tell, and immediately ran to put our gear on also. Greg emerged from operations to say there was a large fire in the park. District and park crews were already on it but they needed help on one as yet unmanned flank.

Since the famous Yellowstone Fire of 1988 all new fires were receiving more attention in an attempt to stem public criticism. The park now wanted eight jumpers and explosives and the Sherpa had come over from Missoula because the Flying Winnebago could carry a lot more cargo than the frisky little King Air. First we were going to get set up on the ground and then West's SMJ base was going to paracargo in explosives for us to blast a section of fireline.

Yellowstone Park has always been a big proponent of water-gel explosives. Rangers use it for a variety of purposes not always associated with fire, such as rock-fall management, trails and carcass removal in the more public areas. Just as on fires the easily handled water-gel explosive lessens the manpower requirement in the remote backcountry.

Using 50 - 85lb boxes of fireline explosives is quick and easy once the heavy lifting has been done. The 50, 75 to 100-foot long sausage-like tubes are then laid along the ground, joined together using tape and detonated electronically by remote control using an exploding-bridgewire detonator (EBW)[*] or old fashioned blasting cap. The result is a blasted line down to mineral soil that has much less impact than a twenty person crew. The soft malleable tubes of explosive can also be wrapped quite easily around small trees, logs and brush to remove any dead or standing fuel.

Missoula Smokejumpers were the first to paracargo fireline explosives for use on the Outlaw Fire in 1974. Since then just about every jumper has wanted the chance to work with it in order to get certified in using the stuff. Logistically, paracargo is by far

---

[*] Originally developed at Los Alamos for the Manhattan Project, creating a more precise detonation than earlier blasting caps.

the best delivery method, removing explosives from the risks, rules and limitations of the public road system. Nevertheless, its use has become so rare outside of the park that it takes years for anyone to become certified. (Ten years later I still wasn't FS certified, even having been trained in explosives as a combat engineer.) Only one of our jumper crew that day was blaster-in-charge certified and only one other classified as a blaster-in-training. Quite pitiful really. Due mostly to misunderstanding the value and efficiency of the product; the lack of informative field guides covering its uses, misevaluating its cost versus manpower and time; and the inherent general ignorance, creating nervousness, in using explosives. But that didn't stop the rest of us from being excited about the prospect of using it. Especially on our first fire!

The plane now loaded and ready with its extra cargo, Bill and Sabino, spotters for the mission, beckoned us onboard. And not to break rookie tradition Steve and I were JPs again, last stick, sitting up front on the cargo just behind the pilots. We looked at each other and just nodded. This was it, our first fire. The moment we had been waiting for since finishing rookie training two weeks earlier. Everything was going through our heads; did we have all our gear; what would the jump be like; and constantly feeling to make sure our gloves were in our helmets, knowing they were but making sure anyway. Repetition, repetition. The plane surged down the runway and we were on our way. As the wings grabbed the air and took to the sky we slid back and grabbed at the cargo straps to steady us. With the town 1,000 feet below us we banked left and flew off into the park, passing over the numerous famous tourist destinations in a matter of minutes.

Herds of widely spaced buffalo sauntered along the river to graze the grasses, while great long lines of silvery steel ruined the aura by cluttering the sides of the roads, each vehicle offloading a little army of plump white humans carrying an array of cameras.

Even from this height we could see some foolish people getting too close to the nonchalant but wary bison. To get that one close-up photograph that would likely impress no one they were willing to risk their lives. Moreover, they were selfishly ruining the otherwise unspoilt view for everyone else.

Every road in the park was a constant stream of slow moving vehicles snaking over peaks and around lakes and rivers. Out of their sight, however, was a huge tract of land. Another landscape containing a world of unique splendor: hidden geysers sprung from the lower basins, their steam soon evaporating in the virgin air; bubbling pools of mud appeared blue, grey and turquoise against the surrounding greenery. And as the hidden valleys and foothills gave way to tall snow covered peaks, visible for miles, meandering streams glistened in the afternoon sun. Those areas were thankfully devoid of, and safe from, the tire trampling hordes of humanity.

It didn't take long for us to see the fire. Over the next valley a plume of dirty white smoke appeared that was getting kicked hard by the same wind that was buffeting the aircraft. This approaching lush green valley contained a vastly different world. Gone were the nonchalant buffalo and metallic rivers. Gone was peace, quiet and tranquility. Here was a valley teeming with raucous activity as a veritable air force of whop, whop, whop, helicopters crisscrossed the airspace dropping bucket loads of water onto torching trees. Beneath the smoke and steam lines of yellow ant-like firefighters dug, chopped and scraped, struggling to contain the flames while they were still able. Larger ships were landing nearby, delivering fresh crews and a mass of unwieldy accoutrements, the beginnings of a fire camp that was already a great hive of activity, all looking frantic and chaotic to an unaccustomed eye.

But it was not frantic. There was some order to the chaos. An arrangement choreographed from studiously examining a thousand such fires over the decades. Fires that most people never knew existed, just like this one. For even though we had entered into a war zone, in the midst of one of the most populated natural parks on the planet, the vast majority of people were still ignorant to the fire's existence. To them, the rising smoke was just a solitary cloud appearing over the horizon, and the subtle whine of helicopters in the distance signaled sightseeing tours. After all, this park existed solely for them, it had been designated such as the people's park, and everything they saw or witnessed must be for their benefit, as if orchestrated. Like Disneyland.

But Disneyland it was also not. Especially not to the recent arrivals. Those valiant young souls toiling near scorching flames in 100-degree heat were like modern gladiators fighting for survival in an arena of fire and filth, entrenched in unyielding effort against nature. Overhead, a few agile helicopters turned and danced, their red Bambi Buckets* swinging wildly beneath on 100-foot cables as everyone together fought to extinguish the next crowning fir. For them it was certainly not Disneyland. It was more than that, better than that. Obscured from public view these pilots and grunts were literally having the time of their lives; gathering stories they would tell for years, making friends they would know for years.

We were all excited to be joining them, privileged even. Our jump spot was a long skinny meadow on the fire's flank with a baldly mountain skirting one of the sides. Both spotters were by the door pointing and chatting, deciding where best to throw us out. We were happy to see a big spot because the keen angle of smoke meant that it was awfully windy out there in Disneyland. Though from our training, we knew we wouldn't be jumping with a count of more than 600 yards of drift on the streamers, no matter how big and long the spot. So we settled back to enjoy the ride.

Inside the cabin we huddled around the windows trying to get a glimpse of the fire and surrounding terrain, as well as the jump

---

* A lightweight collapsible bucket widely used in aerial firefighting.

spot we knew we would no longer be using. It wasn't until the first stick was out the door and away that we realized how wrong we were, and how much misplaced confidence the spotters had in the proficiency of two rookies at the back of the load. The drop point was a good 800 to 1,000 yards from the actual landing spot, and when the first two got sucked from the door they disappeared in an instant. The next stick was already in the door and getting their briefing so Steve and I got our helmets, gloves and PG bags sorted out. The two Westies in front of us were discussing if this was a good idea – something we did not want to hear at this point in the game. But they also quickly disappeared from the hole at the back of the plane.

Not to be outdone, Steve and I sauntered back to the door like we knew exactly what we were doing and cinched our leg straps extra tight, then hooking up before getting a pre-jump briefing. The spotter was calling it 700-and-a-bit-plus yards of drift, with a wide grin. But since the spot was long we would be fine so long as we stayed on the wind line. With that advice Bill slapped Steve out half-a-mile away from the jump spot and I followed. I should have known I was going to get kicked harder than normal when I saw Steve get sucked out of the door so fast. But by the time I realized the math, or the logic of that thought, it was too late. So there I was; spinning like a fucking top over Yellowstone for the whole world to see. No wonder I heard laughter.

Chapter Fifteen

— Rookie God

Once in a while, if one is kind to others and lives a good life, a hand, an angel even, might arrive from the heavens to save you from certain doom. Is there a better reason to live a good life?

– Author

T HE ONE REDEEMING FEATURE about my dreadful exit was as my feet went up and the static line reached its length I got snapped upright with a jolt. And that singular violent whiplash did more good than all the chiropractor visits. I initially saw stars – everything literally went white for a while – but once on the ground, and moving around, I realized my neck was better. It was sore as hell but the relief was oh so blissfully obvious. I could now pick up my packout bag without the searing pain in my skull, and rotate my head without wincing. Within an hour the dull headache that had been my constant companion for weeks was gone.

We stacked our gear on the edge of the meadow and retrieved the strewn cargo. Some boxes had broken apart on landing and there were cans of broken fruit cocktail littering the ground like pavement pizza. One of the chainsaw boxes had been carried too far before being thrown out and was stuck up a tree somewhere at the far end of the meadow. A couple of hikers coming along a mountain trail pointed out its whereabouts – 50 feet up a pine tree.

Usually, having arrived to a fire we would gather our tools and immediately get to work digging line. But for sake of the park's ongoing requirement for a light hand on the land we'd been ordered not to dig but use explosives instead. Contrary to thought, explosives actually do less permanent damage than a crew digging line and the ground recovers more quickly afterwards. So our main job was to scout out our line and wait for the Sherpa to come back from West with its cargo of explosives, plus organize the arrival of bear traps being slung in by helicopters to be used at a burgeoning fire camp about a mile away.

Thankfully, we were to have little else to do with that camp and only visited it one morning when a tantalizing smell of bacon somehow wafted over to us on the breeze, sparking immediate pangs of hunger amongst us. On our way, walking along a well-used game trail in the meadow and through the early morning mist, we could see the camp in the distance, somewhat hidden in the haze except for a subtle snaking row of yellow shirts and hardhats patiently queuing up for breakfast. Those long yellow snakes are a familiar and habitual feature of larger fires, where, almost as a time-honored tradition, scores of firefighters arrive to be herded around camp and up to firelines in perfectly disciplined lines.

We walked along the ranks to join on the end. Along the way watching the young, not yet hardened, faces under their plastic hardhats as they stared at us, wondering who these people were that had emerged from the mist-shrouded trees like ghosts and now strolled casually about the camp in undisciplined groups of twos and threes. Our willful disregard for conformity and uniform caught the attention of those responsible for order, and they also stared, but for a different reason. They deliberated if they should complain about something – maybe our lack of visible Nomex, or no hardhats, or our overly casual demeanor – and make an example of us lest their own charges should feel abused and want to emulate this unsanctioned freedom. To their credit, and possibly good fortune, these ersatz drill sergeants recognized something, and better chose to ignore it.

So we continued to join the queue in silence, being not a word uttered or spoken, the morning chill unbroken, as if deigned by a poetic spirit provoking fear of a vow broken. Once there we stood as we arrived, silent and patient, each in our thoughts, each waiting for a freshly cooked breakfast, though forever moving our feet in a conscious effort keep warm in the wet morning grass. Nearer the food, voices began to murmur, soft stunted tones, while others just nodded, aware of not interrupting or not insulting the religion of the morning. Each knowing there would be a great cacophony of noise to come; conversation, yelling, and barked orders, along with the relentless whirring of helicopters and clattering of tools over the coming hours on the line. But for now we were all enjoying the last moments of peace, and waiting on sunshine for warmth and eggs for sustenance. Other than for that, fire camps are mostly nightmarish places. Jumpers are not made for them and, if keeping with tradition, are destined to hate them.

Fire camps arrive overnight as if by magic and end up being fully-fledged canvas villages, little different to the early railroad towns, and everything gets trucked in from kitchens to showers, from equipment supply to Portacabins. Of course, along with each section comes its own administration, following along as a classic paper driven bureaucracy, often just to say that they had been out on a fire and collected hazard pay and overtime – even though the closest they ever got to fire or smoke was being near a dirty shirt in the queue for dinner. It's all a complete cluster, made worse by the arrival of rules. Because administrators have little better to do than make other people's lives infinitely more difficult.

Fire camp food is contracted and many companies supplying it manage to squeak by with providing the bare basic minimum.

Sure, they abide by requirements, but I've never quite understood how two pieces of white bread surrounding a slice of bologna, an apple and an eight-ounce drink, constitutes a wholesome lunch for a firefighter who can burn through thousands of calories each and every 14-hour day on the fireline. I once shoved my lunch under an IC's nose and asked how he "expected a crew to put in a ten-hour shift on this shit." Not knowing who I was, and in the moment, he said he would see what he could do. What happened the next day? Exactly the fucking same. Some ICs don't give a damn; they're in camp all day drinking coffee and bullshitting with the clean shirt brigade or squatting high over the fire burning up helicopter hours. Backdoor generals are the same everywhere.

Thankfully we had our own little camp, just the eight of us, with food for three days and ambition for a whole lot longer. So after brilliant but chilled eggs and bacon we went back to where there was no bullshit and no generals. Just in time to meet the Sherpa as it arrived to make a pass with another load of explosives.

The wind was still whistling down the meadow as the Sherpa buffeted into the winds at about 200 feet. One after another the bundles were kicked out in twos and between each pass two of us would run out to grab a box each. Lifting the 80lb boxes was easy because the chutes stayed inflated in the wind and after only ten minutes the cargo spot was clear and the boxes stacked neatly in the trees. Once that was done six of us tooled up and headed off to dig line because someone had changed their mind. Leaving behind two jumpers to watch the explosives and help organize some park employees to pack them in. We dug line for about eight hours, finishing our assigned section before getting some rest. In the evening we continued on another section, digging until it was dark. Down in the dirt we didn't feel at all like the glorious gladiators we had earlier admired from afar. Feeling more like subservient slaves as we bowed, swung, chopped and scraped our way along the line, in continuous relentless motion, one tedious foot at a time.

But once our section of fireline was completed and we'd tied in with two other shot crews we remained as helipad managers, organizing all the incoming equipment for our end of the fire. It was one of the easiest fires I had ever had so far and I never ate smoke once. We stayed three nights and eventually got choppered out to one of the tourist car parks. Where a family of fat tourists walked by holding their noses in contempt, asking us disgustedly when the last time we'd had a bath. Gratitude is a wonderful thing, but on occasion in such short supply.

We returned to the base in the evening after first stopping in West Yellowstone for the traditional end-of-assignment per diem dinner. Then, once we had our gear straightened away for the next fire, had filled out our fire-time sheets and, of course, showered to appease the tourists, we headed off into town to meet up with everyone else at the Stage Coach. Only this time we had our own long-winded jump stories to tell.

Other jumpers had returned from the many fires over the district and so with West's complement getting back to normal we assumed the Zoolies would quickly get shipped back to Missoula. But Greg told us that since nothing was happening further west we were probably going to stay for a while. This suited us perfectly, although the missus wasn't too chuffed. I never knew whether she was jealous I was having so much fun or that she really missed me.

After getting off the fire we were now at the bottom of the jump list, working on a rotation where whoever's at the top goes out and everyone else moves up. It's about as fair a system as any, although it does have its quirks that can become quite contentious at times. Not least when a booster goes out and returns to base without ever jumping a fire, and then rotates to the bottom without any fire time and, of course, earning no overtime. I was to enjoy that particular oddity later during the summer, as well as a number of equally strange anomalies, all annoying and all wondrously financially unbeneficial.

Up until the mid- to late-90s rookies were rarely allowed in the loft in Missoula because there were always plenty of older jumpers wanting the rigger work, having themselves, for the most part, waited a long time to do so and being able to pack chutes far quicker than a rookie. In the first year, then, there was very little opportunity to learn the basics of rigging parachutes. (Things have since changed, but in some ways I think the old method better. It gave rookies something to strive for, rather than handing them everything on a platter.) But at West there was no such problem.

Once everything was fire ready – cargo packed, chainsaws refurbished, tools sharpened, personal equipment re-organized and plane reloaded, etc. – and once Jiggs had done with us, there was plenty of time to practice packing parachutes. Miguel and Eric, two other Zoolies, were only too pleased to help and Eric showed me how to pack my first FS chute, but since I wasn't qualified to sign off on it and put it in the shelf Eric opened it himself on the way to his next fire.

Eric was a patient teacher, infusing confidence without really knowing it while instilling a work ethic unbridled among all who worked with him. He was always working. When looking for Eric all you had to do was go to the loft and you'd find him hard at work behind a sewing machine repairing the anti-inversion netting (AIN) on damaged parachutes.[*] On fires, follow the noise and you'd find him with a chainsaw in his hand. This quiet Finnish ox of a man should have gone far in the organization, but it let him down, let itself down and missed the opportunity of having one of the best squad leaders in the business. Just by being there Eric had

---

[*] 1970 British design sewing netting to the skirt of the canopy that dramatically reduced apex inversions and line-over malfunctions. First used on the T-10 in 1978.

the respect of everyone, especially the rookies, who always looked for support, encouragement and experience from veteran jumpers. Eric was always around and willing to provide an uncluttered and honest perspective on the organization, on fire and life in general. Losing people of Eric's caliber and experience signals the end of an era, and that is a sad thought for me. Indeed, it should be a sad thought for everyone.

During a particularly tiresome ethics and conduct class I once mentioned that I would buy the book that Eric had been doodling for years. Every lecture, every boring moment, every opportunity possible, I watched as Eric scribbled away in his blank paperback. We knew he was an exceptional artist – having already published a children's smokejumper coloring book – and when I saw he was nearing completion of this new endeavor I said I would give him $200 for it. Initially I don't think he thought me serious but when I got back from a fire one day I saw the book sitting in my bin, so I immediately cut him a check. Never being one to balance a checkbook I never knew that he hadn't cashed it until I noticed it still pinned to his bin only few years ago. I still have his book. It wasn't a series of doodles at all, but a complete illustrated comic story from beginning to end. Marvelous stuff, and what a talent.

On Eric's last day I had already been long gone, but I showed up at the base to repay the compliment by giving him a copy of my first attempt at a book: *Inside the Great Game*. When people like Eric, Mike, Rudy, Jim, Jim and Jim, Jeff, Andy and Larry retire, to name but a few, those are indeed sad days for the organization.

Before returning to Missoula we had two more fires. One, a three-manner with Miguel just outside of Livingston on the north edge of the Park. Beautiful country. Getting to it early in the day, we lined it right away and spent the next day turning over the hot bubbling dirt before the heat finally dissipated. It had clearly been burning in the litter layers for a long time because the heat was so deep into the ground. Three days later, after rummaging in the dirt with our bare hand for countless hours looking for the slightest ember, we thought it safe to leave and organized our demob.

We packed our gear to a small clearing half-a-mile away where a Jet-Ranger collected us and took us to a fire camp near Big Timber, where we ran into some Missoula rookies coming off another fire. Walt had been the IC and several among the crew of sixteen were rookies already on their second and third jump. It had been a big fire and had gotten a lot bigger.

The jumper rumor mill is remarkably efficient and it took a mere ten minutes for us to learn the latest cluster. This time about a tree frog who had correctly checked that his chute was secure in the branches above him, casually sliding aside his PG bag and reserve as directed, properly tying off his letdown rope, placing it correctly under his legs for friction and then proceeding to unclip his Capewells, and then discovering he had forgotten to thread the rope through his D-rings!

Lucky to have escaped severe injury he came away with only minor burns to his hands and thigh. Then, seeing as Walt was IC on the fire they decided to quickly cut down the tree to remove any incriminating evidence. Keith's escape was certainly fortunate, and inspired in us the presence of a Rookie God.

Rookies do stupid things. Always have and always will. Some born from ignorance and some from arrogance. Some of it, though, is nothing less than sheer bad luck. Whatever is the cause, and for whatever reason, rookies seem to get one chance to survive it.

On his second jump Keith had already used his. I waited until the end of the summer for my season ending injury. One that could have been a whole lot worse (though as I write I know it to have been worse, because it still causes pain 18 years later). That injury put me out for the rest of the season and changed the way I did things for the rest of my life. But I still think myself fortunate.

My early JP and rookie bro, Steve, not to be outdone, was also appreciative of the Rookie God. Being somewhat taller than the average jumper he'd always had trouble getting in and out of the skittish little Beech 99, deservedly dubbed the Puke Box. On his unlucky for some 13th he found himself riding his parachute to the ground sitting atop his cross tie; that little piece of webbing attached to both parachute riser links. To accomplish this neat trick Steve's exit must have been quite spectacular: indeed, a somersault was required. But not surprising since getting someone of Steve's build out the 99 was akin to popping a cork from a bottle. Once his canopy opened he reached overhead for his toggles only to find them underneath his butt, with lines heading off in all directions. With no control everyone on the ground was wondering where he was going, but the Rookie God found Steve a nice big Doug-fir in which to drop him. But that was not yet the end, for he was again fortunate. This angelic-like entity didn't just leave him dangling helplessly up a tree, but stood him up on a branch, allowing him to untangle the myriad loose lines wrapped around his body, which, had he been hanging, would have been taut and almost impossible to extricate himself from. But being on a branch allowed him to do an unencumbered and safe letdown.

Everyone heard about the drama in double quick time because it happened right in front of a herd of squad leaders, even, I think, the base manager! To celebrate the event a little ditty was arranged by Pat and Scott: *Cross-tie Rider in the Sky*, sung to the obvious tune, *Ghost Riders in the Sky*.[*]

Smiley, a Grangeville jumper, had one of the most remarkable Rookie God experiences any of us have ever witnessed. We'd been on the North Fork together and it was great to see a familiar face in the following year's rookie class. But during his rookie season he was jumping in Northern California where the trees are monsters,

---

[*] *Cross-tie Rider in the Sky* (p. 346)

over 200 feet tall. The jumpers were making it into a reasonably small spot when a wind change suddenly blew Smiley into the side of one of these mammoth trees – one of the worst ways to find a tree. His chute barely snagged a branch and deflated, creating an audible gasp from everyone watching in the aircraft as he started to freefall away from the tree at a horrible height. The result, we all knew, was inevitable. Then, at the penultimate moment, his chute caught some air and re-inflated, allowing him to float gently to the ground. It was as if the hand of God had appeared to grab his chute and set him gently down. The relief from everyone in the plane was apparent and immediate. I can only imagine what Smiley must have been thinking while standing in that meadow looking up at that great tree. "Phew!" does no justice at all.

Keith also had an amazing and unexplainable escape on a fire in the Clearwater. Like many in that large Idaho forest it consisted of massive, hollow, old-growth Cedars. Their crew had finished digging line for the night and had moved some distance away from the fire to get some rest. In the middle of the night, when everyone was fast asleep, Keith suddenly bolted awake, jumped out of his sleeping bag and made a run for it. No sooner had he got out of the vicinity when the top of a cedar came crashing down, splintering shards of broken branches everywhere. These massive splinters are quite deadly, spearing into the ground like javelins. Everyone was by now awake and Keith wandered back to find his sleeping bag buried two feet into the dirt beneath the toppled tree.

We say he must have subconsciously heard the initial crack of the tree breaking, but he swears he doesn't remember. Whatever it was, something not easily explained saved him that night. Some people have angels looking out for them. Rookies are fortunate in having the Rookie God.

Chapter Sixteen

— The Zoo

The power of accurate observation is frequently called cynicism by those who don't have it.

– George Bernard Shaw

W E SPENT SEVERAL MORE DAYS at West doing mundane but necessary base chores before dispatch decided they'd had enough of us and sent us packing. A Cessna came to fly us back to Missoula, where we arrived early evening after everyone had left for the day. No matter how hard we worked while away, returning always triggered the same sense; the end of something good, end of an adventure, the end of a vacation.

Roll call the following morning further ingrained that thought. Instead of the casual attitude of West with PT before breakfast we were back to rigidity and discipline. But with almost five times as many jumpers it was inevitable. While away the New Mexico crew had returned, leaving the desert southwest when the monsoons drove them out. For over a month we'd heard of these phantoms jumping in arguably the most challenging and rugged terrain in the country. Now we got to meet these heroes. They didn't seem to be different from anyone else apart from their tans; looking as though they'd just come from a Mexican beach drinking Coronas as they gathered for roll call in an assortment of colorful shorts and Tevas.

Having all the jumpers back meant Steve and I were again at the bottom of the list, and a very much longer list this time. Ed was also at the bottom just below me because he'd arrived back a few minutes after us the previous evening. So it was back to boxes. I started to wonder exactly how many boxes the base could possibly need because the warehouse had scant room left to store them all.

Having everyone back in Missoula gave us time to have a few more practice jumps so that Walt could check our progress to make sure we had improved and not picked up any bad habits. It was the first time many of us we had jumped with veterans as our JPs and soon noticed that although they all appeared to know what they were doing and were remarkably casual in the aircraft, some made the same mistakes as we – and received the same admonishment afterwards.

As I was gathering my gear for the jump, Don came over and introduced himself. I'd seen him around but briefly but noticed that others seemed to think he was the classic jumper. He was clearly good friends with Walt, both living down in the Bitterroot Valley, and looked like he'd used a chainsaw for years since his shirt wore the classic scars of experience. He had seen that we were to be JPs on the practice jump. Okay, I thought, no problem, he's bigger so he goes first, nothing much new in that. Nevertheless, it was one of those little proving moments. Each rookie knew not to screw up on this particular jump, not necessarily because of what Walt would say but because of what our veteran JPs would think.

Good communication between JPs was always stressed, and on practice jumps a few veterans started that process even before suiting up because they knew the jump spots so well. What no one knew, however, was the weather and the pattern the plane would fly. So we thought it rather premature to be discussing strategy beforehand. Better to do that in the aircraft when all the aspects of the jump can be seen first hand and understood by all. Having said that, the strategy being maintained by some of the veterans towards the rookies was easy to understand: "Stay the fuck out of my way" being the most common.

Jim was spotting and he was seen surreptitiously dropping an extra streamer as he slapped each veteran jumper out. A couple of them had been complaining about bad spotting procedures over the past few weeks and Jim's retort was priceless: "Well, the streamers made it in just fine. What's your problem? Toggles?" It was true. Jim's extra streamers had landed only feet from the panel, whereas some jumpers landed forty yards away. There were few complaints after that.

Other spotters have at times not been so good, however, and received justified ridicule lest someone got hurt. Such an instance occurred out of Redding in '92 when a Boise spotter couldn't get a single set of streamers into a spot in a clear-cut. After six failed attempts the spotter then turned to the first two jumpers and said, "I can't get the streamers in but you'll do okay." When asked if they had jumped they said: "Hell no!"

The exact same thing happened a few years later when I was in the door with Jim, and with the same dumbass spotter no less. Jim and I turned to each other, somewhat gobsmacked, with a look of "you've gotta be fucking kidding me," before demanding we try another spot. It's the jumper outside the door whose going to break himself not the bloody spotter. Ultimately each individual jumper must make a personal decision whether to exit the aircraft, based upon experience, ability, and the efficiency of their equipment to counter whatever they find outside the safety of that fast moving tube in the sky.

After the jump Walt walked around congratulating the rookies on improving their procedures. He approached me saying, "better Hubble," even smiling a little. I think it was a smile anyway. Either way, a compliment from our resolute training foreman was always welcome. Seeing everyone do better was probably a great relief to him. He was fully invested in everyone and dedicated to all aspects of training. He well understood that our welfare was largely in his hands and always tried to forestall any encroaching bad habits by 20-year veterans and rookies alike. Cracking my neck on that first fire jump had done the trick for me, releasing me from weeks of pain and I never had a problem after that. No doubt it was a relief to both of us. Having said that, I would never suggest doing it as replacement for a chiropractor!

A few small fires came and went and the list rotated painfully slowly. At weekends the list would change because throughout the summer months we worked a split workweek; some took Friday and Saturday off, others Sunday and Monday, allowing the base to have resources available all through the week, and creating regular discussions about the pros and cons of either. At the time I took Sunday and Monday off since that was the only day that matched Anne's day off. Although with most Missoulians working a four-day week Thursday nights were always the best night to go out, making Friday mornings a little rough on occasion.

However, the Sunday-Monday schedulers did seem to get a little more overtime because if we went out on Friday or Saturday, having moved quicker up the shorter weekend list, we were usually guaranteed to work our days off – reaping maximum OT potential.

It was on this split week that Steve and I finally got separated and my new JP was Ed. Then with the weekend upon us we were finally, as if by magic, back on the load to go out if there was a fire call. At the end of the day on Saturday, almost at the very moment we were all heading home, rumors started, giving us an inkling that something might be afoot in dispatch. Hopeful jumpers arrived at operations in ones and twos, trying to listen in on the phone calls in the hope of that last chance jump. Even those with no chance were hoping for a chance, such is the unrelenting optimism of an eager, money-hungry, jumper. (It's not greed, it's winter survival!) The air was electric and raw with anticipation, a few were even getting suited up, as if to spark *Ernie* into action. Then, to solidify all that pent up hope the siren sounded. Hearts raced as we suited up in the heat of the early evening, everyone with a big smile, not quite believing their luck. Checking we had all our gear, plus iced water and bagels, we jogged across the ramp full of excitement and loaded up into the DC-3 – it having just returned from Silver City – lest someone change their minds. Twenty minutes later we were flying over Rock Creek, east of Missoula, a frequent destination for jumpers over the years. Looking down, the fire was easily visible and spotting around a rock slide. It would only need eight jumpers, to the great disappointment of those at the back. But we couldn't see a suitable jump spot anywhere. After performing a series of low passes over some possible green areas we saw that they were, in fact, all littered with rocks. Not that surprising for Rock Creek! Our foreman and spotter then proposed a timber jump as the only option. So after selecting a nice patch of lodgepoles about 200 yards above the fire we mentally prepared ourselves for another tree landing.

Our last timber jump was still fresh in our minds as Ed and I tightened our leg straps and puckered a little. With our vast wealth of new experience we knew the first branches we hit would snap off easily. But also knew the further down we went the branches could snap us just as easily. The three previous sticks were already among the trees as we drifted down trying to pick out a good one; not too big, not too small, not too brittle and not too thick. But we knew that even with the best intention in the world shit happens and prepared ourselves for the worst. Ed crashed through a tree a few yards from where I was heading, capping it perfectly. I pulled brakes and slid down the trunk of a nearby lodgepole, bouncing to rest a few feet above the dirt. Following protocol, I did a correct full letdown despite being near the ground. Jumpers have hanged themselves on their cords from less height. The top of the tree can get snagged under the branches of a neighboring tree and when it becomes disengaged the tree can bounce back upright, taking the neck of a jumper with it. Four jumpers made it through the tree canopy and found hard ground. The rest of us would have to do a little climbing to get our chutes out later. One of us would be doing a lot of climbing: Richard had somehow found the biggest pine this side of the mountain, and probably this side of Rock Creek.

Before doing that, though, we needed to take care of the fire. We packed up as much gear as we could, placed it into the trees and headed off down hill to retrieve the cargo and get to work. The pilot owed us beer that day. We found both chainsaws stuck in the trees. So as two guys climbed the rest of us broke out pulaskis and started digging, three each side of the fire. The flame lengths were small so we pinched it off at the head to stop it spreading up and then dug down each side. Most of the fire was in the litter layer or creeping around underneath the rocks. Some trees were smoldering but there was little active flame.

Rock Creek is suitably named and our pulaskis grew dull in a few minutes. Cutting line down the sides wasn't too difficult, but at the bottom we had to build a large cup trench in a rockslide to catch any rolling embers, ending up being quite the construction project. But once done and the line completed, at about two in the morning, we were able to relax, enjoy the rest of the night and get some food. We spread out around the fire looking for burning logs and hot spots to keep us warm as it became colder in the early morning, and were stirred into immediate action when a large tree in the center of the fire decided to come down, crashing to the ground in a heap of charcoal and dust. We dug more line around the slop over and left it to cool down.

The following morning we gathered together to hear someone hacking their lungs up. Jeff had caught the flu and looked pretty awful. We delved into the first-aid kits and found some Coricidin tablets that seemed to relieve the worst of it. There's little worse than being sick while on a fire. The sore throat, stuffed-up sinuses and headache are all exacerbated by the constant exertion, and the smoke only makes the symptoms even more intolerable. Packets of Coracedin, Emergen-C, Gatorade, coffee and quarts of tepid water mixed with the latest 'stay awake' sachets of concentrated tea were our perpetual medications. The SMJ adage of sickness being: "If you're going to be sick you might as well get paid for it."

With the fire contained and starting to get beaten down, the foreman let half the crew go and retrieve their chutes. Some chutes were well and truly capped, overlapping several different trees and a real problem to retrieve, eventually coming down torn to shreds, covered in sappy needles and broken branches,. One came down with a big simple tug in the right direction, but not Richard's, he spent half the day in the tree. Someone even hauled his lunch up on a rope because he didn't want to come down for it. When he did finally emerge he was totally exhausted; dry sweat crystallized on his face, his shirt torn and trousers covered in yellow sap. It was a long time before he found another tree. That one was incentive to never do it again.

We mopped up all day with our pulaskis like useless blocks of steel after files became smooth from constant sharpening. Which meant swinging all the more to chop though any roots and crud. I was chopping around the base of a tree when I caught something in my right eye. It snuck by the side of my sunglasses and embedded right below the pupil to become a constant irritant for the rest of the fire. It felt like I had burned my eye, similar to when someone set off a bottle rocket close to my head while at school. It didn't put me in the best of moods and when someone decided we needed to improve the fireline I just about lost it. The fireline was mostly a rockslide! Even Joey complained, and he never complained about anything. Not in those days.

So we hurled our blunt pulaskis against unimpressed rocks one more time and rearranged the line for the umpteenth time. All brilliant stuff. You couldn't make it up. During this rock-bashing, chain-gang routine Keith twisted his knee. The terrain was rough and steep and slipping on unstable rocks was a constant problem. Keith went down and it looked like he'd torn his anterior cruciate ligament (ACL), a common injury while jumping and traversing rugged slopes. Bob called in the medevac chopper from Missoula while two of us carried his 200lbs of muscle up the slope. There wasn't an ounce of lard on him and we were all steeped in sweat by the time we got him up to the rock-strewn helispot. He wasn't happy about being carried, but he was even less happy at having to leave the fire. No jumper wants an injury. It's not only a financial loss but injured jumpers also tend to be treated like pariahs. It's a strange, though not uncommon, trait among such physical groups, where everybody knows how easy it can happen but no one wants to see it, or be around it lest they be reminded of the fact in case the bad luck rubs off on them.

With Keith gone we improved the line a man short until we were convinced the fire was out. Then we packed our gear and hauled it up to the helispot. Once the chopper had slung everything out we headed down to a road to be picked up, which sounds easy except for the hundreds of yards of slick moss covered rocks and a boulder strewn river in between.

Jumpers rarely walk together, almost as if it's a religion. They either find their own way or walk in pairs, something that is alien to most other crews, often confounding and infuriating their crew leaders. On leaving we headed off in five or six different directions and yet all met at the same place. In general, smokejumpers have a good sense of direction because they get a bird's eye view of the terrain before and during the jump. But there's always exceptions. The jump base has, at times, been host to those rare few jumpers who needed cowbells so others could hear when they got lost. One such person turned the wrong direction while walking to a river in New Mexico and ended up 20 miles away in Arizona.

Walking downhill in steep terrain is always tough on knees, especially beaten-up jumper's knees. If not built by man there are few trails that weave around a mountain and few animal trails that don't just go straight down. Contouring is not something animals, or jungle tribes apparently, tend to do when going up or down a mountain. It seems only westernized humans have become used to contouring. During WWII in Burma, when exhausted British and Indian troops were manhandling artillery pieces up muddy slopes in the rainy season, where even Mules couldn't go, they contoured hills to have an easier march. The magnificent Gurkhas, however, just walked straight up. One tired British Officer once asked why they walked up in a straight line. A confused and muddy Gurkha responded: "Sir? But that is the way to the top."

After hobbling down a few rockslides we finally came to the river. It was only 25 yards wide and flowing nicely so we walked downstream and each picked our spots to wade across. On the far side we stripped off our wet clothes and laid them out on the warm sunny rocks while waiting for our ride, more than a little worse for wear. We had beaten rocks like convicts for three days. Our hands were blistered and our arms ached from the shattering pounding. My eye was sore and irritated and I needed to have it seen to when we got home, but for now we sat quietly, munching away on our few remaining snacks while watching the river meander by. It was a satisfying rest.

On the way to Missoula we stopped at the famous Rock Creek Lodge for dinner, known for its raunchy Testicle Festival. But it was too late in the summer for their Rocky Mountain Oysters so we made do with burgers, salads and shakes, and anything else to restore our energy. After filling our bellies we all relaxed and fell asleep on the short ride home. Rather too relaxed for some because the windows were repeatedly opened to remove the foul smelling odor originating from a lethal mixture of spam, dry food, Gatorade, copious amounts of strong coffee and instant tea.

August was now heating up and lightning more frequent. As the days passed we would stand outside the ready room and watch the clouds build up over the mountains. Then, depending on the time of day, we determined whether we would later see lightning from the large cumulonimbus clouds. If they started forming too late the winds would blow them away before having a chance to mature. But if we were lucky, and they started early enough, they would congregate over the mountains and create *Ernie's* wonderful money clouds. We lived by them. Everything we did and all we had was due to them.

Money clouds. Forest Service bureaucrats visibly cringe at the term. Some even tried to stop us from using it! But were it not for these wonderful culminating accumulations during the summer we wouldn't have a job. And neither would they.

During the late '80s Missoula had a single administrative ex-jumper for about 75 jumpers, rotating his time between the base and the regional office (RO) in town. It all seemed to work pretty well. No one seemed to have any problems. Yet in barely ten years administration had grown into a formidable empire, even building its own castle. An empire that inevitably created more paperwork to account for its existence and maintain its survival. From whence it grew even more. All initiated by self-protectionism as each new desk-jockey justified a position by data chunking. And from where did they get all this newfound data? You guessed it! With this massive increase in administration jumpers' paperwork increased exponentially in order to, solely, support the very people who were supposed to be supporting us.

It's an error to think administration is any longer a support role. It is not. It is a parasite that feeds off everything around it, and if not checked it eventually renders its host completely useless. As it once almost did by forcing jumpers to enter their per diem on a slew of hand-me-down computers, some of which had corrupted hard-drives, resulting in jumpers routinely wasting $60 in time fighting with archaic software to get back $14 in per diem. Support that was not, and common sense in rectifying this dazzlingly dumb situation took years. Such is the brilliance and timeliness of well paid administration, sucking the life blood from the sharp end.

This empire, growing before our eyes, led us to believe many of its subjects held positions solely as a courtesy of a government sponsored job placement scheme, and a well-paid scheme it was. The wage differential between people willing to parachute out of planes to fight wildfires in remote forests and the pampered office wallas being fanned in air-conditioned comfort is nothing short of ludicrous. To widen the cleavage between dirt and godliness these administrators had the shameless gall to arbitrarily subtract lunch breaks from firefighters' hours while they were still fighting on the firelines. Where the fuck was everyone going to go? McDonald's? I was once hot-footing it up to a ridge away from a fleet-footed fire when the jumper next to me said: "I suppose this will be classed as our lunch break." He was not wrong; that was exactly the half-hour that was removed from our time sheet. Because of this, and other equally shameful brainless absurdities, we found ourselves having to work more and more just to maintain our same modest salaries. All so the organization could save money at the hot-n-toasty end to pay for the burgeoning administration at the over-indulged soft and fluffy end. Zoolie began to take on a completely different meaning.

People need to comprehend the flaw in allowing administrators to decide where cuts should be made, because even if they live to be a hundred they ain't ever going cut themselves out of anything. If you're on the toasty sharp end, it's your check, your time, your life that suffers, because its feeding time for the parasite. The biggest parasite is always at the top, looking more and more important for every new subordinate it attracts to its nest. Empire building.

A few days after the Rock Creek fire we learned Keith's knee wasn't as bad as expected, but it was still bad enough to keep him hobbling, off the list, and laying low behind a sewing machine in manufacturing. He was naturally disappointed but didn't show it, and exuded the same confidence and sense of humor we'd come to expect from him. It was good having Keith around, although not, perhaps, sitting behind a Singer. Sewing was not one of his most proficient skills.

My irritated eye healed quickly after a surgeon removed a tiny sliver of steel – a small piece of pulaski as a souvenir – so I was never off the list, which was rotating steadily every couple of days. Although we were all near the bottom of it again but watching it hourly to see if it would miraculously alter in some way. The ever hopeful optimists hovering around operations like vultures to the bemused fascination of the operations foreman. "Talk to the hand," he would say, holding up an outstretched palm in defiance.

Chapter Seventeen

— Packouts

We few, we happy few, we band of brothers.

– William Shakespeare

R UNNING SOUTH OF MISSOULA the Montana/Idaho border is defined by the Bitterroot Mountains. Missoula generally jumps the Montana side and Grangeville the Idaho side, although the boundary becomes insignificant during busy periods or when one base or another is short of jumpers. The Bitterroots themselves, however, are far from insignificant. They form a most impressive link in the three thousand mile chain that makes up the Rocky Mountains from Canada to New Mexico. Any lack in height is overshadowed by spectacular rugged peaks, deep canyons and pristine streams. Along with many of the mountain ranges that together make the backbone of the Continent these are steeped in history. Lolo Pass, just outside of Missoula, is now a popular x-country ski area, but originally gained fame when Lewis and Clark used it to twice cross the Bitterroot Range during their Corps of Discovery expedition to and from the Pacific in 1805 and 1806. When they first climbed the Rockies, expecting to see the Pacific Ocean on the far side, the swath of mountains before them forever ended their hope of finding a northwest passage. Not until the construction of the Pacific Railroads was that vision realized in 1869. Eight years later Chief Joseph again made Lolo Pass famous during the heroic Nez Perce 1,170-mile fighting retreat, first to the Big Hole and finally the Bear Paw Mountains of Montana.

Before Lewis and Clark, European and Russian trappers were already dominating the burgeoning fur trade from Canada south to the great northern rivers, mountains and prairies of old Louisiana Territory. Plying their lavish pelts to wealthy Europeans via the Hudson's Bay Company, still very much in existence as the oldest commercial corporation in North America. Although these hardy old mountain men would likely not have survived but for the trade induced tolerance of American Indian tribes already inhabiting this untamed land for centuries. From the Cree in the Plains, across the Crow's great Yellowstone River Valley to the Flathead east of the Bitterroots and north to the Blackfoot, much of whose land now encompasses another national treasure, Glacier National Park. To these proud ancient peoples this land is sacred and significant. And after seeing it first-hand who could possibly disagree. These, and other equally historic tribes across the country have been the great explorers, fighters and custodians of this land for generations, and we, as jumpers, are but fortunate beneficiaries.

The Selway-Bitterroot Wilderness, third largest wilderness in the Lower 48, sitting amidst this region and covering more than 1.3 million acres, is a frequent destination for jumpers from Missoula, Grangeville, West Yellowstone and Boise. Even though it is right on the smokejumpers' doorstep a more pleasant destination would be hard to find. And in that regard jumpers are extremely fortunate. Few people apart from the hardiest hunter and adventurous hiker visit the more remote parts of this formidable wilderness. Which is somewhat evident by the nonchalant attitude of many of its animal population. Deer would often just stroll through our camps without a care, being more concerned with foraging for food. Elk roam the hills and moose are seen grazing the valleys, feeding off succulent grasses along the many trout filled streams and brooks. Black bears generally keep to themselves, but many a jumper has gotten a first glimpse of a bear in the Selway. Tracks of mountain lion are common although I know of no one having ever seen one of these elusive cats in the wild. From the largest animals to the tiniest inquisitive little critters this is home, and they expect us to leave it as we find it. It really is one of the most wonderful and impressive places – and we get to jump it in our own backyard.

A week after returning from Rock Creek our load was only just getting over the bout of flu we had caught from Jeff when we jumped another fire in the Selway-Bitterroot Wilderness, a six-manner with Steve, Bruce, Scott, Morgan and Pat. We jumped a small clearing just below the fire and above a small creek bed. We could probably have gotten away with four but there was no way to know for sure how big the fire was from the aircraft, and since most of the load had jumped a while earlier the spotter kicked the remainder of us out on this one. Then, because we were in the wilderness and not permitted to use chainsaws, the spotter attached a crosscut saw to one of our food boxes.

We dug a quick easy line around the fire and started to mop-up immediately – cooling the dirt and extinguishing all burning fuel inside the perimeter. In the center of the fire were a couple of large fallen tree trunks needing attention before they attracted too much heat, ignited, and caused us unnecessary work. We shared the crosscut work by having a series of competitions to see which two of us could cut through the three feet diameter logs the quickest. Being rookie bros Steve and I were naturally teamed together. After much sweat the log was neatly chunked, some of it to become firewood for our cooking fire. The sweat, mixed with the soot and ash on our faces, made little rivers of dirt that when dry gave the appearance of tiger stripes. To determine the winner we stopped for coffee, only to discover someone had conveniently not timed the event. It appeared to be more of a ruse to see how much effort the rookies would expend on the task. It worked.

In the evening the CNA crew breezed on through and we prepared our hooches. Jumpers rarely carry tents and instead use a small nylon tarpaulin, or poncho, that can be stretched to provide a very basic cover from the weather. Strands of Kevlar are attached to whatever will hold it taut: trees, branches, rocks, tufts of grass, or even an embedded pulaski if nothing else is available. Each fire allows for a different hooch design, depending on terrain, weather and places to tie it down. Then each jumper has a different idea of what a hooch should be – although some evidently have no idea at all. Hooch construction is almost an art form. Some can be modest high-rise, though drafty, mansions, others cramped covert low-lying hideouts designed to limit the intrusion of wind and rain.

A few hardy souls don't bother erecting a hooch at all and, instead, suffer through all sorts of weather, although I never really saw the point of such discomfort for the sake of a two pound piece of nylon. After all, wilderness comfort implies some amount of intelligence, because without comfort morale and effectiveness can plummet – especially when out in the elements for longer than first thought through days of inclement weather. Morgan, however, was having nothing to do with a poncho or minimalism and went to work constructing a veritable shack. It wasn't the sort of thing to be doing in a wilderness, where we were supposed to leave things as though we'd never been, but he'd been doing the job longer and no one seemed too bothered – apart from wondering why he was expending so much effort. He later told us he had simply forgotten his poncho, so full marks for ingenuity I guess.

Bruce had his hooch set up perfectly in a flat spot between some nicely spaced trees. Using his parachute as a bed and a cargo chute for a mosquito net he looked quite at home drinking coffee and reading his latest tome surrounded by silk as though he was in India during the Raj.

Bruce escaped to Alaska the following year. Missoula politics having driven him to greener pastures. Pat left with him and when done with jumping found a job guiding climbs in the Himalayas. What a loss to Missoula. As I write, Bruce has retired from Alaska. One of the nicest, unassuming, smartest people I've ever known. We had quite an inebriated bar crawl in Seattle one winter after he returned from Russia, after being directly involved with Russian smokejumpers. Speaking fluent Russian probably helps in that regard. It took him about eight bars and many more ales before we got through his huge stack of adventuresome holidays snaps.

On this occasion, after emerging from a bar in Fremont, and heading to the Dubliner, someone put their fist in my face. Without breaking stride or conversation I returned the favor, sending him reeling over a bicycle rack and out into the street. When we talked about it years afterwards we realized how funny it must have been, because through the whole episode we kept our conversation going and strode into the Dubliner oblivious to anything. Apparently the guy did apologize, according to Bruce, his excuse being mistaken identity. If that's the case I must look like an awful lot of people because for some reason it happens with all too frequent regularity.

When we were finished I had to call Sara and ask her to come and pick me up. "Are you actually drunk?" She asked.

"I bloody hope so," I said.

Bruce, like many jumpers, is also an incredibly talented artist, both with canvas and sculpture. I hope he manages to channel that talent into something more than pleasure, because 20-plus years of GS-6 smokejumping doesn't provide the financial security that it should. In fact, all jumpers should be better rewarded. Especially those temporary GS-6s who do the majority of the grunt work year after year: prostituting their bodies for a job they love without any benefits or security whatsoever, and with no guarantee of future employment. That unbridled passion is sorely abused, both by the organization that benefits and the administrators making the rules.

We were covered in grime again. Days of constant sweat and dust were ingrained in out pores. Mop up had been an unusually dusty process because the ground had been so hot it had boiled, creating pools of liquid dirt. But after gridding the area we called it out and planned our demob. Although there wasn't really much to plan since we were in a designated wilderness area, which meant we would not get helicopter support to lift out our gear. No amount of asking would get it, except for broken bones perhaps, so we packed and kicked the lumps out of our packout bags ready for an eleven mile packout to the Lochsa.

Everyone has a preference on how to arrange their kit for a packout. Mine was simply to make sure nothing poked me in the back for eleven miles and to keep the weight high. Packout bags are light and flimsy, made of basic Cordura, and provide no natural padding or comfort whatsoever, so we use our parachutes as best we can. The bottom of the bag is filled with the bulky items: main chute, reserve parachute, jump suit, helmet, harness, letdown rope, gloves, and odd bits of clothing, etc. The PG bag usually goes on top with any left over food stuffed down the sides. Water is placed near the top because it needs to be reached easily. The pulaski is carried in the hand, making a good walking stick, useful for when navigating awkward terrain or over riverbeds. The crosscut is then curved and strapped over the top of the bag. The finished product frequently weighs more than 120lbs. And since there are no scales in the woods we just pack, guess, suck it up, and carry it for as far as we need. After which our knees, hips and lower back continue to complain for a further week. Pull-ups are brilliant for stretching out the spine afterwards!

Pat had already set off, saying he was going to scout the trail, but since the trail was clearly marked we figured he just wanted to get ahead and be by himself. The rest of us, meanwhile, placed our bags on the ground, kicked in the last lumps, laid down on top of them, put our arms into the straps and tried to stand.

There was no way in the world all that weight was going to be comfortable, especially with our old packout bags, so we tended to just grin, bear it, get on with it, all the while looking for that sense of humor about the whole experience. I figured the faster I went the sooner it would be over. Bruce figured the slower he went the more he might enjoy it. Everyone generally had a preferred tactic and most tactics fail miserably. Pain is guaranteed. Miles of it.

Beginning the trek, we trundled off down a critter track before finding a trail after a couple of miles where we took a moment to rest and drink some water. We each carried a gallon at minimum and didn't want to run out because we didn't know how long we would be in the woods. If someone got hurt, which would be easy, we could be out there for a long time. Only fools discard water and everyone usually suffers for it.

After a few rocky miles my knees told me that they weren't at all impressed with the trek. It was better going uphill because I could just grunt it out and despite the added exertion it hurt less. It was the downhill sections where we had to be especially careful not to hyperextend a knee under the weight. Our line stretched as we each found our own rhythm and pace, catching up with each other when stopped to rest. There was little point in getting too far ahead in case someone got injured, we'd only have to hike back.

We stopped for lunch by a shaded stream and found company with a group of hikers. They were amazed by the size of our packs, standing so tall above our heads. They were even more amazed, or puzzled, as they watched us struggle to get onto our feet again. The rest by the stream was pleasant but the cool air had significantly stiffened our legs and it took a good half-mile of heavy trudging before they began to warm up to stride again. Our feet soon started to burn under the stress, each step feeling as though skin was being peeled off slowly.

Walking along the traveled trails was actually harder than the deer tracks because they were littered with loose rocks, making it easier to twist an ankle. Decades of mule trains had also left them deeply rutted, made all the worse by the annual spring thaws.

When we got to within a few miles of Moose Creek our pace quickened. Every now and again I could see Pat ahead, which gave me incentive to catch him, just for the hell of it and for something to do to take my mind off the nagging pain in my shoulders. And the sooner it was over the sooner I could sort out my burning feet. Having run for years with a pack I had developed an easy loping action that propelled me forward without over-stressing my knees. So with each bend I slowly gained. Pat was visibly surprised to see this Limey struggling along behind him. He was tall and for every one of his strides I probably took two. It's no wonder he hiked up Everest, for after eleven miles under 120lbs he looked like he was out for a stroll in the park. I was ready to kip for a week.

As we gathered together one at a time at the lake we stripped out of our sweat soaked clothes and went for a swim, leaving our stinking clothes on the grass to dry. It was chilly but inviting, and the water soothed our aching joints like an ice bath. At one end an unconcerned moose sauntered quietly along the bank in solitude, at the other, six filthy men bathed in the cool clear mountain water.

My knees were sore for days afterwards and someone even asked why I was walking like John Wayne. Just stepping off the curb was painful. I tried to jog around the wood shaving running track by the units but it was too early. The result was the same as after playing the Durham Police at rugby during my college days. They had shredded us, clearly relishing the opportunity of doing so, and it was days before the residual pain wore off. The game against the Durham police had been worth forgetting. This, though, had been something to remember. It had been brilliant.

If nothing else, packouts are undoubtedly character building. While training strives to make them easier, determination is what gets people through them. To accept the challenge and accomplish the task is what separates those who can from those who just don't want to try. Rookie training, to some extent, is designed to instill that character by training people to conquer a little bit of adversity. So that when called upon, ability is personally unquestioned. Only in trying and finally succeeding does a person gain the self-respect that motivates the production of intense effort when required for the constant challenges involved in such occupations, and, indeed, later in life when things don't go according to plan, as they most assuredly will not. Respect is often associated to environment and, therefore, needs to be earned in that environment. But once earned it is often infinitely harder to maintain. All that jumpers do gives them a credibility unrivaled in most occupations and that too is a perpetual proving process. All these traits, encapsulated, create morale, which is unquestionably *the* most important collective attribute in any organization. If a group of people have morale they also possess camaraderie. The two are largely inseparable. Those who endure will appreciate the significance and understand the privilege and pride of all who wear that invisible badge.

No matter how short or long a time since their last packout a jumper will endure the pain to get the job done. That is what they do. A question arises, however, when injuries occur because of the political requirement not to allow helicopters or motorized tools into wilderness areas. Notwithstanding the individual issues, one injury can have far reaching consequences; financially, practically, and morally for the organization. Those are management decisions and managers should fully accept responsibility for injuries when they do occur due to those decisions and not pass that burden onto the injured. Even when indirect accidents occur because numbers are reduced due to injuries elsewhere. These points need to be constantly assessed, as well as the moral implication of risking a person's health for what is basically an ideal.

Weird though it may be many jumpers actually like packouts, enjoying the baseness of the challenge. One AK jumper practices packouts under immense weight for his regular fitness regime, so he clearly enjoys them more than anyone! But in hindsight, I also know that without proper preparation it is possible for them to do irreversible damage. Is it, then, worth risking harm for the sake of a political decision based on an ideal? I suppose everyone makes that choice as and when. Given the choice again now, I would unquestioningly do the exactly same and haul that pack around the hills again and again with little qualm. Others, equally, may not. I found it challenging, and in the challenge I find the fun. Then, is it really a political decision, or is it actually, in itself, a moral one, born of history, tradition, respect for the environment and, above all, personal pride?

Apart from the occasional traumatic injuries that are inherent to jumping and firefighting in general (jumpers hitting the ground or pieces of the ground hitting firefighters), there is little doubt that many firefighting injuries occur due to poor conditioning. Here is a dilemma, because most of those on the ground doing the majority of the grunt work are seasonally employed. While maintaining off-season fitness is an absolute necessity for those on the elite crews, it is not such a priority on other crews. That members of the elite crews spend countless hours chucking weights around the gym, or pounding the trails and pavements, for no other reward than to be part of that elite for a few months during the summer, is testament to their drive and fortitude. I know of few other occupations where people volunteer so much of their free time to maintain a level of fitness that directly benefits the employer. In this case the U.S. Government.

Scant appreciation is ever given to this selfless act. Indeed, a few in the organization, even, quite astonishingly, a smokejumper base manager, have tried to curtail, and even halt, smokejumpers, hotshots and helitacks from having the privilege of regular, time honored, one hour physical training sessions during working hours. And for a while these sad deluded dolts even succeeded because other dolts wouldn't, or were too inherently weak, to stand up to them. Whether this stemmed from petty jealousy or a longstanding bitter dispute wasn't made clear. Whatever it was, it was gross incompetence. If firefighters on the more elite crews didn't possess the individual incentive and wherewithal to keep fit, their injury levels would quickly surpass that of the lesser crews because they are more frequently asked to perform more rigorous and more difficult tasks in more unforgiving terrain. Eliminating PT would be a travesty and the organization's effectiveness would dissolve beyond repair. One just has to compare these elite crews to others, where it is not uncommon for crewmembers to remove themselves from the line just for having a blister! This is simple stuff. And yet some people, once in management roles, either get a sudden attack of amnesia and completely forget what it was ever like, never did understand, or conveniently absolve themselves of responsibility to those below once they get promoted. Preferring to, instead, suck-up to everyone above them.

Missoula's particular PT argument was only laid to rest when it was universally agreed that all FS employees could also have an hour of PT. Yes, this even included administrators, whose hardest job was stepping in and out of a swivel chair. Now being allowed PT – which, for most of them, amounted to a sedate stroll around the park smoking a cigarette – the administration's overt disdain for firefighters' PT, obviously born of jealousy, finally dwindled. The whole sorry episode was ludicrous and only allowed to occur because middle managers in positions of power did not support their subordinates, the very people who made them look good. It was a fundamental failure of middle management, something that is still endemic within the FS hierarchy – conveniently cloaked in the auspices of an all-encompassing bureaucracy in which no one is ever personally responsible or accountable for anything. Senior managers still only hire clones, or drones, that they know they can control, those without dissenting views – the opposite of diversity. The grunts on the ground are then left without recourse and remain totally unsupported. And yet these loyal people continue to spend their winters trudging trails, year after year, all so they can return to a job they love. That is where true dedication lies. It is forthright individuals such as these who provide the muscle, intelligence and reason as to why firefighting succeeds – despite the great millstone round their necks that is FS bureaucracy.

Failure in firefighting is usually attributable, either directly or indirectly, to a failure of management. And yet it is the grunts, the working firefighters on the ground, who suffer when managers spit out a host of new reactionary rules – usually involving less hours and less pay – to disguise management complicity in a tragedy. It's a spiral to disaster.

A common theme since 1994 is to keep limiting the hours that firefighters can work. Managers simplistically think accidents only happen when firefighters are tired. I once worked almost 1,200 hours of overtime from April to October in 1994 and was not tired once. Physically drained we may have been but nothing that four hours of sleep wouldn't cure. We were never mentally tired, we were mentally exhilarated! A day off is what made us tired. If we had been tired we would have asked for a day off. We're all adults. Yet since 1994 firefighters have seen their hours steadily curtailed so much as to be almost worthless on some fires. Indeed, one hour after jumping a fire in 2000 we were told to bed down because we had already surpassed our allotted sixteen-hour limit. The fire was still burning, of course, and we could have put it out quite easily. Except for the fact that only half the crew was allowed to work. The logic is unfathomable. One middle manager could have stood up and said this is bullshit, but no one did, not one. Instead, in this instance, we were made to step down for the night. And, ironically, almost got run over by a bunch of cowboys in pick-ups coming to fight the fire that we weren't allowed to fight. Little did they know that firefighters can no longer fight fires when they like, but only when faceless bureaucrats say they can. It's not altogether a good message to send to the indigenous populations when their homes and possessions are in danger of being incinerated.

If firefighters ignore the rules they can be fired. In fact, many in personnel are only looking for an excuse to fire those who would call such an order bullshit (cannot have ~~diversity~~ dissent in the organization). That's why the LAMB is so prevalent in the FS today. Burgeoning personnel departments are no longer supporting those doing the work but are self-sustaining entities, a law unto themselves. Pushing views that are completely alien to the ethos and ethics of the general firefighting community and vigorously suppressing the ability for firefighters to function effectively.

At the height of summer we got a booster from Alaska. It was the first time many of us had jumped with squares onboard. Walt was the foreman on a load taking us to the Lolo. We had been hit by lightning heavily the night before with over a hundred strikes, many of them starting new fires. The DC-3 was split evenly among square and round jumpers, with some of the rounds coming from Redding, California. The first fire we flew was going to take six. The spotter asked the squares if they wanted it but because the spot was so tight in amongst the trees they declined in favor of the next one – there were plenty of fires to go round that day. I hadn't been expecting to leave the aircraft and was relaxing, ready to watch the squares, when I was called back to the door. Grabbing my PG bag and helmet I got ready quickly. Every motion was routine by now, perfectly choreographed so that straps were tightened, helmet was on and cage snapped into place with a gloved hand holding the static line clip on nearing the door. All done in a few bumpy steps as the aircraft bucked and kicked in the unstable roller-coaster air. With a few fleeting glances through a window I tried to gauge the terrain and spot we would be landing in.

The spot was indeed tiny but it was nice and close to the fire. The only other spot was a larger meadow a couple of miles away so we decided on the smaller one. Walt hooked up with Don, his JP. Jim, the spotter, placed Walt's foot in the door and he braced himself. "GET READY!" Followed by a hard slap and they were gone. The overhead steel cable rattled in succession as each static line became taut before flapping in the breeze after the break tape snapped, releasing the jumpers from any connection to the aircraft. Jim looked back, saw both canopies inflated and said: "Jumpers away" into his intercom before hauling in the deployment bags. The pilot, hearing that, banked the aircraft towards the open door, and got set for another pattern. I tightened my leg straps once more and gave the all telling thumbs up to Ken, my JP, letting him know that I knew where the jump spot was, knew what we were going to do, and that I was okay and ready to jump.

Hooking up behind Ken, giving my clip a comforting tug on the overhead cable, I turned my back to the assistant spotter so he could grab some loose static line, making sure there was no chance of it getting wrapped around my head. He slapped my pack, letting me know that he had what he needed and wishing me luck.

Ken had his head out the door watching the first two squeak into the clearing. Now all we had to do was exactly the same thing. "THREE HUNDRED YARDS, LITTLE ON THE GROUND. WE'RE TURNING ONTO FINAL. FLYING INTO THE WIND. THEY BOTH MADE IT IN. ANY QUESTIONS?" We looked at Jim and shook our heads. Then, looking at the assistant spotter he shouted: "YOU'RE CLEAR!"

It was a tiny spot and Walt, my training foreman, would be watching. I had to do well. "ON FINAL!" We jostled around as we readied ourselves, placing our feet exactly where we needed them. "GET READY!" Ken recoiled, waited for a split second and leapt out. I stepped forward, placed my left foot on the door sill, grabbed both sides of the door and heaved myself out in one fluid motion. I tightened, pulled the sides of my reserve into my body, kept my head down and concentrated on keeping my feet together and toes pointed down.

"One thousand. Two thousand. Three thousand. Four..."

It was a decent exit and my chute cracked open nicely, the harness tightening around my chest. Looking up I saw a nice red white and blue canopy fully inflated, with the plane banking in the distance. Ken was below me, giving us good separation. I checked the drift and decided to do quarter turns in the wind cone over to the spot. I did not want to be a tree frog in front of Walt!

Getting lower I could see a few obstacles in the spot; a couple of logs and assorted branches. Lower still I realized half the spot was actually an elk wallow. This left two dry areas, about 20 feet square each, in which to land, one at either end of the spot. Ken picked the north end so I steered towards the south. At 100 feet I turned into the wind and floated down between a couple of trees, picking out a nice patch of ground to plant my feet. I lifted my feet to clear some branches and touched the ground softly, rolling over and hopping up in one fluid motion. Ken looked over and waved.

We were both okay. I quickly collected my chute to allow the next stick to have some room.

The next two were Redding jumpers. As they floated down I packed my jump suit and was just finishing when I heard a loud scream of pain. One of the new arrivals had hit the log and was flat on the ground screaming in agony. Walt was first to him, lifting his leg from the log and trying to untie his boot laces. Then the jumper yelled: "THE OTHER ONE!" The two of us laughed as Walt then lifted the other leg and prepared to remove that boot instead. Often a painful process with a broken ankle. Even so, neither of us had ever seen anyone make such a fuss before over an ankle. He was literally screaming and yelling. Then, as Walt removed his boot he passed out. For a split second Walt and I just looked at each other, half in relief that he had stopped yelling but half in confusion as to why he'd been screaming so much? With him out cold we knew we needed to check on his breathing so I moved up to position his head and discovered that he wasn't!

It was all becoming quite unnecessary really fast. As things tend to do when they go tits up. I raised his head back slightly and placed two fingers alongside his jaw to widen his airway, and he immediately took a breath and woke up. Again, Walt looked at me with an expression of: "What the fuck?"

With all this excitement we hadn't paid much attention to this jumper's JP, who had landed okay but was up to his knees in the elk wallow, and seemed to be sinking. His leg pockets were full of mud and water and dragging him down even further. Don was there trying to haul him out, finally grabbing the back of his harness and dragging him out on his backside. Somewhere there is a photo of the whole episode. Shakespeare would have been proud; it was like a comedy of errors.

The aircraft was still above and waiting to drop cargo but was now lining up to drop another jumper who had replaced his PG bag with the trauma kit. Within a minute or two he had made it safely in, bringing the kit over so Walt could wrap the ankle in ice and stabilize him for when the chopper came in. Walt was an expert at wrapping ankles; he'd been on the ski patrol at Lost Trail for years, though I doubt if he'd ever had as much of a problem as this one. The guy was still making a fuss and clearly in shock. We placed an oxygen mask on him hoping that it would settle him down, which it did, but then realized one of us would have to go out with him.

Life Flight wouldn't get into the spot because it was too small so Minuteman Aviation sent a Jet Ranger that was already working the area. We carried him to the chopper and I got in the back with him. I was disappointed at leaving the fire but someone needed to monitor the guy in case he went into shock and passed out again.

We lifted off and headed to Missoula, finding a larger spot to rendezvous with Life Flight and landing about 40 yards apart so the pilots and I could carry the injured to the awaiting ship. Once he was off to hospital I got back in the chopper and headed back to Missoula. It was barely an hour since I had jumped and I arrived back before the DC-3. Jogging over to the ramp I waited for the pilot to shut down the engines before wheeling the steps to the door, ready to watch Jim's expression when he opened it. He didn't disappoint. He did a quick double take and laughed. "Quick trip Hubble!"

I went straight into operations, explained what had happened, and since I hadn't actually set foot on the fire I was placed on top of the list again. There was already a jump request and everyone was suiting up. Darby, the last jumper on the load, expected me to bump him off, but seeing as he was a rookie I decided to let him go and agreed to catch the next one. It was a busy day and there were going to be plenty more, but I also needed to sort out my second set of jump gear since I had never used it. A week later Darby told me he wished I had bumped him off the load because he hurt his ankle on the jump and had to be medevac'd off as well!

I ended this eventful day on a brilliant three-manner with Fred and Larry, two great old salts of smokejumping, jumping late in the afternoon on a steep slope in the Selway-Bitterroot Wilderness, literally only a few yards from the fire.

When we arrived little did we know that the area was already inhabited. Although it didn't take long to find out once we had the fire lined and stopped for something to eat. A telltale trail of debris led straight to the destruction inside of our packs. Something had been rummaging around and discovered the assortment of snacks we all carried. This was not only a crime of opportunity but a well-organized attack. Waiting for us to turn our backs, unconcerned for our possessions while working on the fire, these little critters had opened every packet of nuts, chocolate and biscuits we possessed. These woods were not simply home to a family of chipmunks, they were home to a veritable colony of the little devils.

And it got worse at night while trying to sleep. We could hear them scrabbling everywhere. When we had our food better secured they seemed adamant to just annoy the crap out of us. I swear there was one inside my sleeping bag and I woke twice to shake it out. I put my clothes beneath my sleeping bag and yet one of the little devils managed to chew into the top pocket of my fire shirt to open a packet of Emergen-C. I hope the little bastard had shits for days.

The fire lasted two days and Chuck even managed to persuade a passing helicopter to sling out our gear, which was a dubious and unusual undertaking in a wilderness. But great for us because the only way out meant climbing several hundred feet to find a trail. It wouldn't have been fun for the old guys. All three of them.

When I eventually got back to Missoula Walt showed me the picture of Don hauling the Redding jumper out of the quagmire. It was a classic. It's a great shame that some idiot saw fit to steal the jumpers' photograph album later in the year. We lost hundreds of wonderful pictures and the memories they instilled. For one reason or another many of the people in those photographs were no longer around. We never discovered who stole it, but rumors abounded, ranging from a tourist to even a thieving jumper. Whoever did is a prat. You know who you are.

Chapter Eighteen

— Jump Season Ends

I've had a wonderful time, but this wasn't it.

– Groucho Marx

A MIXTURE OF LARGE CREW ACTION and smaller two to eight man fires persisted steadily throughout the summer and the jump list continued to rotate nicely As the season wore on and the hot summer sun dried out the northern forests we found ourselves increasingly heading to the Panhandle. The open-range grass fires in middle and eastern Montana and the high alpine fires around Yellowstone were now being suppressed by local crews, aided by helitacks and hotshots who had migrated home after being released from across the south and west.

The Panhandle contains a vast swath of beautiful scenery but I never much enjoyed the repeated journeys to fires up in that part of Idaho. The timber is taller, older and thicker, and the terrain steep with countless wet draws and valleys. It looks fine from the road or from the plane, but once in the middle of it we invariably couldn't see anything after plunging into the unrelenting gloom beneath its dense tree canopy. Gone were the breathtaking views of the sub-alpine meadows, the magnificent vistas of the Pintlers, Beartooths, and Bitterroots, and the sweeping open expanse of the prairies with their broad scarlet sunsets. In the Panhandle we were always too low to see the sun for trees or the view for mountains.

Finding a suitable jump spot was also a neat trick. Inevitably they'd be so far away from the fire that it would take another hour or two just to reach them, hiking through thick eight feet tall alder brush and over logs the size of automobiles. That, or traversing old clear-cuts stacked with unburned slash and bristling with spindly Doug-firs. All the while carrying everything we needed, knowing a cargo drop nearer the fire would mean a lot of tree climbing for the rookies.

In late August and early September all we did was rotate to and from the Panhandle. We might well have settled in and created our own spike base for all the times we went back. After all, there was a suitable airport just outside of Libby where Steven Spielberg had filmed his romantic retardant adventure *Always*. It seemed to work for him, even though he had jumpers digging line surrounded by flame on every side. By the end of summer we knew the airport intimately after having flown out of it so many times, dirty, sore, hungry and exhausted after days of digging and bushwhacking our way back out of almost impenetrable forest.

Looking out of the windows of the DC-3 we could see that this time at least there was a jump spot reasonably close to the fire. A little pale patch in an endless carpet of dark green. Two by two the jumpers left the door with a whoosh and a clatter. I hooked up behind my JP, got the "YOU'RE CLEAR!" yelled into my ear and leapt out the door as easily as if I was hopping off a bus. Floating down I could see the spot littered with parachutes. What I couldn't see, though, were any people. Then I realized that what we were jumping was not a nice flat meadow but a brush field full of alder. Being careful not to land right on top of another parachute I was immediately gobbled up by a huge alder bush. As my feet hit the uppermost branches I slipped, losing my balance and sliding down the slippery branches until finding the wet ground beneath. There was no room or time for a proper PLF, just an untidy crumpf into the dirt. Then, as I knelt on the ground to undo my harness a heavy branch swung back and clipped the side of my head.

I pushed apart some branches and looked up to see if the next stick was coming down. I didn't want a size twelve smokejumper boot landing on my head. But I couldn't see anything except for a tall tunnel into a blue sky. Unwrapping myself from a tangle of parachute cords I unzipped my suit and took off the sweaty Kevlar, just as a stream of shouts erupted to warn those now above us to stay away from "HERE!" Hardly an accurate or descriptive request since the airborne jumper had no clue who was shouting what or from where. I could see Ed some feet away gathering his chute beneath the branches just as a set of legs appeared above him. He dove to one side at the last minute just as a body crashed beside him. The 'Hammer' had arrived. At a lean 200lbs my rookie bro Don was pushing the limit on weight but he was youthful, fit and strong. He had to be. Because his nickname was an indication of his landing technique.

It was a complete mess but it was as funny as hell, and there was abundant profanity and laughter all over as we fought to force the unforgiving brush to surrender our gear. Then, once bagged, we dragged it through the mass of interwoven branches to the edge of the spot, where we had a slightly better view of the proceedings. Indeed, it was daylight here, and we could see the alder brush was a good ten feet tall and covering the entire spot. The only way to not land amongst it was to hit a tree, as someone had already done because a parachute was delicately dangling from a large Doug-fir right on the perimeter. It was the only visible chute and the spotter enquired to whom it belonged. No one knew and no one owned up.

The first thing an IC does on hitting the ground is to check the size and activity of the fire, so that we can get more jumpers or equipment as necessary, such as chainsaws and pumps, while the aircraft is overhead. Our foreman, Jim, emerged from the depths of the forest and asked if everyone was out of the spot because the plane was circling and ready to drop cargo. We said yes, except for whoever's chute that is, pointing to a large fir.

"Oh, that's mine," he said. "Wind shear."

The pilot did an amazing job of dropping our cargo into that tiny hole because only two containers from fourteen snagged trees. Nevertheless, since we had parachutes in trees the last pass was to drop spurs, which arrive with only a small stabilizing drogue and no parachute, since it's pointless having a parachute on something the sole purpose of which is to get other parachutes out of trees, because it needs to get to the ground no matter what. So all eyes were upwards as the bright orange box came spiraling out the door and hurtling toward the ground. It flew across the spot at 60mph and slammed into a couple of trees before tumbling to the ground. Triggering rookies to scramble to collect it while the rest headed off into the forest to fight the fire.

There wasn't much smoke at all. It was just wafting gently in the breeze and occasionally drifting up through the canopy. Most north aspect fires are wet in this area, and just rummage around in the dirt looking for something dry to burn for survival. A few are probably never even noticed and eventually go out on their own. But with timber value being so high in this part of the world any fire that is noticed is suppressed immediately. They tend to go out easily, however, once worked, because there is always plenty of cool wet dirt around, but it's digging deep enough to find it that can be the hard part. The old growth is surrounded on the ground by feet of needle litter, and countless intertwined roots buried in the dirt often behave like rubber when hit with the average pulaski. And if there are soft rotten logs lying around the fire can continue to burn for weeks, even until the snows arrive.

Fires do take off in the Panhandle, though, and when they do they roar. The southern and western aspects dry out considerably throughout the summer and a single well-placed spark can ignite a catastrophe. The Kootenai is loaded with fuel, both lying dead, standing dead and live ladder-ridden trees capable of lifting the fire high up into the canopy. Once there, away from the confines of the ground, it'll go whatever direction the wind goes. Which is usually straight up, but when it's run out of up it can be pushed back down into the valleys by the prevailing winds to start the process over again. The fires can also creep slowly downhill when pushed by the evening katabatic winds or when firebrands get deposited far in front of the active fireline. Fire devils are a common sight on the steep forested slopes of the Kootenai as conflicting winds whip flames into mini tornadoes that dance across the steep slopes and incinerate everything in their path. When large fires, or a collection of fires, start to create their own weather a conflagration blow-up, a firestorm, becomes increasingly possible, and nothing on earth can stop it. Such events thankfully occur infrequently but when they do they can produce tragic results to people, property and environment. Dozens of large fires across the Bitterroot Mountains in the summer of 2000 provided such a conflagration opportunity, but the wind event needed to trigger it never materialized. Even so, many hundreds of thousands of acres were burned.

After we finished digging line we chopped, sawed and bone piled to burn up all the available fuels within the fireline. Anything unburned was thrown outside, large punky logs were broken apart causing steam to mix with the smoky air. Smoke always permeated the air. When the fires were out they still smelled of smoke, albeit stale smoke. Our bodies smelled of smoke. Even after showering for days we still smelled of smoke, it was ingrained in every pore, every crevice. But we learned to like it. It was better than cow shit and it disguised the stench of the great unwashed around us.

After two days of back breaking work we were literally filthy. Imagine a couple of kids playing in the dirt for an afternoon, times ten. Add sweat from days of exertion, thick charcoaled encrusted hands swatting bugs and itching scratches, eating dry food for two days, drinking gallons of stale tepid water laced with Gatorade, tea, or Emergen-C, followed by cowboy coffee and chocolate, and you start to get the picture – and the reason why smoke ain't so bad.

Once the fire was out a couple of sawyers went to the jump spot to cut room for a net and organize our gear for extraction. Others collected sleeping bags and hiked them up to be placed in the sling load. The rest of us got on our hands and knees and did what we do; feeling every inch of the fire with our fingertips. Occasionally there was an audible "aw shit" as someone burned a finger on a hot spot. Dirt can get so hot it literally boils. These areas can usually be easily seen on the surface because the dirt is like dust and tiny gnats tend to hover around the warmer air above them, but when hidden under recently turned dirt the fingers can get a nasty surprise when bitten by the hidden heat.

Satisfied that we now had the fire out we sorted our PG bags, grabbed our tools and headed off down the mountain, in the usual eight different directions. Joey Rule #1: 'Never get separated from your PG bag.' It never, but never, goes in the sling load and it never, but never, goes in back of the other truck, even if you know that truck is going to the same place. Accidents happen and people get separated. It doesn't get left with anyone or get left anywhere. A jumper without a PG bag is useless.

There were no trails of any description on the mountain so we bushwhacked through alder, over and under logs, down draws and over ridges. Traversed steep slopes that made our feet scream until, two hours later, we reached a road. One by one the stragglers came popping out of the forest at more or less the same location. The direction had been easy; down. But there were numerous places to get disorientated in the dense forest that all looked the same. If someone had inadvertently walked a little too far east they might have missed the switchback on the logging road entirely and kept bushwhacking for a further two miles before finding another road. Thankfully we didn't have anyone requiring a cowbell this time.

A couple of local district pick-ups arrived and we all piled in clinging to our PG bags. An hour later we were having dinner in Libby and waiting for the DC-3 to come and pick us up.

Three days later a couple of pick-ups arrived and we all piled in clinging to our PG bags. An hour later we were having dinner at a familiar restaurant in Libby while waiting for the DC-3 to come and pick us up. There was a sense of déjà vu among us.

After another trip back from Libby, Ed and I found ourselves as JPs again over one of the last split weekends. It had taken us a while to crawl back up the list but now, at last, there was a call for a fire on the Nez Perce. The Grangeville Twin Otter came over to refuel and pick up four Zoolies to complete their load. Ed and I were seven and eight, the last stick on the plane. We flew the fire, dropped four and headed off to find another. But had to turn back to give directions to the jumpers on the previous fire because they had lost their bearing walking to the fire in the hills. After steering them in the right direction we, once again, headed off to the next fire. Only to run short of fuel before throwing a single streamer. So we turned for home.

Arriving in Grangeville the light was fading so it was too late to try again. We'd fly it in the morning instead. Ed and I stayed in a motel overnight and made the most of cheap Olympia beer at the Triangle. It never really dawned on us that there were rather a lot of Grangeville jumpers in the bar that night. But realization sank in the following morning when we saw that the jumpers coming back from days off had bumped us down the list. So instead of being three and four, we once again seated ourselves at seven and eight. We were getting to know Nels, the pilot, quite well at this point, seeing as our jump position had us permanently seated right behind his cockpit.

We returned to the fire we should have jumped the previous evening and quickly dropped six. There was no way to justify eight since six was already pushing it. Again, Ed and I were the last two on the load. And again on a plane short of fuel so we landed in Missoula. While sitting on the ramp in our jump suits we were quietly informed that Grangeville dispatch had released us back to Missoula. Meaning that we were now back at the bottom of an even longer Missoula list after having been little more than tourists flying over the Bitterroot countryside. It was the classic bone load.

After yet another week of crawling ever so slowly up the list I finally found myself on the load going to a local fire just outside of Missoula. The Sherpa circled a small clear-cut with a log landing nearer the top. It was a nasty place to jump since there wasn't much leeway for error with the only spot being a hard-packed road among a sea of stumps and slash. Jim threw the streamers and lined us up for the jump. Todd made his way in and Eddie, his JP, landed hard nearby in a slash pile, banging his head hard. I hooked up behind my JP who was already in the door. It was to be my last jump that season and very nearly my last jump ever.

Making my turn onto final I watched incredulously as my JP flew directly in front of me, and instinctually doing what had been drilled into us all though training I made an immediate hard right turn. I should have thought a little longer and, instead, made a quick jogging left. It might have saved me. Because that right turn placed me with no chance of ever reaching the jump spot. I sailed down hill in down air and cracked my tailbone on a 6-inch log that was sticking at an angle a few feet in the air. Someone said I broke that log clean in half and it felt as though I had broken my back in half too. After several jumper EMTs had packaged me up on a sled they carried me up over the slash to the log landing from where I was airlifted to St. Pat's Hospital. An X-ray showed it was not too serious even though I was in a lot of pain and could hardly walk. Though the disconcerting thing was feeling as though I'd had a corncob shoved up my backside. My tail bone was cracked.

Anne picked me up from the hospital and I spent the next few days flat on my back unable to move. Going back to Chris, my chiropractor, he thought I had torn the ligaments on my spine and put me on twice-weekly therapy to heal the damage and stop scar tissue from forming too thickly. I slowly got some painful mobility back and returned to do some light work at the base because I was getting bored to death at home.

So I ended up alongside Keith, behind a sewing machine and building hose bags for the warehouse. However, being unable to sit for any length of time for fear of seizing up I soon went to the loft instead, where at least I could stand up while packing parachutes.

Fires were winding down by now. The weather patterns had visibly changed, signaling a definitive end to the fire season. From now on the only action would be from hunter fires and they would likely be few and far between. To keep people working, operations asked around the local districts to see if anyone could use a few jumpers. The results were promising. There was work for anyone who wanted it in a variety of districts all across central and western Montana and Idaho. Many districts were run by FMOs who were ex-jumpers, creating a network that worked well for everyone. Not least the districts for getting much needed help after many of their crews had returned to school. It was certainly good for those of us not attached to any other source of income, unlike the teachers among us who had already left to return to full-time employment. Working was a whole lot better than being laid off, which was the other option. Being laid off, though, was still just on the horizon for everyone without an appointment.

Not knowing what to do for work over the winter made many of us nervous and we started looking around for any opportunity going. There was nothing available on base, with every job taken up by those with appointments. But that didn't stop a few from persevering and being a thorn in the side of management. A couple of the foremen did try hard to justify funding in order to keep a few temporaries on, although none of them were rookies. Seniority naturally played its part, as did the cribbage board in the loft.

After some internal politics were resolved, and appropriate funding arranged, the warehouse agreed to take a few jumpers to help recondition fire equipment. Gary and some of the foremen had been instrumental in securing this opportunity for us. They at least tried to help the temporaries who might otherwise have had to leave, find other jobs and not return, which would mean wasting the organization's investment in training. Though this effort was more than would happen a few years later when a manager deemed it more important to save money, solely to return some of his budget, rather than keep jumpers employed for a few extra weeks. Maybe there was a bonus in it for him, who knows? There had to be some incentive involved in order to screw people over; the very people that made him look good.

The decision to willingly lay people off, even though money was available, was done by shortsighted, inept management devoid of any organizational ethos, personal ethics or morality, as well as an inherent lack of ability to instill morale. Compounded by a self-serving desire to look good in front of superiors while being a hindrance to those they were supposed to support. It was a pitiful, though classic, example of upper management being allowed to act like puppeteers in a once strong and independent organization. It destroyed morale immediately, thereafter remaining disgracefully low until management changed several years later, by which time they had successfully cruised to retirement on the backs of others.

But losing all respect and credibility they might have earlier earned from those now struggling beneath them in an unforgiving and arbitrary authoritarian environment.

Missoula had, in effect, become like Redding in the mid-90s; a laughing stock among the greater jumper community. Even more embarrassing, rookies in at least one class during this sad woolly period were forced to give each other back rubs and foot massages. While spring training once involved all jumpers being persuaded to hold hands in a circle to tell each other their secrets. Many, albeit mainly new, jumpers went along with this inane bullshit, instigated by non-fire personnel who were always eager to bring their private life's baggage to work. Jumpers who bought into it, willingly or otherwise, likely knew that it was the only way to get ahead in the suck-up environment that the modern, burgeoning, power-crazed personnel departments create these days. Embarrassing is a gross understatement when describing that woolly period during the late '90s. Threatening, puerile, abusive and manipulative, arbitrarily selective, protectionist, incompetent and grossly mismanaged are better descriptions. Insane is also apt, since anyone would have to be insane to think jumpers would be open to such crap. Maybe when they start wearing leotards to jump through fucking circus rings they might be.

Chapter Nineteen

— Snookies

This new cadre of corporals know just enough to be dangerous. Not just to themselves, but us too. Watch them like a bloody hawk sergeant.
– Unknown Commanding Officer, Royal Engineers

W ITH WINTER ON THE WAY, Don, Jeff, Rogers and I ended up doing eight to fives in the warehouse sharpening pulaskis, shovels and axes, along with a couple of temporary warehouse workers in the infamous grinding room. It was noisy, dirty, monotonous work and we spent the whole time cocooned in personal protective equipment; overalls, gloves, plastic goggles and hearing protection. We peered through grimy scratched goggles as we held a variety of edged tools against an assortment of grinding stones. The incessant high-pitched squeal was excruciating and rattled our brains. While some tried to listen to music blaring loud on their Walkmans others tried books on tape. Ironically, even in deafening form, it added a background of calmness to the otherwise chaotic noise and somewhat broke the monotony. In an attempt to infuse some humor I made copies of Monty Python sketches. When three of us listened to the same track simultaneously we would erupt in laughter in unison, which inevitably confused the other workers into believing that we were laughing at them. We weren't. But it cheered us up no end as we listened to the lyrics over and over:

Some things in life are bad
They can really make you mad
Other things just make you swear and curse.
When you're chewing on life's gristle
Don't grumble, give a whistle
And this'll help things turn out for the best...
And...always look on the bright side of life...

Thank God for Eric Idle.

While grinding away we would watch quite enviously as the permanent jumpers left the base early in the afternoons to go skiing at Snowbowl. Some would just grin and wave, knowing full well our predicament. Our jealousy was obvious as they worked flex-hours and left wearing an expensive assortment of North Face jackets and Patagonia fleece to ski the fresh powder in the clean air above Missoula. We were determined to do the same the following year. In the meantime, though, we needed money, so we sharpened pulaskis, cherry picking the best edged *True Tempers* to set them aside for the smokejumpers to use the following year.

Two evenings a week Eric, Don and I went back to school for Emergency Medical Technician (EMT) training. The point had been made clearly by Gary, the base manager, the previous season, that any future promotion would rest solely on an ability to provide longstanding value to the jump base. And since there was a dire shortage of EMTs it was strongly suggested that we should attend if we hoped to further ourselves in the organization.

It was a lot of time to volunteer without being paid a red cent but we considered it worthwhile and learned a lot in the process, thinking it would stand us in good stead with the organization in the future. That was the plan anyway.

The more enjoyable and memorable moments were always the practical sessions, where previous students would volunteer to act injured and be made up with blood to look like a horrendous accident victim. One station in particular was done in secrecy so that the next person would not catch wind of the task.

When it was my turn I walked into the classroom to see a woman bleeding badly on the floor, motioning me forward asking for help. I went over to assess her wound and apply pressure when a man came up from behind pointing a Browning High Power at me. I looked him in the eyes – as you do – to see if he was serious, instinctively decided that he wasn't and turned to help the woman.

Needless to say, I failed. As did all the other jumpers on that station. Collectively we were the only ones in the whole class that did fail that station by staying calm and aiding the injured woman. To me, it demonstrated what drives those who choose to occupy such a profession. They're strong minded, assertive and willing to risk life and limb to help others, and do so by natural instinct often without thought for their own wellbeing. Looking into the eyes of the person holding the gun we each instinctively saw a charade. The spurting blood, pain and anguish, however, looked real, and we went directly to what was the reality of the situation rather than the pantomime. But since no one knows exactly how they will react in an unknown situation, without the advantage of prior training, everything might be very different. But neither is a real situation a pantomime.

As winter progressed into spring the snows departed, slowly retreating back up the mountains from where they began. The pile of blunt pulaskis dwindled and the grinding room soon fell silent. We still had a month before the new jump season started and some of us still didn't know if we would be requested back; funding was always tight and we were constantly told that there were never any guarantees. But in endless anticipatory hope that funding would be available we all stepped up our pre-season training. After inserting hex screws back into the soles of my shoes I started running the icy trails on Blue Mountain again. While at home I kept up a regular routine of push-ups, pull-ups and sit-ups as I watched bad TV in the evenings. I even managed to squeeze in a few days x-country skiing on ice and slush before it melted off the hills.

Confirmation of summer work arrived in March and we all made appointments to see a local quack for a pre-season physical. There was already a collection of jumpers waiting when I arrived at the clinic early one Monday morning. It was clearly a conveyor belt. Read this. Touch your toes. Piss in this cup. Bend over and don't be surprised! I don't think anyone ever failed it, even though I can think of a few who should have. Including me ten years later when I showed up still holding my guts in barely ten weeks after having the second of two major abdominal surgeries – one of which had only recently closed up and stopped oozing pus.

"No worries," I said, in need of work. "It's better than it was."

All returning jumpers have to retrain and we arrived for early refresher in the middle of April. It was completely different from our last visit to the units. Almost a vacation. Except for when the slamulator left us with the annual stiff neck again. During the first two mornings we did all the regular units: letdowns, emergency procedures, PLFs and exits, with time on the parachute simulator in the basement if we thought we needed it.

Walt was in his usual role overseeing the jumps, which were always the bright spots in refresher after having to spend so much time in classrooms being lectured on Ethics and Bleeding Conduct. Real moronic stuff, with topics that made even some of the tutors embarrassed. And as well they should have been. These were early days, however, such insulting condescending classes were soon to become the mainstay of refresher after various members of the organization deigned to subject everyone to their personal variety of psychobabble. In effect, forcing everyone to endure insufferable bullshit while they performed a portion of a twelve step program.

Despite this, we were all glad to be back at work. It was good to see old friends again, and see them all healthy and in one piece. Injuries had healed and jumpers were fit and yearned to get back to doing something worthwhile after the long winter's rest. Although it was readily apparent that one or two rookies had slackened off their fitness regime, as was evident by their expanded waistlines. Such a waste of effort. But it was a common trend among those not naturally inclined to fitness. With the inevitable results that, unless exceedingly lucky, or young, it would eventually mean a change of career. Preferably before an injury removed the choice altogether.

Now that more of us were qualified EMTs we were expected to put on a variety of first aid classes for the other jumpers. Most of them obviously knew this stuff after doing it for years but we went through the motions anyway. As always, the fun part was doing the practical first aid scenarios on jumps. Where an injured jumper would be in a tree and in need of extraction – hopefully without further injury. It was a great learning process in a fun atmosphere, and involved everyone being increasingly creative and knowledgeable of the skills more associated with rock climbing. Everyone, not only EMTs, took part, because each of us could be called upon at anytime to help in any situation. We relied on each other to be willing, knowledgeable and proficient.

If someone was very seriously injured and in a lot of pain we always had the option to call an emergency room physician at St. Pat's Hospital, to request advice on treatment and get permission to administer morphine. To do this we would first insert an IV and then administer morphine as recommended through the drip line. To gain proficiency in inserting IVs we practiced on each other during refresher. Ken quickly picked me to be his partner because I had skinny arms and my veins protruded, providing him an easy target. He, on the other hand, did not, and it was by sheer luck that I didn't turn Ken's willing arm into a pincushion, as some of the others were doing to their unfortunate partners. Poor Bob looked as white as a sheet as he left the room for fresh air – one of the last people anyone would have suspected to become faint at the sight of blood. Though maybe it was the thought of getting stabbed three and four times before his partner found a vein. The looks on faces said it all but no one uttered a word. Instead, looking off into the distance and silently willing their partner to "get it right this time."

If a needle is inserted incorrectly it can damage the valves in the veins. After many IVs over the years the veins in my forearms are now rearranged somewhat differently. But the cause of that resides more with the English National Health Service and not with any jumper I know. During one stay in an English hospital I regularly removed and reinserted my own IV so that I could take a shower each day without hindrance from tubes or IV frames. On one occasion it was a matter of necessity because I was unable to bend my arm without sticking myself. A nurse had inserted the IV too close to the elbow and every time I turned over while sleeping I got pricked again as the plastic tube punctured through the vein, waking me up repeatedly through the night. On another occasion a nurse was so worried that IV fluid was swelling my arm that she kept returning to reinsert it, inevitably turning my arm into a bloody pincushion. After an hour of this I got rather annoyed and asked the doctor why. He quickly informed the nurse that she was not looking at swelling at all, but at muscle!

We were more accepted into the smokejumper clan this year. During our rookie year the veterans had had a chance to get to know us, to see how we worked and see how we played. In only our second year, as snookies, we still had a lot to prove and tried to maintain the work ethic that we had developed during the previous year. Such as always looking for something to do for fear of being yelled at and given something to do that we did not want to do.

Practice jumps took us back to Ninemile and Little Stony, as well as the Horseshoe on the ridge opposite the jump base and the ankle busting, knee torqueing Field of Shame in the back 40 – the hard flat field behind the units. Not our favorite place but a quick and easy place to get a jump done in short order.

We jumped the Horseshoe on Thursday afternoon. The wind had been picking up but there were hundreds of acres in which to land if we missed the spot inside a circle of trees. Most of my load had made it in by the time Joey and I stood in the door. A few chutes were dangling from the sides of trees on the periphery but everyone was on the ground. I looked down at the ground as the plane turned onto final. The spotter placed my foot in the door, pulled his head in and yelled the familiar "GET READY!" And slapped me out.

I heaved out the door and stayed tight with my hands each side of the reserve and my head tucked down. I watched my feet, conscious of keeping my toes pointed down, and felt the slight tug of the static line as it pulled the chute out before giving me a final jerk as it settled down for the descent. Looking back I saw Joey's chute inflate above me with a pleasant whoof. I steered to the right of the wind cone as he steered to the left. Our weights were similar so we stayed at the same altitude for the whole descent, quartering backwards and forwards to maintain our positions on the wind line. A strip of trees lining a draw separated us from the spot and the increasing wind was battering the draw and creating an up current. Neither of us could break through it. We kept trying to get another fraction of forward speed until losing too much altitude and deciding, instead, to drop into the 2,000 acre roll-your-own spot just outside the circle of trees. It was better than risking a tree in pride of trying to get the main spot. We both had fast and hard backwards landings. The wind was definitely picking up.

The last stick was above us and they never once got close to making it in and landed a good 70 yards further away. Stepping out of our suits into the drying wind was pleasant because it instantly warmed the sweat on our backs, created by patches of nylon inside our Kevlar suits. We gathered our chutes, chained the cords and stuffed everything into our bags before hiking over to the others.

As we unloaded our gear back at the base we watched as the DC-3 turned onto final ready for the next load to jump into the spot now a mile away. The plane was following a different pattern now that the wind had changed. A couple of parachutes inflated and floated down into the hole in the trees and out of sight. It looked like they were getting in. The second stick also disappeared in the same area. One parachute on the third stick didn't disappear, however. It caught some wind and started to fly like a kite, straight towards Interstate 90. Then, almost the very last tall tree on the hill caught the parachute's AIN and deflated it, leaving the jumper dangling. Sarah got a couple of hours overtime extracting her chute that day. She likely couldn't have helped it. The wind had increased just as she exited, and being lighter than her partner she had literally floated away on the breeze. If it wasn't for that last big tree on the hill she might well have made it all the way back to the airport – arriving on runway 29 a few minutes before the Northwest Airlines flight from Great Falls. Now *that* would have been a story!

After refresher, early season project work started for all those not lucky enough to go to Silver City, New Mexico. That lucky group had been selected as soon as the jump order was pulled. But before that there had been some heated discussion as whether to allow second year jumpers to go as well. The winds and terrain in the mountains of New Mexico had always been considered too hazardous for inexperienced snookies to deal with. Whether this was a legitimate reason we did not know. It wasn't thought to be a problem a few years later so it certainly advantaged seniority at the time. But since we were new, and had no choice or opinion that was going to be listened to, we didn't think much of it. Instead, we settled down to picking sticks, thinning trees and burning details on local districts while waiting for the weather to warm up so we could have some fires of our own.

Don and I began the year at number two and three on the list. Which meant that, without a doubt, the first fire that came along we were sure to be on it. And we were. A dozen of us ended up on a one day pounder to Ninemile. After which we all rotated to the bottom again. It smacked a little of the previous year's bone load.

Having finished picking up every stick in the district, just to prove to us that a jumper's life is not all silk and glory, we got hard at work in the loft. Jumpers manufacture just about everything they use apart from their boots; from Kevlar jump suits to the bags on their backs, from parachute harnesses to tree climbing harnesses, slings for helicopters, cargo chutes for the military, and just about anything else anyone could possibly dream up. The jump base also provides equipment for other fire crews. So all this manufacturing creates a need for people who can sew. Sew well and sew often.

Sewing is a prerequisite to being a parachute rigger. A rigger needs to know how to build, maintain, pack and repair parachutes. This can involve an awful lot of sewing, literally miles of it, sitting at a machine for hours every day for days. Proving once more that a jumper's life is not all glory, but can involve a lot of silk. A by-product of this much needed talent, along with the necessity for the jump base to own an assortment of sewing machines, is the ability of jumpers to produce virtually anything they need. Or, indeed, anything that anyone else needs also.

When jumpers are not out on fires the manufacturing room is a veritable production line where the primary product is the PG bag, because every single wildland firefighter in the country needs to have one in order to carry their mandatory fire shelter. Apart from water, this shelter is the easiest thing to reach. Inside the PG bag's main compartment is anything the firefighter chooses to carry plus any personal protective equipment not currently being worn. There are some side and top pouches to carry things like the Ten Standard Firefighting Orders, just in case you get bored.

The main reason we make so many PG bags is because people fail to abide by Joey Rule #1.

Over the years jumpers have improved this bag of tricks until it has become virtually state-of-the-art. Stealing ideas from the military, civilian and other firefighter organizations, jumpers have developed a low-slung backpack that can endure almost anything that the environment can throw at it, except, of course, fire. A few bags have even survived freefalling after plastic snaps have failed during opening shock, although the contents never fare too well. But yes, it still burns. So if you leave it in the wrong place, Joey won't be happy but those in manufacturing will be.

It takes time and practice to master even a simple Singer 101. The machines are decades old and finicky, and new jumpers spend countless hours sewing nothing but straight lines on the most basic parts before becoming proficient in the eyes of the foreman, and progressing to more complex parts of the production line. Soon, though, everyone can do almost anything. Which is all well and good because the unwritten jumper ethos states that all jumpers be proficient enough to do whatever is needed whenever it's needed.

The loft is the other place where sewing machines rule. Many people have literally spent weeks sewing mile upon mile of rip-stop nylon while making test chutes for the military or when repairing our own shredded canopies. Proficient sewers sound like they're operating machine guns, only stopping to replace an empty bobbin. Jumpers also use large freestanding heavy-duty thumpers to sew 1/8-inch resin coated webbing into harnesses. All done under the watchful eye of the loft foreman who designates responsibility among both the master and senior riggers – those who make up the core of the jumping organization.

Spring is usually an especially beautiful time in Missoula. The taller peaks that surround the town hold onto the last of the winter snows while the foothills grow lush and green with fresh spring grass. The air is cleaner and the breeze gets steadily warmer each day. Anne had her quarter horse stabled in Arlee, just north of town beneath the majestic Mission Mountains. So to make use of the fine weather one weekend we borrowed a horse from a friend and joined in on a Steak Ride that was organized by a local riding club, taking us into acre upon acre of private property neighboring the National Bison Range. Most of the riders were proficient, having ridden for many years. But there were a few that seemed uncomfortable after we left the main trail and headed into the hills.

Anne, her friend, Ron, and I, were ascending one rocky slope when we heard a loud scream behind us. Someone had fallen. It was a slope ridden with protruding rocks and I could only imagine what would happen if someone fell backwards onto one. Jumping off my horse on reaching the supine person a couple of local EMTs were already taking stock of the situation, or making it look as if they were. The young girl was clearly in a very bad way. She was sprawled out unconscious after having fallen backwards off her horse, hitting one of the bare rocks with her head. I immediately moved to stabilize her head and neck since no one had yet thought to do so – a primary requirement to protect her from further injury should she try to move. While holding her head secure I received some very strange looks, almost as if I was invading their territory. I ignored the looks, told them I was a jumper EMT and explained exactly what I was doing. Someone had already called for St. Pat's Air Ambulance and while we waited we tried to make her more confortable and monitor her vitals as best we could.

But while this was going on we noticed someone else had also fallen. This one dislocating a collarbone about 30 yards away. So a land ambulance was also on the way for her. The pleasant morning had turned into a complete cluster in a matter of seconds. All to be made worse by ignorance. Many who take EMT classes get little chance of any real practical experience and often find themselves out of their depth when a real accident does happen. Whence they often steadfastly refuse to admit ignorance and, instead, feign confidence, which in turn leads to defensiveness. Thereby creating an arrogance that pervades an already bad situation.

As Life Flight approached in the distance it was suggested that one of these EMTs hand over his radio to Ron, an ex-U.S. Air Force survival course instructor, obviously someone well versed in emergency helicopter operations, but it was ignored. Leaving the pilot unaware as to where we were on the great open expanse of ground beneath him.

The EMT saying, "Your off our left side," didn't help much. Neither did, "We're down here by the horses. Look for the horses."

"Tell him we're off *his* left side," Ron suggested, instead. "A thousand yards off his nine o'clock."

The suggestion was again ignored. It was unbelievable. I'm not certain if the radio was eventually unceremoniously grabbed from this lunatic's hand, but I began hearing better directions being relayed to a much-relieved pilot who was unsuccessfully scanning the fast moving ground for a few brown horses against a brown landscape full of Hereford beef cows and horses. For where some people have gnomes, Montanans have horses. They are the great Montana hay-burning knickknack.

As this priceless communication was underway the paramedic in the helicopter was trying to discern the status of the girl's injury and her vitals. I had both hands full stabilizing the girl's head so I asked one of the others to take a pulse once again and relay it, but before I finished asking the man with the radio said: "We have no way to take vitals at this time," trying somehow to portray that he knew what the hell he was doing. Yet in that one sentence proving he didn't. Looking at the person taking the pulse I asked if it was strong, but got no answer yet again – the strength of the pulse at different locations can provide a rough gauge of blood pressure. I asked another EMT to check for eye dilation, clamminess, etc. But again, these were not relayed to the helicopter either. "I know what am I doing," one of them snapped at me. Clearly she didn't, but I let it go since expert help was almost there and this was no time for a confrontation. We were outnumbered by incompetence anyway. The paramedics soon arrived and were allowed to take control of the situation – what a difference a uniform made.

Clearly, in their eyes I had stepped on their territory and they weren't going to listen to anything or anyone. It was a dismal performance by a few individuals doing more to protect pride than helping a person to the best of everyone's ability. Although it was not to be the only time I encountered such an attitude among small town EMTs. Thankfully, however, most are well trained and very proficient, but we more easily remember the worst, which isn't all bad because remembering the worst is often the best lesson.

Looking back, those EMTs did get the girl to hospital in time, which is paramount. And I think I was more critical because I was fortunate in that I worked with more competent people all the time, and thus expected cohesion and professionalism from everyone I encountered. Jumpers often forget how good they have it.

I explained this event to the city firefighter who had originally trained us in our EMT class. He was not surprised. Nevertheless, I had used my EMT training already. And as a group we were to use that new training even more through the summer as the infamous *Glass Class* (1992 rookies) proceeded to break themselves with willful abandon all over the western United States.

Chapter Twenty

— Broken Bits

I then realized my appearance was a bit odd. My right leg was no longer with me. It had caught somewhere in the top of the cockpit as I tried to leave my Spitfire.

– Douglas Bader

ONCE THE WEATHER WARMED UP sufficiently over the mountains, inducing those wonderfully tall towering money clouds, we started to roll. The summer then saw us going all over the western U.S., from New Mexico to Alaska. In the Lower 48 we flew to Arizona, California, Oregon, Colorado, Utah, Washington, Idaho, and Wyoming, and probably more that I have since forgotten. I began in Redmond, Oregon, rotated back to Grangeville, Idaho, went to West Yellowstone, Montana, and then Winthrop, Washington, where I landed on, and slid down, the side of the steepest, rockiest, highest, most magnificent mountain I've ever jumped, before heading back to West Yellowstone again – all the while having the most brilliant time of my life.

The work was relentless and at times exhausting. But it was also exhilarating, challenging, rewarding and, most of all, a whole lot of fun. This really was the best job in the world. Mission after mission saw us high over terrain like nothing else on earth. Not a day passed by that I didn't appreciate the fortunate and privileged position that I was in; coming from a suburb of London, one of the most modern, built-up, inhabited places on earth, to the vast empty expanses of North America. The contradiction was immeasurable. The streets of London were of another life entirely. Even the farm seemed long gone, tucked away in distant memory. The aura of the mountains was absorbed into every pore, convincing me that I had never really even lived those lives. London was now such a distant memory that I could only imagine it as if from a book. Although I could always remember my father working in an office for years so his family could survive – for in England it was survival in those smoggy days, and maybe still is for many. I couldn't imagine ever going back. What could I possibly do in England after this?

Dry lightning was creating havoc all over northern Montana and Idaho and a fire close to Glacier National Park was attracting crews from across the country. Then another was seen a few miles away. The district had been pounded and didn't have enough local resources available to deal with them all. So as a last resort, since all their people were already out, smokejumpers were disgruntledly requested from Missoula.

Jumpers are often considered the final option and only called upon when local crews are heavily committed elsewhere. This was the case in Glacier. The FMO at the time was not a fan of jumpers: professional jealousy, territorial ambition, inane internal politics, or some misplaced notion of elitism, who knows? We suspected it was the latter, but didn't much care because there was nothing we could do about it. Later, however, another more sexist reason was suggested, which was that they didn't like jumpers because it was a profession dominated by males. It didn't surprise me in the least, I had already witnessed that archaic appreciation. And still see it to this day, in this wonderfully entitled age we've created of reverse discrimination under the dubious auspices of Equal Opportunity.

Ambitious people strive for the top no matter what job they're in. Provided they have incentive, morale and drive, they will go for success. For ambitious firefighters that goal is to be part of an elite: hotshots, helitacks or smokejumpers. Not necessarily in that order but it often works out that way. Some people seem to get jealous of others' successes in these fields. Whether due to a personality flaw or some inherent hatred, who knows? It's often more than simple envy, however. Those few who try and fail rarely hold a grudge towards the elite crews – sure it happens, but not often. Those who do hold grudges have more than likely never even tried. Or never tried hard enough, and forever burden themselves with an inherent dislike of elite crews. For they sure don't burden us.

That those with such flaws never forget and find themselves in positions of seniority is a travesty. But they do, and fire camps tend to be where they congregate to congratulate themselves. All the grunts are happy just to get along while those managers spend time plotting how to make one crew's life more miserable than the next, simply because they showed more ambition, incentive and ability to be considered elite. The elite crews are the organization's mainstay and it would dissolve to putty without them. Anyone who has ever held a pulaski looks up to the these crews, not only for guidance and experience, but because they provide something to strive for. That's a good thing. Ambition is always a good thing. Incentive is always a good thing. And if served right, appreciated and allowed to develop along with a good dollop of perseverance, these standards and values are the catalyst to morale, which is *the* best thing any organization can hope to attain. It is a great shame that some managers consistently just don't get it.

Approaching the fire we saw that we were going to be busy. It covered a couple of acres of flat ground and sloped timber, with its tail on the top of an escarpment overlooking the foothills. Don was my JP again and we landed close to each other having just missed the same small tree, acting like a magnet for some reason. It was windier on the ground than expected but everyone was finding dirt. Todd finding more dirt than anyone. I didn't see his landing but by all accounts he failed to turn into the wind and hit the slope with an almighty crack. Leaving him in agony under the impact.

By the time we reached him Ken had control of the EMTs and was already calling in Life Flight. Ken then handed the EMT role to me while he continued to communicate with dispatch. Without doubt Todd was in severe pain. From our initial assessment, and him telling us the location of the worst of the pain, we thought he might have broken his hip, which contraindicated our initial plan to use traction. Removing all his jump gear as carefully as we could, and using it as padding, we slid the sled beneath him as smoothly as possible. At the same time another EMT was initiating an IV. It was a long, time consuming process because we were taking great care not to further aggravate the injury and cause him further pain. Yet he didn't complain a bit.

Once he was secured on the sled the paramedics arrived and after carrying him 100 yards up the hill we placed him in the side of the waiting helicopter. The paramedics were excellent, dealing with injuries like these every day they should be. Thankfully we usually didn't have to.

As we were putting Todd onboard I noticed another jumper also getting onto the helicopter. I hadn't seen Sonny for being so busy with Todd, but others had bandaged his face after he had cut it open on the broken cage of his helmet, after having driven full force into a tree after apparently making the same mistake as Todd, and not turning into the wind. So even before starting to fight the fire we had lost two jumpers. Two rookies that should have been doing all the fetching and carrying. The *Glass Class* was well on its way to gaining a reputation. And not a particularly good one.

It had taken a couple of hours to sort out the injuries, clean the debris off the battlefield and get over to the fire. But once there we started digging line immediately. Eight hours later, at midnight, we caught a break for some quick dinner, finding individual spots of flame to cook our meals and make coffee. When we finally tied the line it was seven in the morning. We'd been digging for 15 hours. Now stopped, we started to get cold. The morning air was cool and damp and our clothes were soaked in sweat. To warm ourselves we mingled around a couple of cooking fires, waiting for water to boil before making coffee and oatmeal, while listening to the latest stories of fires we had missed. You can bet that if you're not on the fire you're going to get talked about at some point. So better be good in that case, better to have credibility in doing some good work, and not get a reputation from being a slacker. Because those guys still get talked about, even 20 years later.

Occasionally we would stand to stretch our aching backs and stroll over to the edge of the escarpment to look at the valley below. Standing there, silhouetted against the passing dawn, we sipped on steaming hot coffee and watched as puffs of smoke drifted up through trees about a mile away. We wondered if it was a spot fire created by an ember from ours, and asked Bob, our foreman, if we should hike down to check it out. But he said the local district was aware of it and was engaged in doing something about it. We assumed that meant they had firefighters on it. But we were wrong. The occasional bright flash wasn't a yellow shirt but active flame. Finished with breakfast, still in need of warmth, we spread around the fire to expend some energy in improving the line where needed before working inwards, turning over the hot dirt and bone piling. Occasionally putting our cups in a hot spot or next to a burning stump for more coffee.

At noon we drifted back to our cooking fire for lunch and yet more coffee – we hadn't slept for thirty hours. The smoke below us was more active now that the shade slid away and the temperature increased. With the humidity dropping the fire would soon break free of the ground and climb the ladder fuels, and we didn't need a fire scientist to explain what would happen if the fire was not soon controlled.

Just then a Neptune P2V appeared overhead. Its deep, two-engine, radial throb all too familiar and reminding us of another age. The pilot was circling and studying the terrain while deciding his best direction of attack before vanishing over the mountain behind us. A minute later he came screaming back. The submarine hunter lost altitude until we were actually looking down on it as it dropped its cargo just short of the largest smoke. After losing weight the old Lockheed soared back up into the air with ease and headed toward Whitefish. At $3,000 a load it was expensive mud.

The P2V refueled, reloaded, and prepared for another run – load and return – and half an hour later it roared overhead again at 200 feet to paint another dull red stripe down the left flank of the fire. After half an hour the other side was painted, the iron oxide in the fertilizer based product marking the accuracy of the drop. The head of the fire was not impressed by all this effort, however, and relentlessly clawed its way up the hill towards us.

Now and again an incendiary Doug-fir could be seen torching out. While the P2V returned time and again; $9,000, $12,000, $15,000. Neptune Aviation was enjoying this fire. Clearly, there were no personnel involved and some bright spark had thought to contain this fire with retardant alone – a flawed and very expensive tactic in this case. A few of us could have quite easily hiked down after breakfast, cut a line around it in a few hours, and contained it. At $12 an hour we could have saved the taxpayer a wheelbarrow full of money. Poor decisions were being made somewhere.

But now we had a decision to make and incentive to make it a good one. Or rather someone else had made a bad decision and we had to make a good one. All our work had been a complete waste of time and the retardant a complete waste of money. The fire below us was still not being contained and it was now growing at a faster rate. In the heat of the afternoon it would stop being a meek little thing, build up a head of steam, and make a run for the ridge.

Two jumpers stopped working our fire and became lookouts. We had already expended enough wasted effort but we continued to utilize our time by better securing the line and extinguishing the interior in case the fire made a run before we left. In which event we would be safe in the burned area of ours – in the black. But that would be folly and wholly unnecessary.

Helicopters arrived to take us off and bring in other crews. They were going to hike down to fight this other fire. In effect, do exactly what we had been told not to. To us everything was back-ass-wards. But it was the district's land and they were giving the orders. The incoming crew would have to be quick and careful. Quick to contain it before the afternoon heat, and careful walking down a ridge under canopy and blind toward the approaching fire. Before leaving, Bob made sure they had reliable people positioned on the escarpment as lookouts, and with adequate communications in an era not yet familiar with individual radios.

There was a lot of fire activity around Glacier and crews were in short supply. But that day someone deemed they didn't want jumpers on their district suggesting which fire to fight so we got kicked off. We got on a school bus in Whitefish and drove straight back to Missoula. I've never been back since. And after that little episode, I never really cared to.

Some fire managers seem to work under the principle that fire strategy is an intellectual game that can be manipulated by whim or convenience. That is fundamentally flawed. Firefighters on the ground develop and use tactics based upon the strategy designed, developed and initiated by fire managers. When that strategy is whimsical tactics become reactionary, resulting in ineffectiveness and injuries, even death. Firefighting is not a board game where rules can be changed arbitrarily. And firefighters would prefer that their lives are not governed by whimsical fortune.

Later we learned that our fire had, indeed, been gobbled up, as had most of the mountain. So although the OT had been good, our efforts had, for all intents and purposes, been a complete and utter waste of time. But more importantly, we'd sustained two injuries on a jump getting to a fire that had been locally mismanaged from the start. One injury being so serious that we never saw Todd work again, and thought he would be lucky to walk normally for the rest of his life. The top of his thigh had completely shattered, sending shards of bone into the surrounding tissue. Every time we saw him afterwards he walked with a cane. Being not yet 25 years old he sacrificed a lot for an occupation he loved but could no longer do.

It was an appalling episode. But one that was repeated a few years later after jumping a fire with BLM jumpers in Colorado. A mixed load – rounds and squares – left Grand Junction for a fire near Rifle. A McCall jumper sustained a back injury on landing but thought to persevere. After working for a while the pain grew worse so he was released, getting a ride off in a passing chopper. Then, after the rest of us had spent several hours containing ninety percent of the fire we were told to stop working and let it go. The district had suddenly decided to turn it into a management fire. As if that was a decision that could not have been made a few hours earlier. Incompetence occasionally reigns supreme at some levels in the organization, by faceless individuals with little or no thought to the efforts and risks that those on the ground face each time they go out. The McCall jumper thankfully recovered better than Todd. But then he wasn't part of Missoula's *Glass Class*.

As summer wore on the morning roll calls were presenting us with more and more broken rookies. There was only one place for the walking wounded and most of them hid their broken, bent and twisted bits behind sewing machines in manufacturing. Although being rookies, not only was their parachute manipulation suspect but so were their sewing skills. Which was evident the following year when PG bags started to inexplicably blow apart at the seams. It seemed that everything was destined to break at the hands of the *Glass Class*.

Being responsible for training, Walt received more than his quota of unfair criticism for the number of injuries. Meetings were held to discuss the matter, which resulted in the inevitable knee jerk solutions common to a bureaucracy. One such solution would plague us four years later when ankle braces became mandatory. But the *Glass Class's* training had been identical to previous years, which hadn't sustained nearly as many injuries. Some of the reason was understood to be that because it was a younger class, exuding youthful vigor over confidence, they assumed themselves infallible and immune to injury. Many were repeatedly making the same daft mistake of running with the wind, that sooner or later will always produce exactly what we encountered – lots of broken bits.

One idea was to increase the number of practice jumps; with anyone not meeting basic proficiency undergoing remedial jump training to try and cure the problem. Walt was visibly worried that he may have missed something. But that was only due to his complete devotion to the job. He was the best trainer we could ever have hoped for. He was not responsible. Youthful arrogance and sheer bad luck were responsible.

The extra practice jumps did seem to help, except for those who got injured doing them. The Field of Shame behind the base always had a reputation for abruptly ending seasons, but this group of rookies quickly found other ways to break themselves. To them it seemed to be almost endemic, like a disease. When not jumping they proceeded to hurt themselves playing basketball, running or swinging a pulaski.

Simple peer pressure is what eventually sorted the problem. The rookies slowly started to realize, one by one, that they didn't know as much as they thought. During one practice jump on Razor Ridge, with hundreds of acres to land, veteran jumpers split up to critique and mentor each rookie. Most rookies took it in the spirit it was meant, but one or two argued their point by making excuses as to why they had performed some totally inexplicable maneuver.

"Now just wait a fucking minute," a squad leader suddenly interjected. "You've been here for exactly how fucking long? Five fucking minutes, that's how long. And you're giving these guys, who've got hundreds of jumps under their belt, excuses as to why you fucked up," he went on. "They all know why you fucked up. You're a fucking idiot. Now pluck your head out of your ass and listen to what he's telling you. Otherwise you're going to be just another fucking statistic... Fucking rookies!"

Profanity-laced peer pressure can be a wonderful thing.

The *Glass Class* was one of the biggest classes in the nineties, but those remaining to the end of the decade were few. Sadly, the two who got injured and were forced to leave the Glacier fire have since died. Sonny survived the Colorado fire of 1994 only to die of pneumonia of all things. Todd fell down a rock slide while trying to regain his fitness by hiking alone in the Olympics, breaking his leg again and bleeding to death. Dying, he wrote a last message to his family on the inside cover of his Bible.

Todd is remembered in better times for one pithy remark he made to Gary, the base manager, during rookie training. Gary was doing what he liked to do: verbally joust with his subordinates. And as a senior paratrooper in the army he could have probably gotten away with it because no one would have dared retort. But smokejumpers are different, and this was not the military. Gary was running around the track and stopped briefly at the units to watch the rookies' progress. As usual, one squad was doing push-ups for failing to get properly suited, to which Gary made a typical off the cuff remark. Todd, sweating profusely in his Kevlar suit and helmet, looked up from behind his cage in mid-push and said: "Are those your legs or are you sitting on a chicken?"

Undoubtedly the best base manager in the '90s could dish it out but couldn't always take it. He made a fuss, which inevitably only made it worse. Several people were called to his office for the summary bollocking, but that obviously didn't help much either. It didn't even stop when Todd was on leave, but continued unabated with clucking on the loudspeaker. It eventually escalated to rumors of phone calls and only ended when Gary moved on. But even then it didn't really end. Instead, it transcended into something far more resilient, far more lasting – smokejumper legend.

Gary was an active base manager and close to the jumpers he respected, he tried to be one of them, and by doing so he was able to forestall the bullshit coming down the pipeline. And by actively jumping he was seen as being one of them, which in turn opened him up to friendly teasing. It was completely anathema to jumpers that the base could ever have a non-jumping base manager, but that is exactly what happened a couple of years later. To be the boss of jumpers you have to *have* respect and credibility, not just to have *had* it, and that only comes from being an active jumper; going out on the occasional fire, joining in on practice jumps. Anything else is a fucking bureaucrat, and jumpers already have enough fucking bureaucrats breathing down their necks. Problem is, non-jumping, desk-thumping fucking bureaucrats get to pick base managers. And when they do, everything goes tits up in a heartbeat. Which it did.

Chapter Twenty-One

— Summer's End, Twice, and Again

*Sunshine is delicious, rain is refreshing, wind braces us up, snow is
exhilarating; there is really no such thing as bad weather, only different
kinds of good weather.*

– John Ruskin

I T HAD BEEN A GOOD YEAR for those who had survived
it in one piece. We had been working steadily all across the
northwestern United States since spring. Fighting fast open
range fires on the prairies; unpredictable scrub fires in the basin;
smoldering valley fires; resilient coal seam fires on the plateaus of
central Montana and northern Wyoming; and, of course, the messy
jungle-like fires of the Panhandle. We'd seen lush forested slopes,
aspen covered foothills and barren rock-littered escarpments. From
high sun-tipped alpine meadows that surveyed the world to hidden
dark damp river bottoms. Fighting fire on lands carved by the great
northern rivers: the Yellowstone, Musselshell, Missouri, Madison,
Beaverhead, Clearwater, Lochsa and the Salmon. We had seen, we
had jumped and we had conquered. It is said that even sent to hell
smokejumpers would put the fire out.

Our last fire that year saw six of us reinforcing a fire deep in
the Bitterroot. Six had been on it for a day but the fire had doubled
in size during the afternoon and they requested an additional six to

guarantee the safety of the surrounding forest in what was a scenic well used hunting area very likely to burn. On our second day we were almost out of food after sharing ours with the original crew – two of their fire packs having disintegrated when a chute failed to deploy, perhaps because a rookie hadn't tied it off correctly. Since the fire had been staffed for three days and we were likely to stay for another two we requested a fresh food drop.

Steve, the loadmaster foreman, went to the local grocery store and picked up the usual list; constituting a range of items from steak and potatoes to bread and jam; from milk and eggs to orange and apple juice; plus cereal, fresh fruit and fresh ground coffee. It was securely packaged into several coolers, boxed in bubble wrap, strapped with parachutes and turned into paracargo.

Within a few hours the DC-3 was overhead dropping it under an assortment of green, white and orange cargo chutes. Dinner that evening was drastically different to the preceding days, and indeed the preceding weeks. Instead of sharing packets of dry food we had succulent steaks, baked potatoes and vegetables. Followed by fresh fruit, ice-cream for those that wanted it, and ground coffee. For breakfast we had steak and eggs, cereal, toast and jam and more fresh ground coffee. This was the life! And it came just in time because our energy levels were sagging after the recent rationed servings and the previous weeks of dry food, sodium soaked Spam and Gatorade.

Ironically, along with the fresh food immediately came cooler weather and the fire started to die. By mid-afternoon it was clear the fire no longer needed twelve firefighters. So after talking with the district it was agreed that eight would demob while four stayed behind to monitor and guarantee the fire would be entirely out. As strange as it was to those of us staying, with the long Labor Day weekend approaching, and the chance to maximize overtime, most of the jumpers decided to go.

Eight packed their kit and left the following morning, leaving their jump gear with us while they hiked out. We already had slings and were expecting a chopper to come later in the day to pick up their gear. In which case it would arrive at the base before them. As sometimes happens, though, the chopper was resourced elsewhere at the last moment, leaving us with a dozen sets of jump gear and the eight relying on their second set should they be lucky to find another fire. But with the weather deteriorating that didn't seem likely.

So now we were four, and had food for twelve.

For that first day alone, Larry, Don, Joey and I, had steaks for breakfast, lunch and dinner, and were hardly making a dent in the larder. The fire was looking really good by now but the district, nevertheless, requested we remain for yet another afternoon, just in case, even though the weather was getting decidedly chilly by this point. But we were okay because we had all the extra cargo chutes and eight more sleeping bags to keep us comfortable. The joke was the district only asked us to stay to eat more of the food.

It was just as well we had our winter gear because we woke the next morning to eight inches of damp snow. During the night our tarps had steadily become lower and lower under the weight and we kept having to shake them to get the snow off. When it got light no one stirred, there was no point. Instead, we held onto our bladders for as long as we could under the warmth of a couple of cargo chutes. Only running out when necessary in bare feet to relieve ourselves before quickly hopping back into our warm bags.

Hunger and boredom eventually got the better of us and Larry and I started to look for dry kindling to build up the cooking fire for breakfast. Since it was late in the season we had already started to carry more fleece and a thicker jacket, and this morning we were glad of it. It was bitterly cold digging out the food from the boxes now buried in the wet snow and a bitter wind howled viscously down the valley. There would be no helicopters for a while.

With the campfire finally kicking out some heat, and my eggs boiling nicely, I walked back to my hooch to pick up a coffee mug and noticed no movement of any kind from Don's hooch. I asked if he was okay, got a quiet murmur in reply and left him alone. I did notice, though, a strange crevice of melted snow outside his hooch.

Don finally arose when he smelled the bacon cooking.

"Finally need a piss, Don?" We asked.

He didn't understand our point, so we explained that because there were no footprints around his hooch he hadn't been up in the night like the rest of us older guys.

"Didn't want to get up," he said, rubbing his hands near the warming fire. "Pissed into my water bottle instead."

"And emptied it at arm's length?" I asked.

"Uh huh."

Problem was, he'd emptied it on the uphill side. Hence the little crevice winding its way back underneath his sleeping bag.

Due to the snowstorm the district was now determined to get us out of there quickly, they didn't want anyone stranded in their forest. Not that it would have been bad because we had enough food to last a week or more and almost all the comforts of home. But they were adamant. So instead of waiting out the weather and being available to sling out all the gear we arranged to leave that afternoon, walking out with only our PG bags and sleeping bags, which seemed to make sense because a mule train was coming to pick up everything we left behind – twelve sets of jump gear, half a dozen coolers of food, cargo chutes and chainsaws.

Once we got down from the mountain the weather improved a little and the sun even attempted to poke through the thick cloud layer. Going down the trail we transitioned from snow to mud to walking in a stream, and passed one of the mule trains on their way in, despondently trudging along the muddy trail as mules do while resigned to a thankless task. We likely wouldn't see our gear for a few days, but after getting dumped on we wouldn't be needing it because the season was very clearly over.

Waiting by the trailhead we looked back to the mountain. It was plastered white, like a tablecloth had been laid over it. Lower down, a grey-white misty haze hung delicately around the steep forested slopes, indicating the dramatic change in air temperature. Every once in a while a brilliant shard of sunlight poked through to impress upon us the brilliance of the new snow now clinging to the drooping branches of thousands of trees. Up there, in those higher elevations, winter had arrived once again. Where it would remain until the spring thaw.

Then it rained. And it didn't stop raining for a whole year.

With me gone for so much of the previous summer, mostly to West Yellowstone where I seemed to be becoming a season ending Westie, Anne decided that she was better off somewhere else and left me just before Christmas. It was quite out of the blue but there was little I could do about it. People make their choices and live with the consequences. She'd made hers and mine was to get over it the only way I knew how. I traveled to Europe and went skiing.

The Pyrenees. Andorra especially, was always a destination of mine ever since leaving the army. It was dirt cheap, devoid of large crowds and filled to the brim with duty free. Half the Scotch on the shelves had to be fake there was so much of it. There were gallon size bottles of every brand imaginable and many I had never even heard of. The food was delicious also. An American who owned a bar just outside of town served up the largest most succulent steaks I'd ever seen. After spending all night there we'd come away with change from a twenty. But what made Andorra so good, except for the occasional Spanish or French holiday, was no lift lines. That's what made it perfect. I never saw the point of going skiing to spend two hours a day waiting in line, and here there were none.

Bob came along and we both had a blast. We hit the snow perfectly. A few days before we left we heard that the slopes were bare and started to get nervous at having wasted our money, but then it snowed like crazy, leaving the sun-drenched mountains blanketed in pure white powder, the weather perfect and the snow excellent. The brightness of the reflected sun was so fierce Bob finished one day looking like a beetroot, and had to cool himself by sticking his head in a sink full of ice.

The fantastic skiing, the idyllic scenery, the wonderful people and the abundant cheap food and alcohol were taking my mind off seven years of marriage. Then to help matters I met a wonderful girl, Lorne, and spent the remainder of the holiday skiing with her. It was bloody fantastic.

Bob stayed with my parents for a while in Devon, southwest England, before going back to Missoula for work. He had a 6/13 appointment so he could work a little longer through the winter. I obviously didn't have an appointment so stayed in Devon. I love Devon. Or more to the point I love Dartmoor, covering 300 square miles of peat and granite. Its hills created from ancient volcanoes, and the grey granite which breaks through the peat are the tors that dot this remarkable landscape. As Montana is considered the Last Best Place in North America, so Dartmoor is to me in England.

I would run a ten-mile loop going up 1,200 feet, down 500 and back up 600. The hills were always deserted in winter except for a solitary ice cream truck, its owner obviously out for the same reason ice fishing is so popular – to get away from the wife. The higher paths, made over decades by cattle, wild ponies and sheep were rocky and uneven, and yet the lower peat paths were soft and spongy from eons of rain and decay. An old stone railway line, used to move granite from the moor in the 1800s, traversed the hill, running down towards the lower vales which were filled with wood smoke from chimneys of cottages 400 years old, giving the misty hollows a Dickensian quality. The moor remains forever the perfect backdrop for *The Hound of the Baskervilles*, the famous Sherlock Holmes adventure by Sir Arthur Conan Doyle. But long before novels, granite quarries and stone railways, the moor was inhabited by various humans since prehistoric times. The remains of their lodgings still evident if one knows where to look, buried in the peat and hidden under the sheltering gorse below the tors.

I was only ever in Devon during winter so I always ended up running in the miserable weather typical of the moor at that time of year: howling wind, mist, cold rain, sleet and snow. The running kept me warm, however, and the 50lb pack protected me from the incessant wind and driving rain against my back. After a prolonged period of rain and as I was running along a familiar trail the ground suddenly gave way beneath me. I instantly fell a couple of feet and slipped on a sharp rock, tearing up my ankle. The pain was excruciating but I didn't want to look. I knew that if I stopped I would never reach the car a few miles away through the driving rain. There was no one around for miles and I urged myself on and kept going, hobbling over rocks as best I could. I could feel my ankle swelling and stopped briefly by a quarry to soak it in the icy water before continuing on, limping as quick as I could up the muddy path towards the car. I was losing body heat even with the effort and there was a great temptation to find shelter and rest. But that would have been the worst thing to do.

Reaching the car I offloaded the pack, put the car in neutral, and coasted all the way down the hill towards home. By this time the ankle was swollen so badly I couldn't even use the accelerator. I hauled myself out of the car and hopped to the house.

"What did you do now?!" My mother said in exasperation. She had become used to my self-induced injuries over the years and was no longer a great proponent of sympathy. But I knew she cared. Deep down she cared. At least I think so.

This latest injury really couldn't have come at a worse time. I had been training hard to be ready for the jump season and now I couldn't even walk. My ankle was twice its normal size. There was nothing to do but ice it, wrap it and rest it, and hope for the best. After two weeks it could finally bear a little weight and I started to exercise it by doing a few simple stretches. But when I picked up any weight I still couldn't stand on it. It was immensely frustrating because I was losing fitness daily, the very fitness I relied on for jumping. It's more than a little ironic that we train in order not to get injured while jumping, and yet get injured while training.

I returned to Missoula in March, still limping and clear to all that I couldn't run. I was getting depressed, first refresher started in a month and I didn't know if I could make it. The run during the PT test is never up for discussion, it has to be done no matter what. It's also part of the test that most older veterans dread. No matter how agile or resilient we were in our earlier years, age has a habit of catching up, especially when the process is further advanced by injuries. Up to now I'd never had a problem, but I was beginning to understand what I'd been hearing. The run can be a bitch.

Lorne was traveling to Mexico and since I couldn't do much I decided to meet her in Playa de Carmen, just south of Cancun. It was great to see her when she met me at the airport She was radiant and drop dead gorgeous after being in the Caribbean sun. She projected health, exuded sexuality and bounced along with the vitality of life, unlike the pasty faced hop-a-long next to her. We caught a taxi and found a secluded cabana a block from the beach. It was idyllic and just what I needed. We spent our time strolling along the ocean shore, sunbathing naked on deserted beaches and enjoying wonderful Mexican food while reveling in each others' company. At the end of each day we'd return to the cabana, shag like rabbits and relax in a hammock. It was the perfect vacation.

At the end of two glorious weeks Lorne went off to finish her trip while I returned to Missoula. Refresher was to start in a week. Mexico had been good for many reasons: thanks to Lorne I was completely over my marriage; I had met a wonderful girl; and the jogs along the beach had healed my ankle. I could run again. It was still sore, and I still couldn't run with my pack, but I could grunt out the PT test run. The rest would come with time. And there was always plenty of time after early refresher.

That year there was plenty of time all the time after refresher. Missoula was washed out. Not a single plane left the ramp on a fire run in 1993. We tried once but a chip light in the cockpit said it couldn't. It was probably wet. The fire would likely have gone out by itself anyway. Nevertheless, all the local crews were racing to own it. The morale of the previous year plummeted. No one was earning. No one was excited. There wasn't even a rookie class that year to infuse a spark. Someone had obviously had a premonition. Incentive to do anything evaporated. Those unlucky to be on the first load were fire ready all season long, having to wear boots and Nomex, just in case. "In case of what?" was the question. "In case Noah came by and the Ark was on fire?"

Then it was wisely suggested that since the aircraft was sitting in a hanger 200 yards away – and would likely need a kick start – the load would have plenty of time to get ready. But by this time we knew boots wouldn't be necessary, nor would an airplane. We had given up, especially after Todd added the perfect snippet of wisdom to the notice board: "The longer you wait, the longer you wait." That pretty much summed up the summer. And to top it off even practice jumps were curtailed.

Instead, we were farmed out to the districts. They had sticks for us to pick, trees to thin and trails to maintain. The tree thinning and trail projects were fun, though. They at least got us out into the mountains, even if everything was soaking wet. The jump list was juggled so everyone had to take a turn on project work, because at the beginning the same bottom group was consistently going out, leaving others to grow fat and lazy behind the Singers.

The upside of having all jumpers on base, though, was that all jumpers were on base. We used this strange new thing called free time by organizing volleyball, tennis and ultimate frisbee. It was strange to organize an event and actually have everyone show up. Normally half would disappear to a fire. In busy years Rudy was often trying to get me to join in a tennis tournament and would put both our names down for the local open. It was a guarantee that at least one of us wouldn't be around for it. Instead, we'd be stepping out the door somewhere in Idaho.

With so many bored jumpers around town trouble was bound to happen sooner or later. There was too much youthful tethered testosterone and no release on the horizon.

We arrived to another dull roll call one Monday morning to find Gary mildly pissed off. A jumper had got into a fight over the weekend at one of the local bars and had buried someone's head in the sidewalk. As soon as it was described we all pretty much knew who had done it. Gary likely did too. And we suspected, too, that the head that hit the sidewalk probably deserved it. While Gary was glad to know there was a jumper who could handle himself – most being more used to receiving than giving – Gary still wanted to make a point. But Gary was a realist, and suggested that if such things were going to occur it might be better not to advertise where we came from by wearing smokejumper t-shirts all over town. The logic was sound. He then asked the anonymous individual to meet him in his office after roll call to explain the situation, but only because the police were involved, having been informed by the bar owner that a jumper had finished a fight.

Mark emerged a little later smiling. Apparently, some mouthy guy was shoving Rogers, who had just sustained a back injury from a practice jump on the Field of Shame, and Mark stepped in to stop it. Seeing more fodder through his alcohol-induced state, the guy took a look at Mark, weighed-up his options, and had a go. A poor choice. The go part was very short by all accounts.

Coming from a ranching family, where his brother had tested for Olympic wrestling, and spending every hunting season guiding in the backcountry of the Bob Marshall Wilderness, an altercation in a bar was probably pretty trivial. Mark was another of my rookie bros, and one of the most forgetful minded people I'd ever met. In West he was known for always looking for his wallet or his keys. Before rookie training he even forgot to bring his boots. Instead having to borrow someone else's in a hurry before going to rookie camp, where he got blisters the size of dollar bills. In the mid-90s, when disillusion set in, thanks to weak managers being driven by a powered-up, agenda-driven, personnel department, Mark left to concentrate on a carpentry business instead.

He also seemed to be more than a little accident-prone, as his scars prove. While on a job in Chicago he apparently plugged a 16-penny nail through his hand with a nail gun. Supposedly staring at it more in bewilderment than surprise, he casually reached for some pliers to pull it out. Those working with him suggested that he instead go across the street to the Emergency Room and get it checked out. They then watched as Mark waited at an intersection, unsure of whether to continue across the street toward the hospital or turn round and go back to work. He was having second thoughts and weighing up his options. What those options were he would not say. In all likelihood he thought the hole in his hand too trivial or the hospital too unnecessary. That, or he forgot his wallet.

I jumped with Mark a few times out of West. He seemed to like it there for a while, being removed from the perpetual LAMB becoming ever more prevalent in Missoula. On one occasion, when we were in West's Twin Otter flying east of The Grand Teton, the small emergency door in the fuselage Mark was resting against suddenly blew out. Literally blew out, falling 2,000 feet never to be seen again. Mark almost followed it, only stopping himself by grabbing onto the cargo straps. He had a knack for being wherever and whenever something happened, and was good to be around for that reason. He was also one of the few willing to call bullshit on bullshit. It was a sad day when that got too much for him. Well, maybe not for the management, which neither of us much cared for – the feeling being mutual I'm sure. But it was a bad day for the organization. The fact that management never realized it is proof of how blind they invariably were to raw talent and hard work.

Simply by being base manager Gary was a target to criticism. But he knew how to manage, understood the differences in people, the diversity, and didn't go out of his way to admonish the whole group when one person was at fault: 'Praise in public, chastise in private.' It worked, is so simple, and yet many managers prove incapable of grasping the concept, even though it is fundamental to morale, respect and, therefore. good management. Whether liked or not, jumpers never failed to appreciated that Gary would always stand up and support those under his command – the lowly GS-6s, the grunts – no matter the problem. He knew who made him look good and was smart enough to look after them. His last year was a bureaucratic battle, you could see it written on his face. The desk-bound personnel department was getting too influential and too deeply involved in jumper politics, trying to erode the jumper ethos as a matter of intent. Gary attempted to curtail this erosion but future managers folded under pressure and sold out. The early-90s were arguably the last best years in Missoula.

They weren't the last best for fires, however, because the late-90s and beyond saw jumpers being increasingly busy. But by that time the original jumper, hard-charging, gung-ho ethos had been all but destroyed, replaced, instead, by a woolly personnel induced philosophy more attributable to a kindergarten on occasion.

The longstanding jumpers were disillusioned and increasingly complained about the behind-the-scenes politics affecting us all. Twenty-year veterans more easily saw the warning signs and were getting steadily discouraged, and looked for ways to get out of the immediate jumping hierarchy. Preferring, instead, to do what was previously unheard of; going to large fires to take positions as crew bosses, division supervisors and helicopter managers. The reason for being a smokejumper was to get away from large fires, to stop them from occuring. Our motto being: "Be a jumper: get out of the Forest Service."

All we wanted to do was get to fires quickly, put them out and go on to the next. Maybe even in the same day. Two fires in the same day was not unheard of. I heard of someone in Alaska even managing three. Once signed up and available we were expected to work all summer long. Taking a break was out of the question and considered unnecessary. Time off was unheard of. But we didn't want it anyway, we just wanted to work. Work hard, play hard and earn enough to see us through the winter. This meant working a lot of hours and we chased those hours with a passion. Not only did our very future rely on it but we had the jumper ethos to uphold.

But that passion was soon looked down upon. Managers tried to forbid us to even mention OT. It became a dirty word. The very reason why we were there; the reason we could feed, clothe and take care of our families became a dirty word in their eyes. It was ludicrous. These desk bound hypocrites – those who earned far more – were given free rein to initiate this thinking, which became the antithesis to everything that was paramount to our ability to function effectively and efficiently. And no one did anything to stop it. Slow years bring out the worst in people. Always those who have little more to do than justify their meager positions by inventing new and more complex rules. And this year that's all administration seemed to do. It certainly wasn't going to support us or our cause. They made that plain from the start.

'Supporting us?' Now there's an oxymoron.

Since there was nothing happening a few of us volunteered to go to the North Fork for a burning detail. They needed jumpers so they could complete their fall burning schedule. The following day I loaded up the Subaru and headed back over to Canyon, exactly where I had started. Chuck had left and Bill was overseeing the burning as acting FMO. They never did give him the full position – more inane FS politics – and he left soon after. But it was good to see him again. He had been instrumental in getting me hired into jumping and he seemed chuffed that I had made it. Pete was also still there, but working a different part of the district so I didn't see him again.

Over the next week it was back to prescribed burns. Not the type we had done before, but smaller units on less steep ground. It was restful after a summer hiking over mountains. I got to work with James for the first time outside of loadmasters. He continued to impress everyone with his love for the job and his astounding work ethic. Every time there was a slop-over James was there eating smoke. I would jump in and out of the suffocating smoke to breath some fresh air for a minute or two but James just carried on regardless. The smoke often reminded me of the tear gas test we'd had in the army, where we were herded into a bunker, locked in, told to remove our respirators and take a deep breath. If it looked like anyone was holding their breath they got a good solid punch in the stomach for their efforts, after which they'd have to breath all the deeper, gagging and spluttering up mucus the instant they did. It hadn't been a particularly pleasant experience so I could never quite understand how James could put up with smoke for long.

One downside of the week was that one member of our crew had deemed it okay to use FS equipment to gather his winter wood. Once back in Missoula it put a damper on our whole experience at Canyon, which apart from that one episode had been fun. Another jumper had also used his spare time to gather firewood, but had used his own equipment. It's so basic and made all the difference.

The end of the season came early and since no fires meant no funding we were laid off immediately we got back to Missoula. We had a day to fill out our termination paperwork, hand in all our equipment and get signed out of the departments. Then that was it. We were done. Season over.

It was a sad drive home realizing we wouldn't be going back on Monday, and not knowing what to do for the winter. We went to the bar to commiserate and figure out what to do. Some were going to do construction for folks they already knew, others were off on winter travels, which sounded pretty damn good to me.

In the meantime I trolled around looking for work on Monday and signed on at Express Services again hoping they might have something. But in reality all I was qualified for was milking cows, shoveling shit and digging ditches. And up to now smokejumping had just been more glorified ditch digging – albeit in some of the best places God created.

On Tuesday I got a call from the base asking if I wanted to go out on a fire.

"Are you kidding me?" I said.

They weren't, and I got to the base in half and hour. An hour later twelve of us were in a van heading to a fire. Once we arrived we cut a small scratch line around it, the first we'd dug all year. It was later improved by remnants of a district crew but it served its purpose, everything else was just pretty work. We clearly worked too hard too quickly because as soon as the fire was contained were off back to Missoula, where we were ushered into the loft and informed that we were laid off again. We could have half an hour to do our time, but that was it; season over – again. Gratitude there was not a lot of.

Once again, we were driving home wondering what we were going to do. Moreover, I was speculating how much longer I could afford to do this job and get perpetually laid off every September or October. I had earned a miserable $8,000 all summer. I was 36 and knew I needed to get a real job real soon. But opportunities for permanent jobs with the Missoula Smokejumpers were rare. In fact, at the time, jobs were non-existent because the government had a hiring freeze on all new appointments and was even offering incentives to those qualified for early retirement.

One jumper who readily took up the offer to spend more time in *Charlie's* without government intrusion a year later was Steve, or 'Mad Dog' as he was known. But before he left, Geno asked if Steve and I would go out to the ramp at twelve o'clock. He wanted to see a Mad Dog and an Englishman out in the noonday sun!

Geno was the other half that got me started in jumping. When he was going though my initial jumper application he examined the section relating to previous jobs, where it says "Reason for leaving." He said he got a chuckle because all it said was: "Barn burned down." That got him interested and he called Bill at North Fork to find out more, who explained that they'd better hire me if they didn't want a Limey on their doorstep every day explaining why they should. So I guess it worked.

Chapter Twenty-Two

— Best and Worst

New lieutenant: *Is there anything worse than a kick in the nuts soldier?*

Private: *Yes sir, two.*

– Royal Engineers on German Crusader exercise.

T HE FOLLOWING YEAR DIDN'T start very well either. While working overseas, trying to make up lost wages due to the previous poor summer, I contracted dysentery and lost 32lbs in two weeks. Since my normal weight then hovered around 155lbs there wasn't much left of me and I looked like a white Ethiopian desperate for food aid. I had no energy and every time I tried to eat it came out immediately. Top or bottom it didn't seem to matter, it just came out from wherever it could the fastest. Getting a flight home was not fun. I spent most of the time either in the crapper or waiting outside one trying to get in. All the other passengers gave me a wide birth, they could clearly tell there was something wrong with me and wanted none of it. The attendants were the same. If they'd had tongs they would have used them, even when filling my cup with water, which was about the only thing I could keep down for any length of time. But even that came out in not so splendid a fashion. I was not a happy camper.

Arriving at Heathrow I forced myself onto the first train home to Devon. Of course, since the privatization of the railway system in the U.K. there were fewer trains and fewer seats on the fewer trains so I sat on my ruck for six hours outside the crapper. When I wasn't sitting on the ruck I was sitting on the can, and watching the tracks thunder past a few inches below my ass. Mother was horrified when she picked me up at Exeter station. I looked like a stick and my clothes hung off me like rags. My face was gaunt and little more than a skull fraught with pain.

An English quack put me on some drugs that after a few days enabled me to eat a little. Or more importantly, keep what I ate down a little longer. I still felt like crap and the pills made me feel worse, but I stopped losing weight – as if I had any more to lose apart from the marrow in my bones.

It is a depressing thing to lose all the fitness you've ever had in life, and wasting all the effort it has taken to get you there. But here I was, barely able to walk up a slight incline let alone a hill, or a mountain. Haytor Rock was so far away. I used to run up it with a 50lb pack in under an hour and now I couldn't make it to the top of the road in a day.

I made two new holes in my belt just to keep my jeans up, my shirts looked like tablecloths and my feet were always sore. I never quite understood that. I was 30lbs lighter and yet my feet thought I was a 100lbs heavier. I had no muscle left anywhere and no energy to get them back.

During the second week of pills I started going to the crapper less. Only eight times a day not twelve. And with home cooked food I was maintaining but still not growing. So the doc gave me another prescription, confident that it would finally do the trick.

A month later I started to put on a few pounds. I still had no energy and barely managed a stroll around the park. But at least I could get to the park without having to take a dump in a bush on the way. My health was improving but not as quickly as it needed to. Refresher was barely two months away and I could hardly carry a light daypack let alone 120lbs of packout bag. The excruciating headaches almost drove me insane. Some would last for days and turn into migraines. It was all I could do just to maintain sanity on some days. With so little muscle my bones grated, my joints ached and the discs in my spine pinched nerves, forcing my back to seize completely and sending shards of sciatic pain down my leg. The nerves in my neck were so tight that every time I turned my head I got a searing headache. Even sleeping was difficult; unable to find a comfortable position with no flesh on my bones and knees and hips aching all night.

How the 14th managed to get though the Burma campaign is mind boggling. There, many thousands succumbed to dysentery and had to fight a war at the same time. After weeks of misery I've heard that some just wanted to die. I know I did on occasion. Apart from having a ruptured appendix a few years later, misdiagnosed dysentery was constantly the most miserable time of my life.

Thankfully, a third round of drugs started to help. I was now only running to the crapper four times a day and even started to put on a few pounds. The easiest way to add weight was to drink lots of Guinness, which somehow also aided the digestion – don't ask me why. Then, as the weeks passed by, I managed to increase my walking and every once in a while would try a gentle jog until becoming utterly exhausted – usually after an unimpressive half-mile marathon. I had no idea how I would manage refresher. This was getting to be a habit of mine.

The hills were the worst because my legs felt like jelly. They had no strength at all. So all through the day I would exercise them doing calf raises, squats and lunges. Then, in front of the TV in the evening I'd do sit-ups and push-ups to exhaustion. After a rest I'd do it all over. I was determined to get fit again. There was no way I was going to let twenty-odd years of fitness literally slide down the crapper, and I was determined to run my old route over the moors before heading back to Montana. Starting slowly, just to maintain a rhythm, I just tried to get over the next hill. Day by day getting a tad bit further. If I found myself too tired, too weak, I would punish myself with a shortcut – the shortcut being quicker but a lot steeper. Strength slowly began to return, but my joints were paying a terrible price for the relentless pounding.

Just before returning to Missoula I managed to do my original run, complete with a 40lb day pack. When I finally reached the top of Haytor Rock I felt euphoric, like Rocky. The feeling of reaching a seemingly unattainable goal through sheer relentless effort is incredible. I tore off my pack and did sit-ups and push-ups on the soft peat in the pouring rain. A family of tourists on top of the rock thought me completely mad.

I spent the remainder of the winter skiing Snowbowl with the regular bunch of ski hounds: Andy, Scott, Joey, Billy, Don and Cameron, and anyone else forced onto the Government Ski Team – those laid off and skiing. Half of us skied conventionally, the rest Telemarked. Andy was the star. Having been weaned on the snows of Snowbowl it was hardly surprising. I was just lucky to keep up with any of them. Cameron said he only skied with me because I made him look good. Which wasn't true at all, he skied with me to pick up the ski bunnies I knocked over.

The snow was great that year. It snowed two to three times a week, each time leaving another few inches of fresh dry powder. Every day was a race to see who could get up the mountain first. After a while, though, I realized that I was treating it like work: getting there early, working hard and staying late. We would rarely even stop for lunch. Just relying on Scott to bring his five-pound bag of peanuts to sustain us in the bar afterwards.

Some jumpers worked off of a lift pass by thinning trees on the runs during the fall, even though the price of a weekday pass was already dirt cheap. Skiing four days a week was plenty for me, especially since the skiing was challenging and consistent, and with a weekday absence of any lift lines.

Refresher was earlier that year, which was great for all the seasonal temps desperate to replenish their savings. Another bit of good news was that the FS had lifted the hiring freeze and there were ten GS-6 (6/13) appointments vacant. Most of those without appointments by this time, and who wanted them, were my rookie bros. So we were finally going to be in the running for a real job. I felt in a good position because I had volunteered a lot of my time in the last few years: I'd done EMT training on my own time; every EMT refresher; worked on my senior riggers license during the weekends; and had taken winter fire classes. I was confident that if I wrote a good application all that extra work would stand me in good stead. Morale immediately improved with this news. The other morale booster was that we didn't have a base manager. Jeff was acting base manager, instead, and he was great; very hands off. Everyone was looking forward to the summer. It was a complete change from the previous year. The base had a great feel, energy infused the air as we anticipated being busy and earning a lot of money over the coming season.

The canteen no longer existed by now. The person running it had put it into a financial hole, and then instead of replacing her and getting someone who could run it properly, they closed it. It was one of the dumbest things they've ever done. For from now on everyone had to either rush down to the airport restaurant or drive into town for a Subway sandwich, all in half an hour.

We did all the normal refresher training stuff except that now there seemed to be even more emphasis on Ethics and Bleeding Conduct. Someone somewhere was really getting into it for some reason. Without food, the canteen was now the new classroom, and conveniently located at the opposite end of the hall to the gym. So for these mandatory classes, once the sign in sheet had rotated, a few would sneak out to pack parachutes or get an extra workout. It was a more efficient use of time than sitting though mindless ethics drivel. The government teaching *us* about ethics – good Lord!

One of the fun parts of training, apart from jumping of course, was always tree climbing. We often jumped into the tree climbing area around Ninemile, just west of Missoula, and it was great being in the woods again. During lunch, right after getting re-qualified in climbing, I was talking with Don about what some of us had got up to in the winter. He already knew a little and I got the impression that he was a little jealous he hadn't been included in what ended up being a poorly planned venture to Azerbaijan – which was at war with Armenia over the disputed Nagorno-Karabakh region.

Skirmishes still occur along the Azerbaijan Armenia border in a small, but little known, conflict that has worldwide implications. Kipling's phrase "The Great Game," brought to notoriety in his wonderful novel *Kim*, was primarily set in India, where for years the British Empire fought to protect the Jewel in the Crown from Russian expansion. The Caspian is involved in a Great Game of its own these days, with large transnational companies and modern imperialism vying for the vast oil and gas reserves in the region.

Much of the effort today is less about the extraction and more about the transportation of oil, and the delicate routes that those pipelines must take to sustain the west's continuing hunger and the new Chinese juggernaut's desperate thirst for more and more oil. In that ongoing saga Azerbaijan is a primary player.

Peace, morality and common sense are easily discarded when vested interests make those decisions financially inviable. Made all the more complicated because Azerbaijan's southern edge borders a thorn in the Middle East, Iran. Without Iran's intransigence the pipelines could follow a more natural course to the infrastructure already in place around the Gulf. But that is not likely to happen anytime soon. So longer, more convoluted, more expensive routes fraught with political and security uncertainties are necessary.

As Americans it was a tricky time to be in Azerbaijan because the U.S. Government had just recently passed section 907 of the Freedom Support Act, restricting U.S. assistance to the Azeris until they lifted the blockade on the Nagorno-Karabakh. Exemptions to this were only made more recently in 1998. Nevertheless, a group of parachute riggers were set up in the defunct Southern Command HQ of the old Soviet Union near downtown Baku. The Soviet base that was directly responsible for running the protracted invasion of Afghanistan that we have since paid for so dearly. A fact made all the more ironic when two senior figures of the mujahedeen paid a visit. I doubt the irony was completely lost on them.

Notwithstanding the embargo, a British consortium, Summit Limited, organized by Lord Erskine, was also clandestinely being set up to supply the Azeris with arms and mercenaries, going even further than the American Mega Oil consortium whose presence in Baku, by this time, had become well known to competing foreign diplomats. Allegations of U.S. involvement were made to the U.S. State Department, which further opened the door for the Brits to quietly fly in advisors on chartered Russian aircraft. Even though it is illegal for a Briton to be a mercenary soldier the Foreign Office turned a Nelson eye towards Erkine's intentions. There was a lot at stake in Baku. And not all of it related to oil or Armenia.

The arrival of 500 to 3,000 Afghan mercenaries threatened to turn an already messy, but localized, ethnic campaign into an even more bloody, and wider religious one, with dire implications for everyone. The Afghans fought like Afghans but against better tactics and weaponry their early gains were soon lost and many of them perished under poor leadership. Against this violent backdrop it is, then, no coincidence al-Qaeda's early beginnings are assumed to have transpired in Azerbaijan. Although scant attention was paid at the time. Not until the embassy bombings in Africa in 1998 did western governments wake up to the threat of a wider Islamic jihad and rather hypocritically blame the Azeris for harboring terrorists. Such was the subjective blindness of national intelligence.

It was a complicated and messy episode. One made worse by ignorance. Some of that ignorance being which was the right side? Other ignorance stemmed from the stereotypical western approach in dealing with people in unknown cultures, that those in charge of personnel in foreign countries are simply not good at it. They seem to think because they can run roughshod over folks at home and get places, they can do it everywhere. But that just doesn't fly. A cursory glance at history shows that this extended region is littered with the graves of people who have made that very mistake.

Don was genuinely interested and we talked at some length about the risks of such adventures. I said that no amount of money was worth risking one's health, or indeed anyone else's either – whether it be by bullet or disease, design or accident.

He agreed for the most part, but added, "But you're jumping, and fighting fires. That's risky too, and you do that for the money."

I remember saying something like: "Jumping really isn't that risky. And I don't just do it for the money I do it because I love it. I go overseas for old-fashioned adventure, fully aware of the risks. Money has little to do with it." But that wasn't strictly true. Money did have something to do with it because I wouldn't have done it for nothing – even though nothing is what I ended up with on this occasion after dousing myself with antibiotics for weeks.

It is sadly ironic (if ironic is the right word), but neither of us knew how risky the summer was to become, or how wrong I was. It was a conversation that would haunt me.

Right after refresher we started doing prescribed burns for Stevensville District, and made some decent early overtime. We worked 12-hour days on the units, preparing boundaries by digging firebreaks, and then igniting and holding in the afternoons. On one trip up to a burn unit, out of the nine in the van, six were going through either a divorce or a separation. Jumping was certainly not conducive to long relationships, especially among the temporaries who got laid off year after year. People gave up a lot to do this job. While marriages were often the largest emotional loss, a home was always the greatest financial loss. And it's no coincidence the two losses often go together.

Some jumpers had been financially stripped raw by divorce: their wives taking half of everything they had after doing very little to warrant it. Mine had simply emptied the bank account before taking off, leaving little to argue about. I had gone to a cash point in Yellowstone the previous year expecting to see a few grand sitting in my account after a summer of work and was shocked to see only $300. Instead of money my wife now had a Montana Hay-Burning Knickknack grazing a field somewhere in Arlee. When I got back to Missoula I went though all the check stubs to see exactly where my money had gone, that which was supposed to support us during the winter. I discovered that she had spent the equivalent of all my wages treating her friends, and new boyfriend, to dinner and drinks while I was away working. So absolutely bleeding generous of me.

I got off lightly, though, stories far worse were commonplace among jumpers all over the country. Yes, jumpers give up a lot to be jumpers. Firefighters give up a lot to be firefighters. And pilots give up a lot to drop stuff. Women like that aren't worth of it, life's better without them and when my divorce came through Cameron took me out on an all-night bender to celebrate. I didn't pay for a single drink all night, just picking up breakfast in the Oxford at three o'clock in the morning.

The burning details weren't too hard and they were great fun, Stevensville was always a good district to work for. They spent the money and hired the right people to get the job done and didn't mess about. We worked for them for a couple of weeks before heading further down the Bitterroot to the West Fork, where we burned some more with the great folks down there. All the districts were trying to get their understory burns finished before summer: burning off the lighter fuels and dead grass and greening up the hills for wildfire prevention and elk habitat.

Between burning details we spent time in the loft, making new jump harnesses and helitack equipment using the big heavy-duty sewing machines. I was happily thumping away on a piece of webbing when Jeff came over to chat. He never came over to chat. I wasn't in his chatting circle so something was up. Since Jeff was acting base manager as well as resident loft foreman I wondered if we had screwed up the harnesses. He floored me. It was the worst news I could ever have expected, and to this day I still think about it, bitterly. Jeff told me that they had to remove my GS-6 6/13 appointment application from the table. It had nothing to do with qualifications, nothing to do with work ethic. Somebody took it upon themselves to remove it simply because I was over 35 years old. I'd never heard anything so bloody stupid in all my life and literally couldn't believe what I was hearing. More astounded than anything I hardly said a word, being utterly gobsmacked! It felt as if I had been kicked in the guts and I thought "Bastards! Faceless fucking bastards." This was age discrimination pure and simple, and someone, a jumper, took it upon themselves to be executioner. The government, one moment lecturing us on Ethics and Bleeding Conduct and the next delivering age discrimination – something it would never condone in the private sector. Fucking hypocrites. I immediately went to find the Department of Agriculture's (USDA) anti-discrimination statement, so bandied about in every catalogue, every leaflet, every piece of self-serving literature, espousing how valuable was the organization and the people within it. Eventually finding one with a disclaimer, in small print, that made the whole statement nonsense, there was nothing 'anti' about it.[*] I thought it better not to know who decided to be a fucking bureaucrat that day and remove my name. For I still had to work with them.

For weeks afterwards the only thing that kept me sane was being busy. And as luck would have it I didn't have much time to dwell on it because we had an unusually early request that year. In the circumstances it was the best thing that could have happened. Twenty of us were going to North Carolina. The DC-3 was being requested as a crew transport and jumpers had been invited along. We were happy as clams, got prepared and loaded the DC-3 for the long slog east the next day, with no idea what to expect. Few of us had ever been east. Those who had had been involved in hurricane cleanup a few years before and were too gleefully telling us about the venomous snakes and alligators "all over the place."

We knew we wouldn't be jumping since we hadn't loaded any gear. Apparently, years before, they'd tried jumping into east coast trees but the hardwoods got the better of them. Not surprisingly really since there's an obvious difference between jumping into a fir and an oak. Oaks tend not to bend, while the human body does quite easily, although not always in the most comfortable direction. This notion had manifested a sadistic urge among locals to shout FIRE! so they could watch jumpers smash themselves into trees.

Britain's Special Air Service Regiment tried jumping into tree canopy during the Malaya counter-insurgency and encountered the same problem. Only they weren't wearing padded Kevlar suits, the trees were hundreds of feet taller and nasty people were shooting at them. Proving that no matter what you do there's always someone doing it tougher.

---

[*] The USDA Anti-Discrimination Statement (p. 347)

Chapter Twenty-Three

— Swamps, Gators and Chiggers

A nation that destroys its soils destroys itself. Forests are the lungs of
our land, purifying the air and giving fresh strength to our people.
– Franklin D. Roosevelt

I CAN'T REMEMBER HOW MANY TIMES we stopped on
the way to North Carolina but it was the furthest many of us
had ever travelled in the DC-3, arriving late in the day to a
hot and humid Croatan National Forest, near New Bern, the second
oldest city in North Carolina, just down the road from Cherry Point
Marine Corps Air Station. Our immediate appreciation was that the
air was sweet, and that the salty ocean breeze was unsuccessful at
cooling the thick muggy air. Most of all, though, we smelled the
smoke, a different kind of smoke. Unlike the brittle-dry desiccated
particulate smoke of the west and northwest this smoke was almost
damp, carrying with it a strange, almost sickly, fuel-like smell.

We were driven to a fire camp temporarily located behind the
local district office on the Fisher Landing Recreational Site, made
up of an assortment of perfectly aligned military green eight man
tents along with a shower trailer, food trailer and equipment trailer.
It was becoming a village when we arrived and the usual collection
of fire camp rats were wondering around with clipboards. It was a
closed camp – meaning we weren't supposed to leave it unless for
work. But that was archaic authoritarian bullshit. No one was

paying us during our time off so no one could tell us where not to go during our free time. We had a quick but thorough briefing by the FMO, taking in fire activity, weather, local topographical nuances and the current tactics employed in fighting the fire. One of the strangest nuances were the ridges that kept being mentioned. On arrival we hadn't noticed a hill for miles. The terrain being flat farmland, flat forest or flat swamp, and the next stop east was the Atlantic Ocean. Where were these ridges? We were told they were very slight raises in the dirt, mostly made up of sand and often no more than a few inches high. So not large enough for a drunk man to trip over. Ridge? A seam in the dirt more like.

With the briefing over we started to get settled and sought out bunk space. Walking around camp it was clear the people were nice and friendly and seemed excited to have us around. Almost as excited as we were for being there. Although we did wonder what they had in store for us to warrant bringing us all the way here.

At night it was just as muggy as daytime and most of us slept quite comfortably outside of our sleeping bags, fortunate that there weren't too many mosquitoes to bother us. We assumed they must have sprayed for them because it was certainly their habitat. The following morning a few of us rose early and went for a run to the mouth of the Neuse River, where we discovered a plaque marking the war grave of the first of the three U.S. Navy ironclad warships, the USS Monitor, which sank off nearby Cape Hatteras during a storm on December 31st, 1862. We then returned to meet everyone for breakfast and tooled up ready for the working day.

Three marine Humvees, complete with drivers, arrived to take us to the fire, which was only a few miles away down a series of dirt roads. Nearing the fire we noticed wide water-filled ditches on either side of the road with acres of scrub wetlands beyond. With all the water around we wondered where on earth the fire could be.

Then we stopped next to a cat line that disappeared into a swamp, covered with what looked like impenetrable jungle.

During the drive we'd seen a few bushes smoldering away in the swamp, but nothing serious, and here there was nothing at all. Apparently we had flown 3,000 miles, first class, to put out a fire in a swamp. But it was explained that the fire could easily travel along the root system of the plants under water, and even beneath the road to emerge on the far side. So our job was to lay irrigation pipes all along our section of swamp to act as a firebreak in the jungle-like vegetation growing out of mud and water. The ground was already sodden and spongy but they wanted even more water. The fires were certainly resilient in this part of the world.

We started carrying 20-foot sections of aluminum pipe in by hand, but quickly realized a helicopter would considerably speed up the process. Otherwise we'd be walking further to and further fro the farther away we got. Todd, our foreman, mentioned this to the liaison officer and we soon got a chopper on the scene; they had the resources and had to use them to justify their availability, so we were 'In like Flint.'* A couple of us organized placing the pipes into slings while another two walked into the swamp to scout suitable sling spots in which to drop them. The rest of the crew followed the sling spots and laid out the pipe as fast as they could fetch and carry. By the end of the first morning we had it finished. It wasn't supposed to happen that way, however. It was supposed to have taken a lot longer. A whole lot longer.

The Incident Commander (IC) came by to see how we were doing only to find us already finished. Describing him as surprised would be an understatement. Describing him as pleased would also not be completely accurate since he now had to find us something else to do. So, after some radio chatter, some deep thought, we built three helispots along the line of the pipe-lay in the off-chance

---

* As opposed to 'In like Flynn.' This was work, we weren't about to get laid.

crews might be needed – apparently local crews never ventured where we were walking for some reason. In fact, as we finished laying out the irrigation pipe a few of the district crew did show up to stare at these western jumpers. One said: "You'd never get me in there." We didn't get it. It really wasn't that bad, and it was fun.

We split into three groups and cut three helispots on our side of the swamp, building the landing-pads from the trunks of small trees we removed. It all looked very professional when finished, although we doubted any of them would ever be used. Here again, though, we had worked too quickly. Inevitably, splitting us up had only led to competition between the groups, each attempting to outdo the others by having the best helipad in the shortest time. Once we were finished, and without having anything else to do, we hiked around the bush to examine and critique the other helispots. One group had been driven to the far side of the swamp and come in from a different direction, but we wanted to walk through it to see if it was really as bad as everyone made it out to be.

We followed the cat line as far as it went and then set off bushwhacking through the rest, getting stung, torn, shredded and soaked through, but generally thoroughly enjoying the challenge of the different terrain. We finally found a manmade clearing where another group had built their helipad. It wasn't nearly as good as ours! After a further few hundred yards we came across a natural clearing, which pretty much made the recently constructed helispot redundant. No one on the ground could have possibly known it was there, not without some serious bushwhacking and thoroughly scouting the area. The helicopter must have seen it, however, but never once mentioned it! Such is unnecessary busy work.

It was getting late in the afternoon and because we were being limited to 12-hour days we bushwhacked back towards the road. In much of the area we could see where the fire had already passed through, but the worry was that it would pass through again. On its first pass the fire had smoldered around the understory grasses, burning the odd bush but mainly staying close to the ground. What they were worried about was that if the fire passed this way again, with everything dried out, and the predominant bush inclined to be incendiary, the re-burn would actually be more severe due to its ability to move more quickly through the pre-dried fuels.

When we emerged from the swamp we were met by more locals who couldn't believe the work we had put in already, and had done so in terrain that they apparently feared to tread. During our briefing the FMO had warned us to be especially careful in this unknown forest because it was so dense, making it very easy to get lost. Apparently a marine aircraft had crashed there once. The pilot got lifted out but when a team went in to check the crash site they got lost. A second team sent to look for the first also got lost, and a helicopter was eventually dispatched to rescue everyone.

The following day we cleaned up and perfected our helispots, for want of something to do rather than anything else. We knew that in all likelihood the spots would never be used but it was professional pride. While most of us were doing this, Wayne and Mark walked through the entire swamp from one side to the other. And if one were to believe the marines and the locals it was a feat not easily done by anyone. Or "anyone sensible" I think was the phrase used. These two had been asked to check out thermal FLIR (forward looking infra-red) sightings of hot spots somewhere near the middle of the fire. The previous night a FLIR aircraft had made passes over the fire and recorded everything. These images were then studied to determine if there were any remaining hot spots on the fire. In this case they had found three red dots, all in a neat line somewhere off to the north of one of our helispots.

After a few hours Mark and Wayne emerged from the forest looking like they'd hiked half way across Burma in the monsoon. Mark's Nomex trousers were shredded so bad they were literally falling off, while Wayne's shirt showed the results of hundreds of unforgiving branches. It had been quite the adventure by the look of them: caked in dirty sweat from head to toe, sodden boots and clothes barely fit for rags. For all their effort, though, neither had found any hot areas, even though they had been in the exact spot; one of few clearings in the area. There *were* deer tracks, however. Leading everyone to believe the three red spots on the FLIR image were actually the body heat of three deer casually walking along a game trail in single file.

The district was getting short of things for us to do and while half the crew started to splash about trying to put the fire out in the swamp the rest of us patrolled the fireline, a 20-foot wide dirt road. We drove around these washboard roads looking very important in a beautifully finished maroon Ford Custom Van, complete with captain seats and swivel chair, and with tools scattered all over the floor. The vehicles must have been the only ones left in the rental lot, although I doubt the company ever realized what they were to be used for. For us it was like being on a vacation and at lunch we even went to town for Chinese food. On the few occasions we tried to eat pack lunches a local gator made out quite well on the ham.

The other group was having too much fun splashing about in an area that had been deliberately flooded and yet where the fire stubbornly persisted. They were literally wading around up to their knees in water and grubbing around like the peasants digging for peat in *Monty Python and The Holy Grail*.

While they continued searching for hot spots in water the rest of us were put to work renovating a campground. I don't know if the funding for this came from the fire budget or what, but we sure traveled a long way, first class, to build a campground. Although it was all good, because for the first time since being in North Carolina we got to work directly with some of the locals. That's always fun. Not until you work with the local people, appreciate their culture and way of life, and try so damned hard to understand their humor, can you grasp what the area and people are all about. With the 'recent' Civil War still being a major part of their history they constantly mentioned, indeed with some glee, that we were all Yankees. I reminded them that they were all damn Yankees to me.

We started improving the campground by leveling off parking spots with new gravel, with one of the locals bringing us bucket loads of crushed rock using a huge Seabee tractor. He made a fuss explaining that this was *his* machine, and that we should not touch it, even though it clearly said U.S. Government on the side. After dumping a load another local on a Massey Ferguson tractor arrived to scrape it around until it was level. Our lowly job, as longtime punishment for being those damn Yankees, was to rake it by hand to make it all look pretty. There was a very obvious pecking order determined by the ability or privilege in operating equipment. It wasn't hard to see that we were at the very bottom of the North Carolina Forest Service food chain.

We took our lunch at the campsite and I hung my hammock to relax. After an hour there was no sign of the locals so I decided to grab the Seabee and get to work by moving some gravel. Machines are machines, they pretty much all work the same, some are just bigger than others. On the farm and in the army I had driven most things so it only took a minute to figure out what lever did what, and I was soon trundling around the campsite and having a blast on the big Seabee.

When the driver did come back and saw what was happening he looked at me as if I had stolen his only child. Not wanting to offend, I quickly got off and jumped onto the Massey instead, and seeing as that driver never did come back, I stayed using it till the end of the day. I had risen in the food chain, only by attrition, but at the same time had insulted the dogma of the pecking order.

Despite the overly territorial appreciation of machinery the locals were fun to work with. They had a great sense of humor and tried to explain the workings of the district to us. It was much different to the northwest, but this was a poor area and the district was probably very under funded, so they had to make the most of it when a fire came long. Fires are known for their great waste and once resources are available they have to be used. While we were fixing their campground there was plenty of money being spent on repeated retardant drops: military C-130s fitted with the MAFFS (Modular Airborne Fire Fighting System) were painting a swath of the swamp red by spewing out 2,700 gallons a pop on each pass from a series of pressurized tanks. This wide, and getting wider, red strip seemed to be a long way from the fire. Firefighting was clearly very different in this part of the country.

Something else different was the quickly learned necessity to be very careful where we sat. Not for fear of alligators or snakes, but chiggers and ticks. We usually rested by sitting against a tree. But after a couple of days a few of the crew started to itch badly and realized they were getting chewed to bits by chiggers. Jeff was literally covered in bites. Already too late for some, we learned to spot where the chiggers were and went elsewhere. But then had to check ourselves for ticks.

Denny didn't check himself well enough and ended up with a large bulbous bloody tick in the crack of his ass. Too embarrassed to go to the medical tent to have it plucked out by a cute nurse, he persuaded Dave to do it instead. As Denny pulled down his pants and Dave peered into the crack of his ass, I reached for my camera to snap the smokejumper photo of the decade. But I was too slow and Dave too quick. It would have made a classic picture for the jumper album! For my tardiness I apologize.

Another insect problem was the fire ants. I stopped to talk to one of the district crew who brought us drinks every day and after I got back into the van to go on patrol I started to get bitten. I must have been standing on a nest. Fire ants were all over my boots, up my pant legs and ripping into my legs like little piranhas. Sitting in the front seat stamping my feet as fast as I could to shake them off. The relentless little bastards chewed on me for about five minutes, only stopping when I removed my pants to shake the rest of them off outside the van. Everett thought it was all so very funny.

When the rental company finally wanted their vehicles back – a good move on their part – the marines stepped forward again to fill the gap. For the remainder of our time in NC we were driven around by these very sturdy marines in three wonderful Humvees: six of us per vehicle. Their commander really had no idea what he was letting those kids in for, because inside of a week we had ruined six months of hard military discipline. They seemed to have fun though! Wayne even asked one of them to prove the Humvee's amphibious qualities by driving one into the lake. They were great kids – heart and soul of the country. I hope we didn't teach them too many bad habits. I'd have hated to hear they ended up doing brig duty because of what we may have persuaded them to do.

The marines picked us up from camp each morning, looking more and more relaxed as the days went by, their initial disciplined rigidity slowly giving way to youthful humor. They seemed to like us and we liked them, not being the civilians their commander had warned them about. We were the guys in the swamp.

During one trip to the fire we spotted a large snake slithering across the road. The first Humvee stopped immediately and Don got out to play with it. Taunting it rather like a cat with a mouse, or an inquisitive child with an insect. Those in Eric's vehicle weren't impressed, however, and suggested leaving it alone "for fear of the snake karma." It was interesting to see the personality differences between the two vehicles: all those in one were happy taunting the

the pain involved, but because immediately after an injury we'd be taken off the clock and no longer paid!

The Humvee did very well in the lake, as well it should given the cost of it and the lake being only shallow. And that was about the only way you could have got any of us into it. It was said to be teeming with alligators. Although they may have been little ones a six-foot gator can still get a snack from a careless thigh bone. We assumed they weren't great pork eaters because after throwing one a ham sandwich it got really upset and chased us back to our truck, lickety-damn-split. God it moved fast! No sooner had we slammed the doors than it was outside, staring up at us with those beady top eyes looking very pissed off. Ungrateful sod.

We spent quite a bit of time down by the lake because it was our 'mobile reserve' point. A fancy term which meant in case of a flare up anywhere on the fire we would be immediately available to go. While there, Mike, Eric and I were watching the lake from an unimproved boat ramp looking for gators. All of a sudden Eric decided he needed a swim, stripping off completely and walking casually into the lake. Mike and I just looked at each other in mild bemusement but watched the banks for anything slithering just in case. Soon realizing, however, that any gator meeting Eric would probably have come off worse. A few minutes later Eric popped his leonine head from the green water and stood up, looking like an amalgam of Thor and Triton emerging from some ancient lagoon.

In the evenings we often sauntered a few miles down the road to the closest bar, which clearly had more resident cockroaches than customers. The cockroaches on the pool table so big the balls bounced off them. Those on the ground were crushed like walnuts. It wasn't great but it was the only beer for miles.

The two girls tending bar were clearly grateful of any human attention. We were never completely sure if they did actually own the place or just worked there because they spent most of the time on our side of the bar. One was as gorgeous as you'd expect from a small poor community: young, poorly dyed ratty blonde hair and extremely skinny; pretty maybe, but not attractive. The other was a house. But it was only a matter of time before the brain deadening effects of alcohol led an inebriated jumper into thinking the house was a cabin, the cabin a sofa, and the sofa worth lounging on.

It didn't take a jumper long to gain the selfless pleasure of the skinny one, however. After winning a game of pool an unnamed someone redeemed a wager by receiving payment in flesh among the cockroaches. Someone else – again nameless to protect them from everlasting ridicule, and maybe even their marriage – ended up with the house. And disappeared from sight for hours.

One squad leader was nowhere to be seen the next day. This was more than a little unusual because he was a decent chap and we expected better. The floating joke was that he had been trying to call all morning but couldn't reach the phone because he was pinned beneath a behemoth pile of giggling jiggling flesh. He finally showed up after lunch looking quite sheepish, asking where were his friends that would allow him to do such a thing. His great friends, of course, had been earnestly wagering on who would first fall victim to that beer induced delusion of loveliness.

Our three weeks in North Carolina were nearing an end and 'Persuasion Wayne' persuaded the district into allowing us a day of R&R before flying home. Agreeing to this proved the district had been happy with our work, and as well they should have been: we had done far more than expected on the fire and helped them renovate a campground in the bargain. So, after of our last shift we said our goodbyes to the marines, packed up our kit and headed off to a hotel near Myrtle Beach.

The beach was fantastic: glorious sunshine, warm sea and acre upon acre of beautiful golden sand, all topped with scores of little bikinis. We swam, played volleyball, walked along the beach and watched the sights, stopping at the various bars along the way. It felt strange to be actively engaged in a summer that everyone else knew so well but we were usually too busy to notice. Summer to us was all about work, and it generally flew by without a second thought as to what other people might be doing. If we flew over a lake on the way to a fire we would, of course, see hundreds of people splashing about, but it was all too remote from us, they just looked like ants. But here, on a North Carolina beach, everything was real. Well almost everything. There was a selection of magnificent enhancements that took on a life all their own, in and out of the water. Personal floatation devices we called them.

Later that afternoon some of us congregated outside a bar on the beach. A very cute blonde waitress seemed to be enjoying our company. Although blind ego lets me forget that we were probably the only ones in the bar. The typical beach girl: blonde, petite, fit, cheerful and drop dead bloody gorgeous. Once she explained she had broken her wrist doing a movie stunt she received even more attention. As the afternoon wore on we started hitting it off and I arranged to meet her later for dinner. I could hardly believe it, such things never happened to me. She was way above my pay grade.

As I walked back to the hotel in a rather cheerful mood I saw Denny ahead of me, a little unstable on his feet after spending most of the afternoon in the bar. On reaching a building site he eyed up a portable toilet since he was obviously desperate for a piss. But he couldn't find the way in. A builder on scaffolding looked down in amazement as Denny went round and around the toilet trying to figure out how to get in! He finally disappeared so he must have found his way in eventually. And since he was with us again in the morning he must have figured his way out as well.

Terri, the gorgeous blonde, arrived at the hotel to pick four of us up for dinner in a bright red Mercedes. She looked outstanding in simple skin-tight jeans and t-shirt. Over dinner we were clearly hitting it off because every now and again she would reach over and slap me. After dinner we went to another bar on the beach and met up with the rest of the jumpers. Some of whom had gone deep sea fishing all day and looked a little green around the gills. Terri and I finished the evening by drinking beer on the beach, just like the movies. Yup, it can be real. It was a great ending to a great day and a terrific ending to a outstanding trip.

As Terri drove me back to the hotel I saw Eric leaving in our rented van. I wondered if I'd missed a call, but on finding my room Dave explained that Eric was off to bail Roger out of jail. One of our ex-jumper friends had traveled a few miles to meet us and had been picked up on his way home. Eric was the last person I would have expected to see driving away at three in the morning, but he was the only one sober who could. The crew had worked hard for three weeks solid and we were enjoying ourselves by spreading the wealth.

The next morning most of us were dragging but we got to the airport in time for our flights back, boarding three separate aircraft following three different routes, typical of jumpers. Wayne and I spent most of the time enjoying the company of a pretty flight attendant who was happy plying us with endless Tanqueray and Tonics, which was to merge into a tradition over the years. After a while she just smiled and handed us a handful of miniatures, only returning to replenish our tonic and the occasional coffee. Flight attendants see a number of jumpers in the summer and generally appreciate what we're about, as long as we behave! While flying with Southern Air Transport a few years later I got to know exactly what they were all about as I witnessed their debaucheries all over South America. Those girls knew how to enjoy themselves before TSA stepped in and removed all the fun of flying.

Arriving back to Missoula was disappointing. It always was after such a good assignment. We had worked hard, had fun doing it, played hard and had earned a lot of overtime; averaging 12-hour days for each day we were away, putting us well ahead of anyone else in overtime. Not that it's ever a race, but it wasn't yet July and some already had over 400 hours of OT. Compared to the previous year of little to nothing it's easy to see why we were all so happy. We could finally pay our bills.

Those jumpers stuck in Missoula were clearly jealous. It had been a once in a career trip. We had been amazed by the resilience of the swamp fires, had seen new and interesting places, met great people and experienced new adventures. It had both cemented new friendships and dissolved old.

It took a few days to get back into the routine: packing chutes, food boxes and sewing dozens of hose bags for the warehouse; the same old same old. In the meantime, though, the list was rotating. People were leaving for West Yellowstone and Miles City, eastern Montana. So the North Carolina crew were back in the top 20 very soon and looking forward to going out again. The summer had started well, it had a good feel. We were motivated, didn't have a permanent base manager and things were purring along nicely with personnel having no direct conduit to bother us. Thanks to *Ernie* everyone was happy, enjoying life and earning decent money. It's what we all lived for.

The same old same old didn't last long because we were in need of practice jumps since not having jumped for over a month. But as soon as the jumps were organized along came a fire call, a load was going to Colorado. We were going suited up so we put our red bags on the Sherpa, emptied our bladders and slid into our jump gear, the first time we'd been in our gear since refresher. The pilots gave the Sherpa a preflight and we boarded for the flight to Grand Junction. It was incredibly hot and had been exceptionally dry all across the west for a long time, evident by the low levels of water in the reservoirs that passed below us, the almost gagging dusty dryness of the air, stunted growth of the summer plants and the desiccation of decaying matter on the ground. The potential for large fires was obvious, and growing steadily by the day. Three of us sat on the floor by the big open door at the back of the Sherpa, savoring the warm breeze blasting past the door while watching the change from lush forested mountains to arid desert scrub as the countryside unraveled beneath us.

We crossed the Snake River Plain, over the Colombia Plateau and into the Great Basin. A massive area of the United States from the Sierra Nevadas to the west to the Wasatch Range in the east. Water in the basin arrives mainly as snow and stays in the region, being unable to cross either range in the east or west to flow to the oceans. Instead, it sinks into groundwater aquifers or flows into the salt lakes via the Humboldt or Bear rivers. Western clouds over California are emptied of rain long before they ever reach the basin by the pressure of Sierra Nevadas. It was a vastly different place to the northwest, a panorama filled to the brim with new places, new fuels, new wildlife. Bringing us new desert adventures.

Many of us had never fought fires in Colorado and we were excited to see what it had in store for us. However, we had no idea how our careers and, indeed, our lives would be affected by events over the coming weeks. It was 1994, and not quite yet July.

Chapter Twenty-Four

— Red Mud and Fire

Action may not always bring happiness; but there is no happiness without action.

– Benjamin Disraeli

C OMING IN TO LAND AT WALKER FIELD we were amazed at the sheer number of swimming pools adjacent to the homes in the suburbs below. This was clearly a wealthy city. The temperature changed dramatically as we lost altitude in readiness for entering the landing pattern at 800 feet, becoming almost stifling hot. After landing we taxied to the northwest end of the runway where the jumpers inhabited a small shack, currently home to about 50 jumpers from bases all over the Lower 48 – BLM and FS – with most of them out on fires when we arrived. The BLM base manager briefed us as soon as we had our kit squared away, giving us a more thorough analysis of the situation than usual. He wasn't expecting us to be around for long and wanted us to be aware, and prepared, for the volatility of fire behavior that we would encounter across the basin. We learned that they had been exceptionally busy and were expecting to be even more so. Resources were stretched. Forest fuels were the driest they had been in years and the weather was forecasted to only get hotter and drier, with no rain expected in the foreseeable future. Every fire was being manned and contained as quickly and efficiently as possible. While the ground resources were being stretched to the limit, the aerial resources – fixed wing retardant and bucket drop helicopters – were working extra hard to make up the difference. To prove the point a magnificent old silver PB4Y Liberator rumbled down the runway a few yards away, the sound of history reverberating from its deep throaty radials awesome to witness. Followed immediately behind by the immense power of a retardant encrusted C-130 as it thundered heavily along the tarmac.

There was a veritable air force on the ramp next to us. It was incredibly impressive. People were busy washing red mud off the bellies of aircraft with fire hoses, others were loading retardant and fuel, some were grabbing a quick snack before their next flight and a gorgeous, blonde, shorts-clad, ramp manager was running around choreographing each arrival and departure. She had obviously been here a while and her deep tan would not have been out of place at Saint Tropez, and neither would she. She was a pleasant sight for the returning tanker pilots and everyone, including her, knew it.

Retardant pilots are easily among the most the courageous of firefighters. Every year we watch in awe as they manhandle their antique pieces of aluminum and steel into situations that would make most pilots wince. Not only are their machines castoffs from a bygone age but most are funded and maintained on a shoestring. Watching pilots heave and weave these lumbering giants around the valleys of the Salmon would make anyone stare in admiration. And not just a few firefighters owe their existence to the selfless skill and professionalism of a handful of retardant pilots over the years. They love what they do because the risks are enormous, as is seen by the growing list of memorials. Scores of retardant pilots have been killed since the sixties and that figure is compounded by the fact that their numbers are already few. Jumpers, especially, have the utmost respect for these pilots because they are often our only support in the more remote areas of the country. They are also our eyes when no one else is available. Retardant pilots live a little of that wartime camaraderie, in that, "the problem with being one of the few is how they become fewer."

Many a firefighter has a photograph of thousands of pounds of red sludge coming down on top of them. It's not always the best place to be but after spending countless hours on the fireline it's almost inevitable. Everything gets well and truly covered in red mud and it drips from the tree canopy like blood rain afterwards. Neither is it at all refreshing as it would seem. If the aircraft is low enough the force of falling retardant can flatten trees and upturn rocks, so being beneath a low drop is not the healthiest of places – unless one is being overrun by fire in which case that sludge can be a lifeline above a 'shake and bake' fire shelter.

Every few minutes a different aircraft thundered along the runway to deliver a fresh load of retardant to crews spread out on the firelines across the Western Slope and wider Great Basin. It felt like we had arrived in a war zone. The converted submarine chasers, vintage WWII, Korea and Vietnam bombers and transport aircraft (P-2Vs, PB4Ys, P-3 Orions, DC-4s, C-130s) were load and return all day long. Hearing the growly throb of the radial piston engines thundering fully loaded P2Vs and PB4Ys along the runway, scratching and scraping to get airborne in the heat and thin air, was an amazing experience. We were witnessing history in action, an aural and visible display of machine and aviation, it rumbled deep into the soul. I could feel my heart vibrate and the concrete beneath my feet shudder as these weary old ships were pulled down the runway and heaved into the air, finally becoming free of the ground and flying almost in slow motion as their great rotating propellers clawed at the thin air to get their massive hulks airborne.

How it must have felt with hundreds of piston-driven bomb laden aircraft taking off from airfields across England and Italy all those years ago I cannot imagine. I can remember my father telling me about the massive bomber formations congregating overhead before heading off to deliver their deadly cargo onto industrial Germany. It must have been a powerful, awe-inspiring spectacle. The survival of these planes is a testament to the resilience of their original design and construction. But we were watching the end of an era, however, because the familiar sight and sound of a PB4Y over a fire would soon be lost forever.

Because of the heat and resulting thinner air the jumper loads were reduced. The bulky Sherpa could only carry six from its usual twelve, giving us plenty of room inside the cabin but reducing our efficiency dramatically. The more agile Twin Otter fared better, carrying six during the day and its normal eight in the evening. The heat was stifling. The air so dry that when we ran during PT the sweat evaporated instantly, and only dripped off once we stopped. Hydration was a constant process and we each carried regularly replenished water bottles around all day long. The freezer had dozens of iced bottles ready to put into our leg pockets to take onto the fires. The base was rolling. It was electric. We loved it.

We would go out on a fire, come back in the evening, go for a run, have a big breakfast, rehab our gear and go out on another fire the following afternoon. I even managed two fires in the same day: jumping one first thing in the morning, coming back on a chopper in mid-afternoon – caked in dirt, sweating, hungry, but always yearning for more – and immediately suited up to board the Twin Otter for another. It was awesome. Our job had a real purpose here. We were being tested to the absolute limit, but being treated well, felt appreciated and were eager to work harder because of it. When Jeff, our acting base manager, arrived to be a spotter he couldn't believe how many hours we had worked. The season had barely started and we were already upwards of 600 hours OT, in July.

The first few fires we had were small, taking between two and six jumpers each, in the high desert scrub among the sagebrush, pinyon and juniper trees. There was never any water but the fuels were usually sporadic so the fire rarely traveled far and did so only by localized spotting or heat transfer. Once we cut out the burning fuel and buried it the fires generally went out quickly. The evening fires were perfect: jump, work hard for a few hours, relax and eat while the CNA crew wen to work, dink around in the morning a little more and then demob after calling it out. The early fires were a little tougher because the heat of the day would make them more active, harder to control and more prone to spread. Those we'd concentrate on containing before allowing them burn themselves out. Then, late in the evening or early morning, when the humidity rose, the fire would dwindle and die. We always tried to demob in late afternoon, right after the heat of the day. That way we'd know for sure the fire was completely out and we could maximize our potential. Demobing early evening also allowed us to grab some much needed food on the way back, before showering and having a few beers. It was also logistically easier if we left the fires later in the day because it saved on resources during the hotter, busier part of the day, allowing jumpers to be available for fires before sending them on a fetch and carry mission.

On most fires we were burning up between 8,000 and 15,000 calories a day, and needed to replenish that loss with anything we could. So when full to the brim with food we would drink beer. Although someone once attempted to stop us from drinking beer, but only because they couldn't stop bringing personal baggage to work with them. Since having numerous abdominal surgeries beer is often the only way I can keep my weight up and dull the pain. It also works great on the joints now that I'm older and still trying to run. Proving "Guinness [really] is good for you!"

Jumping into these high desert scrub fires was sometimes a neat trick because the winds were always more than expected and on most jumps the FS rounds would arrive backwards – often quite fast. The BLM's square chutes were much better in high wind and they used the wide open spaces to fly in, flair the chute and do cool stand-up landings. And then scoff, "Can you do that Zoolie?"

No. No, we couldn't. When the wind was at our maximum allowable we always landed hard – and it was never pretty. During our pre-jump briefings in Grand Junction the spotter would often yell another snippet of thoughtful advice if he was worth his salt: "DON'T FLY PAST THAT RIDGE! STAY THIS SIDE OF IT. OTHERWISE IT'LL FUCK YOU UP! And it would. Getting lee side of a ridge anywhere is bad news, but doing it in Colorado was always a whole lot worse, the down air could cripple a jumper for good. And it's no coincidence that the lee side is, more often than not, the side of the mountain with all those lovely sharp rocks.

But the BLM jumpers rarely got the pleasure of seeing us land like sacks of scattered shit because the rounds often jumped first, not needing so much altitude. But once on the ground, and bruised, there was definite envy when watching a square have a more enjoyable flight and then come in flawlessly for a tip-toe landing.

But it was just a mode of transport, not a sport. Rounds tend to be better in the tight, tall-treed spots of the Northwest whereas the squares are unarguably better on the windy plains. Each has its place. Getting one chute to do both jobs has yet to be accomplished despite a couple of attempts since the '90s. Eventually, though, it will happen. And when it does I doubt the FS program will survive in its present form. It isn't vigorous enough. Not enough vitality: too many years of hiring too many drones have ruined enthusiasm and any aptitude for thinking outside the conventional box.

snake, while those in the others were dead set against it. Especially Mark, who absolutely hates snakes.

Each day during lunch breaks Mark had been constructing a basket from local reeds. He carried it everywhere and whenever he got the chance he improved on it. It was on its way to becoming a good looking wicker basket, everyone was impressed. But one day Don placed a dead snake in it without Mark realizing. It wasn't a smart thing to do. Don was not only pushing his luck with Mark but was tempting fate and risking the repercussions of the snake karma again. It surprised no one that those two didn't get along too well after that. But Mark's dislike for snakes didn't stop him from getting involved anywhere where snakes were likely to be.

One afternoon, a portion of the crew were doing their surreal peasant routine; fighting fire up to their knees in swamp. Getting from where they were in the swamp to the road meant crossing an even deeper dike that had been flooded to stop the fire spreading underneath the road. Mark tried floating across on a discarded oil drum, managing to get halfway before capsizing. No sooner had Mark reached the other side, with water to his waist, than a water moccasin swam menacingly by on the surface, flattening its head in warning to all those now watching this creep show glide across the water. It was like a child looking for trouble.

We came across quite a few snakes during our time in NC, usually hiding beneath the scrub brush, under upturned canoes or discarded construction waste. We got very wary of picking things off the ground by hand and found long sticks to flip things over with instead. But more worrying than being on the ground they often waited in the branches of trees. And with the forest so dense it was difficult to always know what was a branch and what was a snake. No one wanted to cut the trip short due to a careless moment and get bitten by some nasty venomous snake. Not just for

As summer progressed the weather became hotter, the fuels drier and the fires bigger. Another booster arrived from Redding. Air-tanker loads were relentless all day long and semi-trailers of retardant mix frequently arrived to replenish their thirst for mud. They'd dropped over a million gallons so far with no end in sight. We rarely saw the pilots in the evenings because they we too busy sleeping and resting up for the following day, where there would be more of the same. And someone somewhere would be grateful.

I found myself on a steady rotation with Mike, a BLM jumper from Boise. Through my jumping career I would have more jumps with him than with any other jumper, including all of Missoula. He was an avid and practiced Scrabble player – taking the Scrabble Bible everywhere he went. It looked like cheating to me because I had never seen some of those damned words before. Or since for that matter! Mike was the last to wear a steel helmet, rebelliously proud of it and painted it to look like plastic. Steel helmets were banned long ago, supposedly because they conducted electricity. But we knew that if we ever got that close to lightning it wouldn't just be steel conducting it! Gone were the days when a firefighter could boil up water in a hard hat. The new plastic ones were often so hot we drilled ventilation holes in them.

On one of the slower days I had a nice two manner with Dave. We were the last on the load at the end of the day, having dropped everyone else a little earlier. Daylight was dwindling but we saw a small smoke rising from a ridge near some properties. There was a pasture close to it so we geared up quickly to jump it, keen to get out before the light faded. Everything was becoming second nature to us after so many fires. Once we saw a fire we immediately sized it up, took in the terrain and instantly knew how many would go and got ready accordingly. Then we'd stand to the side of the door and watch as the spotter threw his streamers. If he got the first set reasonably close we'd give a quick thumbs up and tighten our leg straps. This time I was first in the door, Dave being one of the few jumpers lighter than me. I placed my foot in the step of the Twin Otter and watched the release point draw close after turning final. I readied myself in anticipation and heaved myself out – my heavy PG bag bouncing off my legs. Our bags were becoming heavier as the season wore on because we were carrying so much extra food by now, having to eat at every opportunity. It was also good to have that extra food in case a cargo box creamed in, as they did on occasion, leaving us with nothing but slime and dust.

For me it was an uneventful flight; being at the end of the day, with the sun going down behind the hills, the air was still. I picked a spot to the side of the field, floated in nicely and did a perfect PLF before hopping back to my feet – nothing to it.

Then a bright flash filled the sky and a loud crack! I wondered what Dave was doing taking pictures already because I didn't think he could have landed yet: being lighter he should still be up there. I looked around and saw his feet touch the ground but do no roll. It looked so slow and delicate, hardly a round landing. Then I noticed his parachute was still vertical, as if someone had grabbed the apex and pulled it taut. It was so strange. Getting closer I could see that his chute was actually wrapped between a pair of overhead cables. The bright flash and crack I'd heard had been both wires touching each other and arcing, shorting out the entire valley! Except for a couple of small burns on the side of his reserve container Dave had squeaked right between the two wires without a scratch!

We dared not pull his chute down because it was still wrapped tightly around both cables, so the spotter had to notify the power company to come and retrieve it, and then reconnect the power to the valley. There'd been a sprinkling of lights further up the valley before we arrived but everything was now black. When we finally got a look at the chute it was covered in little burn holes and the nylon had actually fused together in places. I doubt the electric company ever had to retrieve a parachute from their cables before.

None of us had seen the wires because the whole valley had been cloaked in shade, and when we had transitioned from sunlight to shade during descent our eyes hadn't time to get accustomed. It was certainly another lesson. When we got back to base, after the fire, everyone was surprised, not least the pilot, who said that wires were always the first thing he looked for over a jump spot.

The fire was much more relaxing than the balls to wall we had become used to. It was out in a couple of hours so we spent the night eating just about everything we could lay our hands on before getting picked up the following morning, along with a great story. That's what jumping is all about: having experiences that would make most people cringe and living to tell about it. I just wish I'd had a camera to record it all.

With all the fire activity there were so many jumpers at Grand Junction that there was no room for everyone. The temporary base is only a small shack and a patch of grass. So to give all those who were on the load more room to relax before going out on a fire the rest of us were released to the hotel. The Hilton Hotel. The pool at the Hilton Hotel. Instantly boosting morale from good to epic.

The Blummers (BLM jumpers) excuse for pool standby being they needed a large enough area of clean grass on which to pack their chutes. We, on the other hand, needed to stretch the rounds out before packing, and a couple of us jerry-rigged a piece of floor space in the local BLM offices for that purpose. But after packing ours we went to the pool as well and waited around to be called in after a load had gone out. It was ideal.

The National Weather Service issued yet another Red Flag warning for all areas across western Colorado. Compounded with drought, the high temperatures and low humidity were a recipe for disaster, and when summer storms unleashed thousands of dry lighting strikes across the region over the next few days it stretched already taut resources to the absolute limit. It was no surprise when Dave and I found ourselves onboard the Twin Otter again the next morning, looking for a fire that had been reported near Glenwood Springs. Circling the area a few times, no one was able to spot it. But since the fire was not considered a priority, and with numerous others in the area, we went off in search of another. The spotter tried to get streamers close to a fire on a rugged escarpment, and I think we were all a little relieved when we realized there was too much wind for such a scraggy spot. Then, right over the next ridge, we found another close to some properties that had what looked like a long sandy ridge running down one flank of the fire, so with the high wind we opted for that fire instead. This time the squares positioned themselves in the door first and we climbed to 3,000 feet to throw streamers. So for the first time I got to watch a couple of sticks of squares exit the aircraft.

Instead of a vigorous exit the Blummers sit down and simply slide out. A static line opens a drogue that keeps them stable until manually deploying the main chute. The spot was, as usual, very windy and the squares were using the length of the ridge like a runway, getting spread out all over but getting in fine.

When our turn the ship descended to 1,500 feet, allowing the spotter to throw one more set of streamers and we hopped out. We immediately turned into the wind and quickly discovered the wind was a lot stronger than first thought: almost like our first jump into the park. But knowing that there was a nice sandy ridge below we weren't too worried. Until we hit it flying backwards at a great rate of speed. It was like bloody concrete! We were all so sore after the landing we had bruises for a week. Then, just to make matters worse, I got dragged off into a juniper bush where a broken branch stabbed me in the chest. Sandy ridge my arse!

The SEATs (single-engine air-tankers) were already dropping mud on the flanks of the fire and trying to stop its spread before we got there. The added humidity from those drops allowed us to get closer to the flames and dig direct, making our work easier and more effective. Without the SEATs it would have been extremely hot and heavy work. It was already over a 100 degrees and there was little else to stop these active fires from exploding and going into extended attack, then needing more crews. Our job was to get there quickly, contain them as soon as possible and hand them over to other ground crews already on the way, while we got released to do the same thing somewhere else. It was ideal because we rarely had to do any of the long-winded mop-up. For us it was all glory.

The SEAT tankers were great. They don't carry as much as the heavies, between 500 to 800 gallons, but they make good use of what they have by being incredibly accurate. They're converted crop-dusters and very agile, buzzing around the fire like bees while waiting for a request from the ground. Then they do a quick recon and drop it next time – right on the money. They were the perfect tool on smaller fires because we didn't have to retreat from the area; giving us the opportunity to work close while the flames were subdued immediately after retardant had been dropped. In those days you didn't have to run away from retardant drops. In fact, the opposite was true: a red spotted shirt was deemed a prerequisite for any seasoned firefighter.

Chapter Twenty-Five

— Tragedy

Probably most catastrophes end this way without an ending, the dead
not even knowing how they died...,those who loved them forever
questioning "this unnecessary death," and the rest of us tiring of this
inconsolable catastrophe and turning to the next one.

– Norman Maclean, Young Men and Fire

DURING THIS FIRE WE STARTED to hear confusing radio communications from a nearby fire on our jumper frequency. Things were clearly heating up and voices were becoming hurried and anxious. Then, after a few calls went answered we didn't hear anymore. Just silence. We immediately sensed something bad had happened but no one wanted to bring it up for fear of tempting fate, and without any word to the contrary we continued working the fire. Having got it contained we began bone piling unburned debris in the middle of the fire: an efficient method of fuel removal and a comfortable way of staying warm at night. Jumpers are often found huddled around a few burning logs in the small hours, getting ever closer to the dwindling embers as the morning wears on, and only moving to place a fresh lump of wood on the fire or to relieve themselves in the shadows.

The following dawn, while enjoying an orange, sun-drenched morning's mug of coffee, warming our bones, we were released from the fire earlier than usual. We didn't think much of it at first because the fire had been well knocked down by this time and just assumed we were needed elsewhere. After gathering our gear we sat waiting by the edge of a dusty meadow, leaning against our heavy packs and allowing the sun to burn our grubby faces. Three Suburbans arrived to pick us up and take us back to GJ, stopping off for lunch as usual and taking the opportunity to get some much needed rest by dozing in the air conditioned trucks. Every now and then a shoulder moving to wake up a heavy weary head, and the head bouncing and nodding for a while before once again finding rest. It was a never ending process when three bodies occupied the rear seats of a Suburban. The unlucky one in the middle with nothing to lean against but a stinking sweat soaked t-shirt covering a stinking sweat soaked body.

By this point in the summer we could sleep almost anywhere. Not only crunched tightly in the back of a Suburban or a passenger van, but also on a pile of parachutes, on a tree branch, on rocks and anywhere we could be left alone for a few minutes, even hunched up in a fetal position balancing on a 100lb packout bag. But we would also wake easily and jump right back to work if needed. As we neared the airport we stirred and stretched out our legs as much as possible in the tight space.

There were a lot of people milling around when we arrived. It was unusual to see. In fact, it was the first time everyone had seen everyone else. There were also some new but familiar faces. Some of the Silver City crew had made it up after their season had ended when the monsoons arrived, as they traditionally do after the fourth of July. With so many jumpers congregating rumors abounded, and there was a solemn air of trepidation. Somewhere there had been a problem and some of our bros were involved. We just sensed it.

As more trickled in we started to hear rumors of what had happened. There had been a blowup on a fire near Glenwood, and there were people missing. Fourteen firefighters were unaccounted for. Then another group of familiar faces arrived, looking worn out and shocked, and we watched as they carried the crushed remains of their retardant splattered fire shelters. We wandered over to help get their gear from the trucks. I hadn't seen Sabino since early refresher, when he had kept me company on a slow mile and a half while recovering from my latest injury.

"Good to see you Sabino," I said.

"Good to be seen," he said, shaking my hand solidly.

The look in his eyes and that comment said it all. What he had seen would remain with him forever. They had all been through something that we knew only too well could happen but expect and hope never will. Some of our friends would not be coming home. The only question at the time was who?

Many of the normally voracious jumpers were subdued as we looked around to gauge who was there and who wasn't. We soon had an idea who we had lost. Don Mackey had paid the ultimate price for a job he loved. A job we all loved. From McCall we lost Roger Roth and Jim Thrash. Also, Jon Kelso, one of the nine Prineville Crew to perish was a rookie bro. The others lost were no less our brothers and sisters in the world of fire. We knew of them, we just didn't know them.

Hindsight is the luxury of survivors but suffice to say enough has been written about the events of that day. What is certain is most of us would have done little different. Events overtook them while in unfamiliar terrain, in unfamiliar fuels, and with a blast of unforgiving wind the resulting firestorm caught and engulfed them one by one as they raced for the safety of the ridge. The last man free was Eric, suffering severe burns to his arms, legs and neck, but he survived. He had done what few have managed in those conditions: he had outrun the fire. Everyone behind him perished – even those in their fire shelters. Including Don, who had returned down the slope to muster those left behind. No doubt knowing full well the risk of that selfless act. Yet doing exactly what is expected of a crew leader when things go terribly wrong.

We visited Eric in hospital in Glenwood. Covered in gauze bandages he spoke to us while clearly in a lot of pain. He said he had just kept running for the safety of the ridge when others had stopped, determined to reach the top, and as soon as he reached it he got blown forward off his feet by the blast of the super-heated air rushing up the hill behind him. Apart from his great effort he figured it was that which saved him from something far worse. He scrambled over the ridge to where Sarah, Sabino, and a few others were already safe. Sabino snapped the last horrific pictures of the tall wall of flame as it roared up the hill consuming everything in its path.

An Australian firefighter, having been burned in exactly the same situation, once told me he thought it was like soldiers going ashore at Normandy. Many of which said that they had been so sea sick, so exhausted, they couldn't care less what happened, they just wanted off the damn boats. So they disembarked by the hundreds into a murderous hail of machine gun fire. He'd said the same was true when describing the complete and utter exhaustion of trying to outrun a fire on a steep summer slope in pre-heated air. Admitting how dreadful it might be otherwise is just too hard to contemplate.

No better account of this tragic fire can be found than in *Fire on the Mountain* by John Norman Maclean, son of Norman Maclean, who wrote so vividly about the earlier 1949 tragedy at Mann Gulch in *Young Men and Fire*. One notion I would differ with, however: Norman Maclean says in his lyrical literary way "the dead not even knowing how they died." On the hills of South Canyon they knew exactly how and why they died, because they had exhaustive time to contemplate before they died.

An immediate hold was placed on all firefighting activities, which was why there were so many people milling around looking lost with very little to do. This was strange to us. We had become used to relentless rotational activity, going balls to the wall every minute of every day. And yet strangely, even with the downtime, no one was sleeping, we were simply not tired.

Meetings were held and important people emerged from the woodwork. Yet all most of us wanted to do was go back to work. Not to trivialize the suffering or disrespect anyone, nor ignore the significance and inevitable implications of the tragedy, but we didn't want to dwell or be drawn into the mass of misery that was beginning to engulf the post-fire situation. We also knew the fires would not wait, and would only get bigger and more dangerous in the meantime if were not out there fighting. In life and death most jumpers don't want to be the center of attention, preferring that our friends and colleagues continue doing what they love, and maybe, if so inclined, occasionally remembering over a few beers or while sitting by a secluded mountain campfire when the work is finished. We had lost some people but our work was not yet done. When the work was done, when the season was over, when people were safe, that's when we would do the remembering. And we do remember.

In this, there was a cleavage in attitudes between the various crews. The younger seemed to be engrossed in the misery, almost as if it was expected from them, a duty, all compounded, of course, by obliging peer pressure. To us it looked more like an insincere excuse for emotional indulgence. The older ones just wanted a few beers to remember and toast lost friends before getting back to work. Whether our attitude was solely due to being older, having maybe experienced similar loss in the past, I don't know. Perhaps the very act of jumping – parachuting into forested wilderness to fight fires – we already possessed a keen understanding of risk and accepted it unconditionally. So it's not a surprise when accidents happen, as they are bound to from time to time no matter how much emphasis is placed on safety. A certain risk is inherent to the job and is why many of us love it so much. Alternatively, some might simply possess the age-old more basic desire to 'walk away from misery.' That's how I felt because that's exactly how I was brought up: in an environment that had experienced family loss and witnessed the deaths of dozens of friends and neighbors during a war. While some may find such thoughts heartless, even callous, we each understand the best way to deal with loss and it is not for others to judge how we do it. Just because we don't feel obliged to broadcast it in a grand display of weeping emotion doesn't mean that we don't remember, mourn and respect internally on our own terms, where it is sincere.

One thing to be grateful for, however, was the total absence of the media machine. Whoever succeeded in keeping that parasitical intrusion at bay from firefighters not directly associated to the fire did everyone a great service, and saved many a firefighter from looking completely stupid in front of attention whoring journalists seeking to collect silver from someone else's misery.

No matter how we each dealt with the situation personally, we all knew that a host of pompous, self-righteous individuals would emerge from the woodwork over the coming months and years to use this tragedy against us, to crucify the jumpers and vilify the organization. Especially the grossly misunderstood 'gung-ho,' 'can do' spirit. We were not to be disappointed. Gung-ho was to soon be denigrated and regarded as a detriment by those wet individuals who never possessed it, couldn't understand it, or were jealous of it. How the fuck do you force strong-willed firefighters from being gung-ho? Cut their balls off maybe?

Notwithstanding that the professional fire investigation team, led, as usual, by Ted Putnam, more than adequately analyzed the fire and recommended a wealth of valid valuable changes, various other individuals of dubious qualifications still emerged, and were given free rein to condescendingly scorn and pour more salt on the wounds during the inevitable post-fire re-indoctrination classes. ('Inevitable' because no one was ever likely to turn them down.) It even got to the point of threatening some jumpers with disciplinary action for leaving a classroom after being blithely told they were not qualified to even be in the class and would not be able to take the rote exam. It was a pitiful episode. One instigated by a simple longstanding grudge, backed by a combination of innate jealousy and bigoted hatred of an organization dominated by men.

A psychologist even once appeared, like a snake oil salesman, saying that as a group we had no cohesion, and that he could see it, or the lack of it, just by looking around the room. This insulting prattling prat didn't know us from Adam, had clearly never been among such a group before and obviously knew squat what he was talking about. And so, just because we were spread out across the room, with the usual few lounging at the back, he used insane cavalier logic to back-up a claim that we had no cohesion. I have never seen such a diverse group of civilians possess more cohesion in my life. In fact, I have only seen anything remotely similar in the military: when removing mines, building bridges and digging trenches alongside combat sappers of the Royal Engineers 20 years earlier. Even when jumpers from different bases come together a solidarity exists because we enjoy an unbridled camaraderie and all operate and function in much the same way. We explained as much but this ersatz shrink scoffed at the suggestion out-of-hand, writing it off without a thought to immediately squash any debate. Scoffed, because he had an agenda and wasn't going to stray into a valid discussion. Knowing he would get his money either way.

He was there simply to make himself some money and had successfully persuaded some wet administrator, based on the fire's findings, that we needed an education in bloody 'team building.' The fire's report did, indeed, mention poor cohesion as being a factor in the breakdown of the overall decision making process. But, it was specifically describing the lack of cohesion between the different crews that had been hurriedly slapped together at the last minute to fight the fire, from local district crews, helitack, hotshots and two separate loads of jumpers coming from different agencies and originating from different parts of the country. And yet this expert quack did not touch this issue, which is a common problem among separate groups that are arbitrarily thrown together, no matter how well or proficiently trained each may be. There is a valid purpose to having different crews for different tasks. And it would take an enormous amount of inter-crew training in order for those crews to amalgamate and interact seamlessly. One only has to look at the years of time and effort required to meld infantry with mechanized troops or, indeed, special forces with anyone. Such things take time, money, and regular full-time personnel willing and able to undergo days of training. Several components that seasonal fire agencies do not, and will likely never, possess. Most notably due to the top-down dogma stating that wildland firefighting requires a cheap, forever youthful, non-retentive work-force. *

A day later we were back at work and in the door above a new fire, and thanks to the mandatory stand down the fires had had a chance to grow since the last lightning storm. What we were now looking down upon was a two acre fire in a bug-killed forest that had all the potential for another massive blowup. Jeff completely emptied the Twin Otter: eight jumpers, chainsaws, pumps and all the food and water it carried, everything. We would need it all and

---

* Stated to me personally by Jack Ward Thomas, Chief of the Forest Service, in 1995 to justify the FS's policy on age discrimination. (p. 347)

more. After hitting the ground I checked the fire and immediately requested more jumpers. In an hour everyone who was available arrived; four of them. Then one of the four got injured on the jump and had to be medevac'd off. I had two radios listening on four frequencies and was talking to air-tankers waiting to dump their loads, a jump ship that was still circling waiting to drop cargo, a medevac helicopter taking out an injury and the rest of the jumpers working the fire – most of who were already requesting more help at their individual spots with us being stretched so thin, It wasn't a cluster yet, but it had the beginnings. Things had already started to go wrong and the fire had the potential of being another disaster.

Eleven of us were working gung-ho, balls to the wall, trying to contain a fire that was threatening to consume swathes of forest. And it was a forest for consuming: in all reality if there was ever a fire that needed to burn, this was the one. Once the injured girl was medevac'd there were no other resources available, except for the air-tankers appearing overhead every half an hour dropping loads of mud on the upper flanks of the fire, where Mike was fighting the hottest and more active section.

The tiniest embers would start new fires almost immediately outside of the fireline. Everything was that dead and that dry that a solitary spark could actually ignite the long-dried bark on a stick. The mountain was covered in it and more, it was incendiary. We could feel it in the air, sense it. There was no humidity only stifling heat. No coolness or calm just a hot gusty breeze that was ready to blow embers feet away from the line at any moment.

After completing the fireline we worked consistently trying to keep it contained but it was repeatedly jumping the line even with the *Mark 3* throwing gallons of water on it. We were stretched too thin and almost everyone was calling for help in their sector.

Sonny was the sawyer on the right flank. He was one of two on the fire that had only recently been on South Canyon – and who were all the more aware of the potential for this one. I asked him to drop a tree that was creating a problem close to the line and stayed to give him some encouragement because it was larger than he said he was used to, providing back up because we couldn't even spare people to support both sawyers, everyone was spread out all over the fire and digging like dogs. Sonny dropped his tree perfectly. He had come to us from California, where we got the impression he was a 'bit of a bad lad.' With us, though, he was great. I can still remember having coffee on the main street in West Yellowstone and seeing Sonny walk down the street in a pair of shorts and tank top that were easily two sizes too small. He just loved showing off his physique! Sadly, Sonny didn't survive the winter, and we all went to his funeral ceremony the following spring after he died of pneumonia, of all things.

Smoke obviously harms the lungs and infections can become problematic to older firefighters no longer on the line. I no longer felt it worth going out for a run with a cold as I had repeatedly done in my youth, because the cold would be forced deeper and felt it might cause infection. Since breathing smoke for so many years I was already vulnerable to long bouts of bronchitis. Once I hacked continually for two months after working too long and not taking care of a simple chest cold – it wasn't pleasant. To this day, Sonny's death is a taut reminder to take better care of my lungs.

While on the fire I had no direct contact with either the local district or dispatch and wasn't able to directly explain the severity of the situation, instead, having to walk to a high point a half mile away to relay information through a lookout – and then only able to do that at certain times because people were in short supply. I asked the lookout to relay to dispatch that if they couldn't get more resources here soonest then this fire would no longer be ours.

It became someone else's fire the very next afternoon. The air-tanker overhead tried in vain to stem a flare up high on the left flank, but an ember must have crossed sixty yards of rockslide and sludge to ignite a bug-killed tree on the far side, from where it took off like a freight train. The noise was incredible. In a few hours it consumed more than 2,000 acres, sending up a cloud of smoke that could be seen for miles. No longer able to do anything we retreated to our jump spot to gather our gear.

After recent events panic soon set in among some managers thanks to one of the helicopter pilots. People were spooked. The helicopter pilot was relaying information that he had to get us out of there immediately, with or without our gear. Since I wasn't in direct contact with anyone apart from the pilot I couldn't resolve the situation by explaining that we were perfectly safe and needed to first take care of our gear, and then if necessary we could hike out. But I was overruled from above, by someone nowhere near the fire, so we were told to leave our gear while being airlifted out.

I was pretty despondent and felt that there was nothing I could do to remedy the bad situation: radio communications were dismal, there were no ground resources immediately available, and being post-South Canyon there was a distinct nervousness among many not on the ground – to the point where they didn't listen, or didn't believe, reports coming from crews actually in the situation on the ground. Although not immediately evident at the time, it was the start of a knee-jerk micro-managing process that would eventually first blame, and then destroy, much of the enthusiasm inherent to smokejumpers and firefighting in general. Bureaucrats and pseudo-science-ladened suck-ups with a vendetta were to turn a 'can do' attitude into a badge of disgrace. But blame cannot be placed fully on those promoting that type of thinking, but those high in our ranks who allowed it to happen so easily.

As we debarked the helicopter we could see the massive cloud of smoke behind us. It was a monster, and growing. The fire had taken off like a train, eating everything in its path. The dense bug-killed trees fueled its growth almost as if it was gasoline. Only a change in weather or a natural barrier would stop it now. Losing a fire brings a sense of failure. But we are fighting several forces of nature, and in that we are outnumbered and grossly ill equipped. When taken into perspective it's sometimes a wonder that we are successful at all on the larger more active fires.

As the days afterwards progressed the fires became even more intense and the weather gave us no sign of ever letting up. Alaska jumpers arrived to further boost our numbers, having been waiting for weeks to be released by the state and desperately wanting in on the action in the Lower 48. That's where the overtime was, where the excitement was and, moreover, where their purpose for being was. Jumpers are forever envious of others getting all the action.

Even with this new influx there were still fires enough for everyone and I got another pleasant para-camping expedition with Dave. This time we ended up near Moab in Utah. No power lines in sight this time. After working to put out the spotty fire among stunted Juniper and scraggy brush we sat on an escarpment in the evening and sipped coffee while watching a thunderstorm engulf the night sky across the basin in the distance – the dozens of down strikes creating more work for everyone the following day.

Sitting quietly on the rocks, silhouetted against the night sky, each with our own thoughts, trying to forget the aches and pains of the day, we understand and appreciate our temporary role in this sandstone landscape. We are but a fleeting speck against the more permanent fixture of this vast backdrop and this country's great broad backbone: the length and breadth of the Rocky Mountains. For the minutest fraction of time we become part of its nature, a trace in its history, and are indebted for the opportunity. When our body and spiritual memories of our existence are long gone only dusty remains might linger to fill the crevices of time. Everything else will be as it has always been.

Thanks to the storm there had been several smaller fires in the vicinity and a group of us were all picked up together later in the morning. On the ride back to Grand Junction we came across yet another fire just off the highway, started by the lightning storm the previous night. It was becoming more active in the litter layers below the Junipers as a band of bright sunlight crept down toward it on the hillside. We called it in and all piled out of the Suburbans, grabbing our tools and some water before clambering up the hill to do what we do. We put in a few hours work to contain it and burn off the unused fuel before a local district crew arrived to relieve us. Although how exactly they planned to do that without tools was a mystery. We left them our pulaskis and shovels before continuing back to the airport.

It wasn't the first time we'd seen a crew show up without the means to fight a fire. After jumping the Crow Agency out of West Yellowstone a few years later it quickly became apparent that the local fire crew didn't need us as much as they needed our tools. Although they generously allowed us to finish constructing fireline before releasing us immediately afterwards, minus our equipment, water and food. It felt like a heist.

On returning to Grand Junction we were ordered to take a day off. We had been consistently busy for three weeks and new rules were coming down the organizational pipe mandating more time off for firefighters. It was the start of many CYA processes we were to experience after South Canyon. All of which meant less time worked and hence less money for those who needed it most – the grunts at the lower end of the great FS bureaucratic food chain. It never failed to amaze us that administrators always got off scot free while everyone below them suffer. And when budgets are cut, those who do the work are let go but administrators remain – to do what exactly? But this was only the start, it was to get far worse in the years to come.

Nevertheless, since we were now at the bottom of a very long list at GJ, thanks to the recent appearance of more Alaska jumpers, we didn't mind a day off in this instance. Especially since it was to be a paid day off with the list rotating nicely and ready for us in a couple of days. In the meantime, we enjoyed a day of R&R and watched Brazil play Holland in the World Cup Finals at the Hilton bar surrounded by a bevy of beautiful airline stewardesses.

Chapter Twenty-Six

— California LAMB

There are no bad regiments, there are only bad officers.
– Field-Marshal Lord Slim

COLORADO WASN'T THE ONLY PLACE to see action that summer: New Mexico, Oregon, Idaho, Utah, Nevada, California, Washington and, of course, Montana were also burning up. And with the arrival of more Alaska jumpers to Grand Junction many of the rounds were released back to their respective bases, or to Redding, California.

A Redding pilot, CR, came over to pick up a load of Zoolies in the Sherpa. We traveled jump ready in hope of getting a fire on the way. But despite all the effort in looking we didn't find a single one because we hadn't yet hit the heat of the day when fires make themselves visible. Instead, we got swallowed up hook line and sinker in the LAMB that was Redding at the time.

That's nothing bad against the Redding base – and certainly not against its jumpers, who are no different to jumpers anywhere – but because every base seems to go through a period of enduring an exceptionally high level of bullshit at some point. As quick as it starts it can stop, but it's often kick started, one way or another, by changes in prominent personnel, usually administrators unable to comprehend the uniqueness of jumpers. For whatever reason this year was Redding's turn. Our initial arrival fire briefing wasn't so much to explain the current fire situation, but to demand that we all follow the base rules, for which there were a large growing number according to the frustrated older Redding jumpers. Some of whom went elsewhere the following year.

There were five loads ahead of us so we spent our time on our growing piles of stinking laundry, repairing kit and reorganizing and replenishing our gear. Up to now we hadn't had much time to mend torn shirts, fix snaps on our PG bags or clean the grime from our boots, so we took the time while wearing our usual off-load hot weather attire: shorts and Tevas.

But that attire didn't go down too well. The base commandant didn't like the casual atmosphere and she demanded that everyone be fire ready in boots and Nomex, no matter there being only two planes and us five loads away from going anywhere. A couple of us soon had a young Redding squad leader approach us and tell us put on Nomex and boots. "You've got to be fucking kidding me?" was the natural response. One that never went down particularly well but did succinctly state our opinion. Personally, I never heard another word of it, others did however, and many of them abided by these arbitrary regulations simply for an easy life. Rules that had, no doubt, been forced down the food chain by some lard-ass non-jumping, non-booted, female bureaucrat sitting on a swivel-chair in an air-conditioned office somewhere

After being rushed to Redding for a major lightning bust we watched *Tombstone* more times than I can remember But at least I was comfortable while Redding jumpers sweltered away in 100-degree heat in Nomex and boots for no other reason but to keep an administrator happy. The key to having energy when arriving on a fire is hydration. If you've been sweating all day on base you're hardly going to be in front of the hydration curve after spending a further hour sweating inside your jump gear in the back of a plane.

Anyone dictating such compliance because of some ill-conceived agenda or ignorance is a fool, and is putting a jumper's health in jeopardy. Our old hard-charging friend from West Yellowstone, Jiggs, was always a proponent of hydration and allowing people to be comfortable – even while working them half to death.

We had been brought to Redding but little was happening. A load would go out each day but half would always come back. So the list didn't rotate as best we hoped. But since it was slow, CR, the Sherpa pilot, grabbed me for a couple of afternoons to give me some flight training on the simulator in the pilot's shack. That was a lot of fun and reignited an urge to further my pilot's license. But since I was forever out of the running for permanent employment due to the FS's age discrimination it seemed an expense that would never prove worthwhile. And on the wages I was earning, the same as I would for the rest of my career, without step increases, I would probably never be in a position to afford to fly again anyway. As it turned out, it proved true. Even after ten years, and being involved in training new hires, I was still one of the lowest paid jumpers in the organization. After a while that became a bitter pill to swallow when I was expected to train others who would, in only a couple of years, be earning more thanks only to age and receiving automatic step increases annually and promotions as and when deserved.

Finally, after several more videos of *Tombstone*, we got a fire. It was nothing special, just six of us in the Shasta National Forest. Don and I were wondering if something was missing because since arriving in Redding the level of excitement that we'd all had in GJ had dwindled considerably. The unquestioned enthusiasm that had pervaded every corner and crevice of GJ was absent, and it was readily apparent on this fire. Instead of everyone being gung-ho all we could see was the fire being fought under a restrictive, almost repressive anal-retentiveness, completely taking the fun out of the job. We were digging in dirt as usual but with no banter. Redding regulations had followed us even into the woods, which is exactly what happens. When a base undergoes a major change – for better or worse – that change pervades all aspects of fire. In this case the change was for the worse and it was dragging us down, even in the woods. There was tension in the air and tempers were frayed. We were no longer a tight group but a bunch of individuals doing what the hell we liked. Still fighting fire, still putting it out, but missing the morale, camaraderie and humor that made fires enjoyable.

When we returned to base everyone was gathering in the loft for a bollocking. Regulations were apparently not being adhered to by a certain few people and, worse, far worse, someone had stolen the pop tarts. Oh dear, we thought, how adolescent do you have to be to think pop tarts are a valuable food item on fires? If Missoula had been putting pop tarts in our fire packs we would have wanted someone to steal the damn things! The missing pop tarts summed up our experience of Redding that year, they became legendary.

We were all itching to go. There were other places burning in the Northwest and we wanted to get there. Some wanted to go just because they were tired of getting rashes from the poison oak. But mostly we just wanted to be where the action was, and right now it wasn't in California. Not on load seven, creeping up to six.

Through the rumor mill we got an inkling that Missoula was sending over the DC-3 to pick us up. But first had to make sure they weren't going to get any requests in the meantime. Redding, desperate to make use of every moment of our time since we had been removed from their list, decided to have us all assemble their following year's recruitment brochures. This would seem a strange thing to ask of another base's jumpers, especially disgruntled ones you've just accused of nicking the bloody pop tarts. The recipients of those brochures must have been rather surprised because inside some we placed dollar bills as a bribe, more were scribed with "run away while you can." Others suggested applying elsewhere, like

Missoula or Redmond instead. But by that time applicants would likely have witnessed the full circle of life and the migration of the LAMB to Missoula.

When we boarded the DC-3 we felt as if we were escaping. It was a good feeling, and one of the few occasions where returning to Missoula was a great relief and not a great disappointment.

Most returning jumpers were given a mandatory day off. But since I had already had one a couple of weeks before I was on the list and ready to go. It was also a short list and one consisting of a different bunch of jumpers than had been in Colorado or Redding.

That is what's so good about the rotating list. Those going on fire will sooner or later end up with a completely different group of people. The different lessons and experiences that jumpers have is, therefore, spread out over everyone. It is, in large part, what makes the base, and the diverse group of jumpers it contains, so cohesive a group; since sooner or later everyone knows everything that has gone on everywhere we've all been, and likely learn from each fire accordingly. The rotating list also stops cliques from building because everyone has to work with anyone at anytime, enabling everyone to see individual strengths and weaknesses, likes and dislikes, and can assign tasks accordingly. Moreover, jumping with different people keeps the stories interesting around the camp fire.

Although after a few years stories often get so embellished as to be almost unrecognizable, which is noticed when listening to the tale of an event in which you yourself were the major participant. This embellishment is not needed in most cases, but is no doubt how many jumper legends are born and remain to this day.

Chapter Twenty-Seven

— End of Days

*It seems to me that the natural world is the greatest source of
excitement; the greatest source of visual beauty; the greatest source of
intellectual interest. It is the greatest source of so much in life that
makes life worth living.*

– Richard Attenborough

THOSE WHO HAD REMAINED in Missoula for most of
the summer spent much of their time rotating back and
forth from the Kootenai. When I found myself on the list
it was to be no different, and the following day twelve of us were
heading off to the Panhandle. As usual, the smoldering one-acre
fire tucked under the tree canopy was not too difficult to spot from
the right angle, but a suitable jump spot was proving otherwise.
We finally agreed on a little patch of pale green half a mile away.
Another small brush filled meadow surrounded by large Douglas-
firs just waiting to grab a small piece of AIN netting to make a
jumper's life miserable.

Everyone made it to the ground, except Bill reached it after
first taking out the top of a tree. His chute had capped the tree, but
the top was brittle and had immediately broken away, leaving him
free falling 30 feet to the ground, landing awkwardly and cracking
his spine in the process. To add insult to injury the top six feet of

the tree almost impaled him as it speared itself into the earth right beside him.

Always the realist, and probably the best field medic we ever had, Bill knew exactly what the situation was and took control of the EMTs caring for him. (I know of no other occasion where the patient was, in effect, also the EMT in charge.) While in pain he was, nevertheless, perfectly calm and explained exactly what he expected from jumper EMTs, talking them through how to best position him on the sled that had just been dropped.

The non-EMT half of the load went to resource the fire while the rest of us packed Bill up for extraction. Since we were so deep in the Kootenai, with no roads for miles and no helispot possible without a lot of time and effort in already dwindling daylight, the only way to get Bill out was by requesting the military extraction team based in Spokane. Without them it would have taken us until the following morning to get Bill safely on his way to a hospital, after slogging through the unforgiving terrain in one of the most formidable and thick forests in the country. It would have been no small undertaking had the Army not been there to make that effort unnecessary.

Two jumpers cut a small clearing in the brush while the ship was on its way. The rest of us packaged Bill up and carried him over stumps, holes and logs to the extraction point. Within the hour he was being hoisted to safety 100 feet up in a medevac basket to the hovering Huey, courtesy of the U.S. Army.

Once the ship was away we all went back to doing what we do: digging in the damp dirt of the Kootenai for days. Followed by the now traditional DC-3 pick up from Libby airport after a four-hour hike from the woods.

Some of us visited Bill in Community Hospital the following day, fully expecting him to return the next season, being one of

West Yellowstone's almost legendary and most stalwart jumpers. But instead we learned that his jump career might be over.

Losing longstanding jumpers to injury is an inevitable part of the job. But it is no less dispiriting. Veteran jumpers are those who preserve the ethos, instill the camaraderie and, unconsciously, are instrumental in maintaining the unquestioning morale paramount to the success of the organization. Losing an experienced jumper means losing a piece of history. We lose their current experience and future perspective, lose their humor, laughter and unwavering steadfastness. While friendships may withstand time and absence, we miss their presence when chinking away on the all night digs on those never-ending firelines, around the piles during the autumn chill, and when relaxing over a beer surrounded by friendly banter in the bar afterwards. But more than that, when injury cuts short a veteran career we inevitably lose a piece of ourselves.

No sooner had we returned to the base when another request came in from northwestern Montana. A mere hour after leaving Bill at the hospital we were again looking down onto the vast dark green expanse that is the Kootenai. This time we were a few miles southwest of Libby, over the magnificent Cabinet Mountains and looking for a possible jump spot in the shadow of Snowshoe Peak. At almost 9,000 feet this peak looks over some of the finest subalpine scenery anywhere in the country. For once we would have a Kootenai fire with a view.

The DC-3 circled a nice looking jump spot in a saddle that had a few stunted sporadically placed lodgepole pines. The spotty fire was a few hundred feet below, slowly edging out of the timber in search of drier fuel. A few old logs were smoldering away but there was little chance that this fire was going to go much higher. Once a line was dug above it the fire would have nowhere to go until the downhill winds later in the early evening, by which time it should have been contained.

Instantly summing up the fire while peering from the DC-3's little square windows those of us at the front realized we would not be jumping on this one. Those at the back, however, were getting their gear together and tightening their straps. The first two were already hooking up and leaning towards the door, looking over the spotter's head for a better look at the scene below. A scene they would very soon be a part of. Jumpers ten and eleven weren't even bothering to watch anymore. They had settled back, laying across the cargo as best they could to be comfortable before the aircraft dropped to 200 feet to deliver cargo, whence we would be sitting down securely with seat belts fastened and helmets and gloves on. If we inadvertently plowed into the mountain I couldn't see those things helping much.

However, mountain turbulence is real and dangerous. While dropping cargo a few years later, flying through some unusually violent turbulence in the DC-3, the two spotters found themselves pressed violently against the roof of the aircraft. Once they hit up air again they were unceremoniously dumped hard on the floor. One of them received a severe back injury and was out for the rest of the season. They said it was like being physically shaken around inside a tin can. A tin can 1,000 feet in the air with a large suction hole in the side of it.

On Missoula's DC-3 the seats often faced forward, so we couldn't see a thing during the cargo run, only hearing the plane steadily lose altitude, briefly keep straight and level, and then roar back into the air after a clatter of cables and a whooosh of cargo as it was shoved from the door. After the cargo was done we resumed a normal altitude and circled the fire to relay information, during which the remaining jumpers would routinely stretch out to get more comfortable in the vacated space.

While spotters are tied in these days, many cargo handlers in the past were not, and more than a few have paid the ultimate price by involuntarily following their cargo out the door. However, even when tied in it's not the easiest task to retrieve oneself after exiting the aircraft in a 110mph slipstream. It takes all the strength of two people to haul someone back in. For that, some military aircraft are equipped with a winch should a jumper or spotter be unconscious on the end of a rope or static line not separated from the parachute. If conscious, the jumper is usually just cut away, using the knife perpetually attached to the inside of the door, after which they are forced to rely on their reserve.

With the fire resourced the rest of us went back to Missoula. Being last on the load and heading back to base is naturally a little frustrating since we are always eager to get out and keen to make money anytime we can. But it is as it is and this was not our turn. In that, we are resigned, and settle down to enjoy the flight home. In these situations the best place on the aircraft is right next to the open door. It's nice and cool on the hot days but can be damn cold on most days. But the reward for the chill is the outstanding view, which is endlessly fascinating as we weave through the taller peaks and slip over the crests of lesser ones. One moment the ground can be a mere 100 feet below and then, in an instant, several thousands of feet separate us from everything. As we get closer to Missoula the terrain changes, becoming less rugged but no less enthralling as the forested slopes of Lolo N.F. roll beneath us like a vast green velvet cloak. One can almost smell the great pines and the abundant firs by watching acre upon acre of woods revolve beneath us. A boot pressed against the door frame is all that separates us from earth. The breeze gets warmer as we descend over Blue Mountain and into the valley. In different air we can now smell smoke from fires all over the district. Maybe one of those will be ours tomorrow.

As it happened, we didn't have to wait for tomorrow. *Ernie* was good to us that afternoon and within hours we found ourselves flying off to reinforce a fire already resourced by a crew of Westie and Boise jumpers south of the park in the Teton National Forest.

Missoula was socked in with smoke coming from fires in all the surrounding valleys. Missoula is a sump for smoke as it wafts in on the air currents or simply slips to the valley floor during the cooler evenings. When there is no wind it can stay dormant and linger for days under an inversion, the tiny particulates creating a health hazard for everyone. It's always a relief to get back into the higher air when Missoula is socked in. But today it took forever to find fresh air. As the aircraft continued to climb it seemed as if we were being enveloped in a marshmallow: we knew there was an open door but there seemed to be nothing beyond it, except for a twilight zone full of puffy white stuff. It was quite eerie, giving the impression that we could safely walk out into cushiony comfort.

After a few more minutes we left the valley and climbed over the Bitterroots, where the air was once again invigoratingly fresh. We inhaled it deeply after trying to breath shallow during the flight up. Looking around we could see active fires over the surrounding mountains. Some small, some massive. Some manned, some not. Those not turned into management fires. It was like looking down onto a war zone, where the enemy was a friend as well as a foe, depending on the situation and the ferocity.

As we climbed further over the highest peaks we could see the Missoula valley blanketed under a pall of grey-orange smoke. Looking at it from here we wondered how anyone ever breathed in such conditions. Even though we were used to the smoke, used to it burning our eyes, plugging our noses and filling every crevice and orifice with dirt, this year was truly exceptional. And even up here, high above the lush green world rushing beneath us, we could still smell the smoke of scores of fires. It was quite the year.

We circled a large high alpine meadow a few hundred feet from the fire. It looked perfect. Well worth the wait. The streamers went straight in and the first two jumpers hooked up. On the next pass they were out and enjoying the ride as Don and Mike casually walked back to repeat the procedure. The spotter grabbed the static lines in the bottom corner of the door and dragged the deployment bags in before looking up and beckoning two more jumpers. Once they were hooked up he gave them a quick briefing, no shouting this time: "Fifteen hundred feet, two hundred yards and nothing on the ground. Any questions?" Two black helmets shook in unison. Don gathered his large frame close to the door while Mike glanced back to the assistant spotter. "You're clear!"

"On Final!" Don shuffled his big feet into position, placed his hands down the side of the door, recoiled a little, and waited.

The spotter was counting off the yards by tapping his hand on the edge of the door. He pulled his head in to slap Don out, but he was already gone. Mike took a step and followed right behind.

It was a beautiful jump. On exiting everything appeared in slow motion. As I fell I could feel the lines being pulled from the deployment bag until the chute snapped open with a slight wispy crack, leaving me watching the DC-3 bank off to the left in the distance. Once away from the turbines there was absolute silence. Four red, white and blue chutes scattered over the meadow below marked the spot and I made a few quartering turns to enjoy seeing more of the scenery around us. It was a big spot and it didn't really matter where I steered. Parachute handling was much like driving a car by now, almost subconscious by nature. I just enjoyed the ride and visually inhaled the spectacular surroundings.

Nearer to the ground I could see the grassy meadow sprinkled with a few late blooming flowers, and littered with fresh cow pies. Okay, now I'm going to pay attention, I don't want my jump gear covered in cow shit, I thought. I shouldn't have worried, however. Even in the thin air of 6,000 feet the landing was light as a feather and I had to physically force myself to do a proper PLF. The chute wafted gently over my head and settled softly onto the lush grass as I flipped my Capewells and removed my harness.

It's always a pleasant relief not to thump in, it gets everything off to a good start. There's nothing worse than leaving a jump spot wondering if you've hurt yourself but don't want to admit it.

This time, though, none of us could have asked for anything better. It was a perfect jump with a terrific bunch of jumpers in a truly beautiful part of the world. Every once in a while it all comes together. And at this moment of life, toward the end of an historic season, we were all old enough to appreciate every single moment. It was written on our faces; smiles of approval, appreciation of the last of the summer, grateful to be here, one more time.

We placed our gear in plastic bags and left them at the edge of the meadow in case it rained. Unlikely so far this year, but for the sake of a piece of plastic it was worth not ever having to carry out the added weight of rain.

The previous load were already digging up both flanks and we split up to join each line equally. It was rocky and their rhythmic chinking echoed off the cliffs in the distance, making it sound as though there were a battalion of jumpers and not just six of them. Moments before we arrived a load of retardant had painted both flanks, making the rocks and grass slick underfoot. But it was just as well, there were several small spots outside the fireline that could have taken off into the plush lichen covered timber and free-grazed meadows that adorned the area if not dug up in time. The air was fresh and healthy and years of desiccated lichen hung from the brittle low hanging branches down to the annual snow level.

Lichen is a great starter for a campfire, and as such is equally good at moving a slow moving ground fire up into the tree canopy, from where it can become an uncontrollable wildfire in a matter of seconds, able to cross roads and streams with ease and jump hard-worked fire breaks as though they didn't exist. One piece of lichen catching an ember outside the fire can ruin days of work.

As is common on these fires there was one large burning snag right in the middle: the lightning tree, with a long scar from top to bottom and several four foot splinters peppering the ground 20 feet away. Some story tellers mention bowing in thanks to such trees in some obscure spiritual belief, but we weren't '60s hippies, it was a hazard and it had to come down. The chainsaw roared to life and we positioned ourselves to chase the hot splinters that would break free and fly everywhere when it crashed to the ground.

No sooner had it fallen than eight of us were chopping off the burning chunks and throwing them back up into the fireline. The larger pieces were smothered with dirt to cool them down while we continued to burn everything else within the fireline. Don thought he saw a chunk break free and go down the hill and went bounding off after it lest it start a fire below us. His effort rewarded when he found an ember a hundred feet down the hill and buried it, and staying to check for any small smokes before coming back up. We didn't want to be surprised by a fire below since there were dozens of dry logs just waiting to burn scattered among the cured grasses, which could easily ignite and engulf our fire completely. As had happened a couple of years earlier near Glacier.

A few of us waited for Don to walk back up, but ready to go down should he find something larger to take care of. We sat in the cup trench and watched the scene above, instinctively mapping the last remaining pockets of fire in our heads. Once Don was back we zigzagged up through the fire to extinguish the last few smokes. It was dirty inglorious work, but necessary. Looking up we watched a flock of migrating geese come into view above the valley to the north. The gaggle forming an unequal wing as they passed directly overhead, with an occasional high altitude honk persuading an out-of-step goose back into the draft. It would not be long before they were over the mountain and into the next valley. Perhaps they were there already.

By evening the fire was looking good and we settled down to some much needed dinner. We had two campfires a few feet apart and the group split up evenly in no particular order. At this time in the season everyone was well prepared, in that each had collected an assortment of favorite foods from previous fires and different bases throughout the summer. Mine was a simple dried mince and potato mix with generous helpings of Tabasco to add some spice. Others seem to prefer the fancy new Italian style dried pasta dishes for some strange reason. There's no accounting for taste.

There were no stolen pop tarts only good old-fashioned Spam, which always provides for a highly imaginative display of culinary delights among some of the more adventurous campfire cooks: sprinkling them with an assortment of MRE jams and marmalades before frying or grilling slices to perfection, and sharing them with the group. Further adding a social element to the quiet camaraderie that is the wilderness jumper campfire experience.

While dinner around the fire is relaxing and the conversation enjoyable, for the most part, food preparation can often follow a strict regimen. Many get particularly finicky about simplest things: like how the campfire is constructed; where their cup is located on the fire; whether water is at a rolling boil, and not just fool's side-boil; even the preferred method of cooking a can of beans. In this, some simply open the lid while others prefer to bleep it; dent it, throw it on the fire and wait for pressure to force out the dent. The latter is easier and less messy if the timing is right. But if timing is off a little everyone can get covered and very upset when the can explodes. Those not too familiar with the process are often nervous when someone else is bleeping but not paying attention. Although it's often hard to know exactly when someone is paying attention because everyone is usually so laid back, giving the appearance of having no concern whatsoever.

Most of that stems from the complete satisfying relaxation only possible after a good solid hard day's work. And so, while sipping scalding hot coffee from grime-ridden mugs, burning lips on the edge of enamel cups, and picking soot from of our eyes with burned fingers, or trying to find a comfortable spot in the dirt for our backsides, we reminisce over past fires and discuss what we shall do over the winter when we all get laid off.

Conversation naturally varies depending on those around the fire. If women are there the dynamic can change dramatically and the conversation often less coarse. If only men, no subject is out of bounds, no language too offensive, and no ridicule too sharp. And absent women (not all of whom are female, if you remember) often bear the brunt. There are some brilliant women jumpers, however, who do mix in and swear a torrent like ruddy sailors. While others have been heard to brag about sexual conquests when it suits them and then complain vehemently of sexism when it doesn't. There is a continuity about men's campfire conversation – anything goes. When women are present men have to be almost psychic to know what is acceptable for that particular moment, and understand that anything they do say might come back to haunt them later. Then, of course, there are *those* times, when bears get the scent and come a roving, and when it doesn't take much to light the touch paper.

In any event, whatever the talk, everything gets washed down by lashings of strong coffee. And, like our food, by this time in the season many of us were carrying real ground coffee. None of that dried powdered crap. We'd heat a couple of gallon cans of water to just before boiling and add the grounds, stirring it in and allowing it to stew for a while. Before pouring we'd add a few drops of cold water to settle the grounds. Cowboy coffee to perfection.

The relaxation at the end of a day, leaning against a rock or a log with a cup of steaming hot coffee in hand is ideal. The wildfire will likely have subdued by now, leaving numerous scattered small fires burning fitfully on the mountainside as the remaining pockets of fuel are consumed in the dusty black dirt. An occasional gust of wind might hoist an ember into the night sky, where it dances in the breeze like a firefly before cooling and gently falling back to earth as carbon. A branch of a tree cracks and falls, sending up a small cloud of dust on the cool evening air. Another piece of wood gets chucked onto the campfire. Someone after a last cup of coffee. A flickering yellow glow fleetingly revealing the circle of tired dirt encrusted faces. Everyone stares into the new flame, silent in their thoughts, content in their world.

This year, our thoughts steered often to those we had lost. Not searching for reason but simply remembering. For who they were, what they did, what we would miss. Their names remembered for now but their ghostly presence around the fire fading with time as the jumpers who knew them dwindle on the summer firelines. A natural process, true of anyone who retires or otherwise leaves the jumper ranks. Larger than life legends might traverse generations, but with time, humble smokejumper stories drown as new people emerge with fresh ideas and new stories of their own. However, we all live with our memories, our personal recollections, and the best we shall take to the grave. In those last waning days our memories of friends, places and glory should provide solace, with no regret whatsoever for a life well lived and a job well done.

For as a collection of ordinary people we are fortunate to have lived a life brimming with adventure, in a landscape teeming with unparalleled splendor, with the unending enduring camaraderie of those many people we call friends. Look around you. Examine the faces of the fire. Remember them. Appreciate them. For when you are no longer there, or they no longer with us, you will miss them.

A relaxed body slides down a rock. Someone edges closer to the fire. Conversation become subdued, until but a murmur. A foot shifts a rock, a shoulder rubs into the dirt to get more comfortable on unforgiving ground. Collars are raised against the chill. Snoring occasionally masks the gentle spit, crackle and pop of the fire. Eventually silence and stillness. Wilderness tranquility cocoons the evening as jumpers slowly migrate to sleeping bags or huddle ever closer to the warmth of the fire, to sleep the sleep of the exhausted under the stars.

Long toward morning the chill night turns decidedly cold late in the season and the remaining wood is thrown onto a fading fire. But soon someone will rustle up more and rebuild the fire to boil the first water of the day. The eastern mountains are silhouetted black against the coming dawn. The orange glow behind becoming more pronounced by the second. On reaching the peak the glow turns pale and bright as it rises above a distant valley far beneath the behemoth rocks that are the Rocky Mountains. Coming from dark an initial pang of brilliance brings the first welcoming warmth of daylight and stiff bodies begin to stir. Slowly at first, almost lethargic, allowing aching joints time to warm. One by one we stoop our bent and broken backs to pour coffee, then sit to savor the view in quiet solitude as another morning begins in this great unspoiled landscape that we rather selfishly call our jump country.

Afterword

You have enemies? Good. That means you've stood up for something, sometime in your life.
— Winston Churchill

THERE ARE FRIENDS WHO UPDATE me from time to time about the goings on in smokejumper world. Things have changed, some for the worse but hopefully more for the better. Whatever the changes, smokejumpers still provide this country one of its most valuable resources. As I write, jumpers are busy in New York helping to clear thousands of downed trees after *Storm Sandy*. But only those with full-time appointments. Others, those perpetually abused temporary seasonal employees, limited to 1,040 hours per year, with no insurance, no benefits now or in the future, have been laid off and not allowed to return until next year, even though their presence and the skills they possess would be invaluable to the people and City of New York. That hourly limit is written in stone, inviolable, it cannot ever be broken. When a jumper once arrived to work early in the spring, eager to climb trees in New York, he was yanked off a fire in the middle of a fire assignment, 1,040 hours later, during one of the busiest seasons ever. That's one of those idiocies that remain the same no matter what: the willful abuse of seasonal workers and the national waste of highly trained personnel.

I provided the National Smokejumper Association with its very first website. Someone else is apparently saying they did, but that's bullshit, I have paper to prove it, and was asked to censor someone else's writing on an external link within days of it being gifted to them, proving that blind ignorance is everywhere. It was an early website, circa 1996, yet it was the development of that very early simplistic site that enabled me to get a real job that I didn't much like but one that lasted 14 years. A few years later I created an informational jumper website while working for Microsoft. Then between 2000 and 2002 I developed a professional smokejumper site that allowed jumpers anywhere to enter and edit information to keep jumpers and the public informed and updated, much like a modern WordPress site, only many years earlier. It could store each jumper's red card qualifications, every parachute record, each jumper's individual jump record, and every incident record, along with anything else they would ever need; such as documentation storage, PowerPoint and video presentations, the latest fire and fire weather data, lightning charts and a wealth of easily accessible, easily updated, safety information. All this data could be entered, edited and retrieved from anywhere, unlike the archaic, simplistic, cumbersome, time consuming Excel system the base was currently using, and has been using for years since. It also allowed jumpers to upload their own photographs to share with others, write their own articles and put forward ideas. A company I once worked for valued the site conservatively at $100,000 in 2003. The only 'G' time used was for importing all the data into the database. All the design, development and functionality was accomplished privately, on my own machine, in my own time. Hundreds of hours worth. In addition, I put in at least half an hour every single morning fielding emails from people either in the media or hopeful rookies. So it was also a very simple, easy to use and yet remarkable recruitment tool. Ten years later there is still nothing like it.

Talking of recruitment: in 2002, during one of those brilliant Ethics and Bleeding Conduct classes, someone asked if Bill was correct in saying that cash awards had been awarded to people for recruiting minorities under the Forest Service's, almost fanatical, EEO hiring process. The suggestion was immediately quashed and quite vehemently denied by the personnel department, which said, and I remember it quite clearly: "You shouldn't believe everything Bill tells you." Not a lie in the literal sense, but certainly a typical oft-used administrative obfuscation.

No, it was indeed a lie. Because Bill was right. Many among us knew he was right. The irony of that lie, right in the middle of an ethics and conduct class, was not lost on veterans long ago tired of the repetitive force fed bullshit who were hunkered down at the back of the room. For until that year the jump base had a plaque, in public view, right above the water cooler, congratulating the base and personnel for successfully hiring minorities. Everyone knew it! Not satisfied with that snippet, though, I left the room to search for Paul, a jumper actively involved in recruitment, and asked him, point blank, if he'd ever received a cash award for recruitment. He admitted that he had, to the tune of around $1,500 to $3,000. That, when people were literally queuing up to join the organization. But obviously the wrong people, or the wrong color of people anyway, and maybe even the wrong sex too.

Such lies, to those who put their health, even their lives on the line, and deserve better from those who do not, is appalling. To tell even such a small lie, especially such a nonsensical, meaningless, albeit protectionist, lie from a position of power shows the gross disconnect that exists between jumpers and administrators, as well as the gross lack of respect frequently shown towards those who do the actual field work, that which is the sole purpose of the Service.

For spending countless hours building a modern online tool that would help not only the Missoula jump base, but all others as well, I received the astounding sum of $500. But even that I didn't really mind, because being a seasonal I was long used to getting screwed.

The priceless piece of this saga, and the reason for mentioning it, came one winter morning, when I was not working, not on the payroll, and had little intent of ever going back. I got a call from operations informing me that a troublesome female administrator had taken exception to the caption beneath one of the photographs. To put it in perspective, the photo was of two jumpers climbing a large cedar, using old-fashioned ropes and spurs, with one jumper on either side lifting, in turn, the flip rope of the other. The caption said something like, "wish this had a skirt on." Oh, the scandal!

The site was on a private server, completely unconnected to the government, no one was getting paid a penny to run it, and yet an administrative bitch in a cubicle apparently had so much clout that she threatened to close down the Smokejumper Visitor Center in Missoula if the photo was not removed.

Since no one else was apparently willing to remove it, not least the person to whom it was attributed, though I never knew why, and since we all live in America with, uh hum, free speech an' all – or so I thought – I was not in the habit of subjective censorship. Especially not because of some faceless, self-righteous, moralizing bitch working in a cubicle. But a second call was then made to me, strongly requesting that I remove it because the issue had reached the higher echelons of the Forest Service HQ in Washington D.C.. "What?" I said, "those fuckers have nothing better to do?" It was the last straw with me. I removed it all and left a message:

> After removing everything that people over the years have ever complained they didn't like, for whatever their personal reasons... and to be fair to everyone's sensibilities in the future, you now have a non-functioning website. For this, you can thank equally non-functional bureaucrats in swivel chairs, who have little else to do but endlessly complain about the very people that provide them a living - the smokejumpers.

It left them with nothing but a blank white page, with $100,000 of work, and untold savings in time, down the crapper because a few people were too feeble, too pussy-minded, to stand-up against some obscure power-crazed bitch in a cubicle. Too quick to satiate and appease blind ignorance simply because it's easier. Easier just to sit back, collect the annual step increases and hang around until retirement. Smokejumpers deserve better than that. Maybe one day, when someone finally grows a pair, the outfit might gain back its independence and be run as it should, without impregnable bureaucratic incompetence, by people who don't care about a little confrontation when needed, aren't too sensitive, don't get offended by a little appropriate cursing and are willing to stand up for what is right. We all know who these people are and who they ain't. So what's the bloody problem?

The problem, in the public sector at least, is that there's little incentive to do better. A few people strive to get ahead, but then only hire those they know they can control. Long gone are the days when good, tough managers willingly hired a variety of strong personalities. Diversity now means color, not thought; culture, not ideas; and sex, not character. It means conformity when there is no tangible measure of improvement, no bottom line, and, hence, no incentive. Mediocrity thus reigns supreme because those who are driven, have a desire to improve, are seen as a threat and are rarely given opportunity to excel, unless they're willing to sell their souls by buying into the bullshit and spend time brown-nosing their way up. While others stagnate in a pool of mediocrity or leave.

In government, crap really does float to the top, especially the turista type. Once proved by an agency-wide memo, from a high-ranking manager, that once stated, in a last ditch effort to save face no doubt, that morale went from the grunts upward. So basically insulting everyone beneath him. Stupid, stupid, stupid. High paid bloody stupidity. Did this cretin think morale would improve after such an inane statement? Problem is, such notions are, sadly, not infrequent among administrators with scant ability or experience in managing people, those thrown into the job because they are weak, subservient and amenable, and will do whatever a boss tells them, even if it's stupid, stupid, bloody stupid.

The subtitle of this book should probably have read 'Fighting Wildfire in the Rockies and Bullshit in D.C..' But some poor dears seem to get offended by the word bullshit. No coincidence, I'm sure, that those most offended by the word bullshit are either those most responsible for it and, therefore, the most indebted to it, or those too wrapped up in their own heads to be oblivious to it.

The majority of people seem to look at the world through rose tinted glasses because it provides an easier life; ignorance being bliss. Some see the world as being cloaked in camouflage; the dirt and bullshit there but inwardly hidden and easily forgotten. A few, though, willingly see the bullshit for what it is, and are appalled at the apathy of the rose-tinted-camouflage brigade for it is they who allow it all to perpetuate by ignoring it, ignoring the incompetence and ignoring the trouble that it brings. Those instigating bullshit always rely on a weak audience so if the masses would just stick their heads out from under the camouflage the world might be a better, cleaner, more honest and more sincere place. The same can be said for the smokejumper organization.

In the Crimea a Russian officer is reported to have said British soldiers were "lions commanded by asses." *The Times of London* then turned it into the more lyrical "lions led by donkeys" that we know today. A phrase that gained notoriety when describing the shameless incompetence in leadership during WWI.

I hope the smokejumper organization never gets so tagged. But if it ever was to be, I hope the firefighting grunts, women and men, would fight on regardless. Like the lions they could be if left alone to be.

Lastly, writing is thankfully not yet a science, it is much an art. Like a painter chooses colors the writer chooses words. The trick with each is to put the paint and insert the words the right order in. So if I've upset sensitive souls with the abstract order of words, or the occasional use of profanity, I'm actually quite pleased about that, because I'm not responsible for personal sensibilities or the wonderfully colorful English language.

For when a jumper sees himself landing in a rockslide, or finds himself bouncing down the steadily thickening branches of a pine, he doesn't say "oh dear," he says "shit" or "this is going to fucking hurt!" When he finds himself spinning like a top over Yellowstone for the whole world to see, he says "goddammit!" That's a normal occurrence and real life to these people.

Would I do it again, knowing that I'd have two herniated discs, occasional debilitating back pain, a piece of webbing holding my stomach together, abdominal pain for the remainder of my life, no retirement or health benefits? You're goddamn right I would, in a fucking heartbeat. Only next time, knowing how I'd end up, due to administrative callousness and blind incompetence, I wouldn't be so bloody amenable.

U.S.F.S. Smokejumping History

(abridged, from a collection of USFS documents)

*All parachute jumpers are more or less crazy – just a little bit
unbalanced, otherwise they wouldn't be engaged in such a hazardous
undertaking.*

– Evan Kelley, Regional Forester, Region 1 (1935)

T HE UNITED STATES FOREST RESERVE ACT was
signed to law in 1891, allowing the President to establish
Forest Reserves from land in the public domain. Thereby
entrusting to the U.S. Government vast tracts of pristine lands
across North America, to be managed by the Division of Forestry
within the Department of the Interior, so that the land be preserved
for use by future generations for the public good. In 1901 this
division was renamed the Bureau of Forestry. The Transfer Act of
1905 then placed the bureau's management under the Department
of Agriculture, whence the name changed once again to what we
now recognize today; the U.S. Forest Service (USFS).

The Weeks Act[*] of 1911 was largely a result to the great fires
of 1910 that burned an estimated eight billion board feet of timber,
allowing the Secretary of Agriculture to purchase lands in order to
protect the nation's waterways, and use state and federal resources
to fight forest fires.[†]

---

[*] Congressman John W. Weeks of Massachusetts introduced the bill.
[†] The 1910 fires left the newly formed Forest Service with debts of $1.1 million.

The United States Forest Service first began using aviation for fire detection in California in 1917, fourteen years after the Wright Brothers' historic first powered flight at Kill Devil Hills in North Carolina.[*] Colonel Hap Arnold, himself a student of the Wright Brothers' aviation school, one of the world's first military pilots and later head of the U.S. Army Air Force during WWII despite, ironically, having a fear of flying, did much to help the USFS's development of aviation in fire management by cross-sharing his military knowledge and flying experience.

As is still the case today, a few forward-looking imaginative individuals were always eager to test the boundaries of space and time while more than a few were just as eager not to. While some instantly saw the advantages of furthering the Wright's pioneering exploits in getting men and material to fires quicker, more orderly, and in one piece, others equally deemed the enterprise too chaotic and crazy. It was, after all, early in the world of aviation, where the majority of aircraft used were still fragile-looking biplanes pieced together using wood spars, horse glue and cloth. Nevertheless, new innovations, rapid improvements in technology, and the advent of newer more resilient monoplanes meant that it was only a matter of time before aviation played a pivotal role in fire fighting.

Early tests in the '20s saw the USFS dropping water and foam onto fires using an assortment of jerry-rigged apparatus such as tin cans selected to break apart on impact, and paper bags – and even oak beer kegs attached to parachutes. While such techniques were disappointing other roles had promise and aviation's future in fire management was realized.

The first promising role was aerial photography, which began on a large scale in 1925. Followed by free-falling basic supplies to firefighters on remote fires in 1929.

---

[*] Kill Devil Hills is located 4 miles south of the Wright Brothers' base at Kitty Hawk – the name most people remember as the location of the first powered flight.

Emergency parachutes had already been used successfully to save pilots and balloonist spotters during the First World War, but it was not until the 1920s that the use of non-emergency parachutes became popular by early adventurists in a sporting role. The Soviet Union, especially, became a mecca for primarily European sports parachuting enthusiasts in the late 1920s through the 1930s.

In 1934 the Intermountain Regional Forester, T.V. Pearson, attempted to advance that role in the U.S. by proposing the use of parachute deployed firefighters, and to convince bureaucrats in the Washington Office several demonstration jumps were performed near Ogden, Utah, by professional parachutist J.B. Bruce, barely two years since Amelia Earhart had caught the nation's attention by flying solo across the North Atlantic, proving the strength and reliability of the modern, twin-engine, single-winged aircraft that would eventually become the mainstay of the organization.

Nevertheless, in July 1935, Regional Forester, Evan Kelley, replied:

> I will remind you that you wrote some time ago about J. B. Bruce's scheme of dropping men from airplanes for firefighting. I am willing to take a chance on most any kind of a proposition that promises better action on fires, but I hesitate very much to go into the kind of thing that Bruce proposes. In the first place, the best information I can get from experienced fliers is that all parachute jumpers are more or less crazy – just a little bit unbalanced, otherwise they wouldn't be engaged in such a hazardous undertaking.

Despite Evan Kelley's innate bureaucratic assertion, someone somewhere must have thought air delivery of men and equipment an interesting concept, even if not a new one – the Soviet Union was only one year away from performing their first fire jump, on June 16th, 1936, afterwards becoming fully operational across the whole of the USSR.[*] That Soviet lead might well have been the catalyst needed for the USFS and its sluggish bureaucracy to catch up. Because after Kelley's letter, the Washington Office initiated the Aerial Fire Control Experimental Project (AFCEP), tasking it with experimental dropping of fire retardant chemicals and water onto fires. Although these once again proved impractical, the road was paved to begin using parachutes to at least deliver cargo – and subsequently firefighters.

Four years later the AFCEP changed tack and instead placed all its efforts into personnel parachute jumping. Led by David P. Goodwin, Assistant Chief of the Division of Fire Control, the project was moved to Winthrop, Washington, where employees of Eagle Parachute Company of Lancaster, Pennsylvania, acted as consultants. After test drops using 150lb weights, 7 experienced jumpers and 2 locals made the first of 60 successful jumps from a single-engine, 5-seater Stinson, jumping into the rough terrain in the mountains around Winthrop. The parachute was a basic 30-foot diameter, round backpack, designed to face into the wind.

While modestly steerable, this early canopy nevertheless had very poor penetration, and the lack of any deployment bag created such a severe opening shock that it required jumpers to wear a stiff elasticated leather waistband as protection against abdominal injuries. Leather ankle braces further protected jumpers from the high rate of descent into rough and inhospitable terrain. And since the parachute was only moderately steerable, a felt-padded, one-piece jump suit and football helmet, complete with face cage, was used to protect the jumper during inevitable and often unavoidable

---

[*] In 1936 the Soviet Union had already installed 559 training towers at 115 separate locations, recording 1.6 million training jumps. Whereas a year earlier the U.S.A. had only one 125-foot free-drop tower – in New Jersey. The Soviets were, literally, leaps and bounds ahead of any other country, with over a million civilians taught how to parachute by 1940.

tree landings. In which event they carried a rope in a leg pocket to tie off and abseil down.

A year later, after effort had been spent developing equipment and parachutes, the first season of the Parachute Project began: six smokejumpers were set up in Winthrop and seven more at Moose Creek, Idaho, with the experienced Frank Derry, Eagle Parachute Company's west coast distributor and loft operator at Mines Field – now LAX – acting as an instructor and rigger for both bases.

Major William C. Lee, U.S. Army,[*] visited the Region One[†] jumper training camp at Seeley Lake, Montana, in June that year. After which he incorporated many of the techniques he saw when establishing the Army Airborne at Fort Benning, Georgia. Starting an interagency cross-training camaraderie that still exists today. It was undoubtedly no coincidence that Lee's visit occurred exactly when Britain's Winston Churchill, himself half American and one sixty-fourth American Indian, was requesting the rapid formation of an elite airborne corps to match that of Germany's famed *Fallschirmjäger*,[‡] which had been training for three years prior to the invasion of Scandinavia in April 1940.

The Seeley Lake camp was extremely basic at the time, with two 14-foot tents making a simple loft and a tree used as the tower, where Frank Derry hung a parachute to describe its various parts to those making their first jump the following day. Only 2 jumpers managed to complete all 10 training jumps; Jim Waite and Earl Cooley, the rest having sustained a variety of minor injuries in the process. Bill Bolen initially had problems pulling his rip cord and did aerial somersaults for several hundred feet before managing to

---

[*] Major William 'Bill' Lee is recognized as being the 'Father of the U.S. Army Airborne.' He commanded the 101st Airborne during WWII as a major general and helped to plan the D-Day drops.

[†] The United States is split up into 9 regions, encompassing two or more states (except for Region 10, Alaska), including both forests and grasslands.

[‡] Soon to be known as the 'Green Devils' the *Fallschirmjäger* was actually a branch of the Luftwaffe (air force) during WWII, and not the Heer (army).

successfully deploy his main chute. Jim Alexander encountered a similar problem and badly sprained his arm when it got entangled in his parachute lines.

The first actual fire jump was performed in Region One by Rufus Robinson and Earl Cooley on July 12th, over Martin Creek in the Nez Perce National Forest. Cooley, a legendary figure in the fire world, also had the first unintentional operational tree landing when he ended 140 feet up a spruce tree after his parachute almost failed to open. And yet, according to Cooley, "the only bad part of parachuting into a forest fire was the walk home."

A month afterwards, August 10th, Francis Lufkin and Glen Smith jumped over Bridge Creek on the Chelan National Forest in Region Six. Altogether, nine fires were jumped that year, saving about $30,000 in suppression costs – three times more than the budget for the entire Parachute Project.

In 1941 the Parachute Project moved to Missoula, Montana, simply because it was the home of Johnson's Flying Service, the contractor supplying all aircraft and pilots.[*] It was also cheaper to dispatch jumpers from a centralized location rather than maintain separate facilities across the Regions. Sixteen jumpers trained at Ninemile, west of Missoula, after which they all went on project work. Although only nine fires were jumped that year also, the project was nevertheless proving itself by savings both in timber and the cost of fire suppression. Safety was also improved with the late adoption of the 1920s, Italian developed, static line for the main parachute, removing the need for a rip cord. The larger Ford Tri-Motor ('The Tin Goose') dramatically improved the efficiency

---

[*] Missoula's existing airport, now the fairgrounds, was getting boxed in and so in 1938 the Missoula County Airport Board purchased 1300 acres west of town to construct a new airport, using Works Project Administration funds released through President Roosevelt's New Deal agency. In exchange for the provision of Forest Service equipment to construct the airport, the Forest Service was given a perpetual easement, enabling Missoula to become central to aerial firefighting and fire research.

of the whole project by carrying eight jumpers and cargo, thereby initiating an extraordinarily long history as a smokejumper aircraft, not being decommissioned until 28 years later, in 1969.

With America's entry into WWII the availability of qualified fit personnel for smokejumping dried up as instantly as Japanese silk. In 1942, a few months after Pearl Harbor, only five previous jumpers returned. Inexperienced firefighters were then accepted in order to make up numbers to the required 35. At the same time, the design of the current operational parachute was improved with the addition of Derry slots; six-foot slots in the silk five gores apart, greatly increasing the chute's stability, maneuverability and forward speed. Frank Derry later patented this design improvement in 1944, after adding the modification to previously non-steerable, military reject Nylon canopies that boosted the USFS's dwindling supply of silk due to the war.[*]

The following year was equally bad for available manpower, with only five jumpers and an instructor. However, with thousands of troops fighting in North Africa, and the rush to get thousands more trained for combat in other theaters around the Mediterranean and the Pacific, requests were made from some of the 12,000 draftee conscientious objectors among the Civilian Public Service (CPS) camps. Camps that allowed lawful religious conscientious objectors – under the 1940 Selective Training and Service Act,[†] and originating from the nonviolent peace churches (Mennonites, Hutterites, Quakers, etc.) – to serve their country in some capacity

---

[*] Prior to the war all parachutes were made from Japanese silk. With the threat of war, America had been stockpiling silk but could not produce nearly enough herself, so the military was also testing other materials, such as Rayon, but it wasn't until after the development of Nylon, by DuPont, tested for parachutes in 1939, and entering production in 1941, that an alternative material proved reliable and durable enough for military use in various climes. The last silk canopies being manufactured (on a large scale) in 1943. (As late as the mid-90s it was not unusual to see 1940's silk canopies hanging in the Missoula Smokejumper loft – for cargo use only, of course!)

[†] Also the Burke-Wadsworth Act; the first U.S. peace-time draft in history.

other than militarily, without wages, mostly in forestry, agriculture and firefighting. Seventy candidates from the CPS arrived to train at Ninemile to become smokejumpers while supported financially by their congregations and families, with minimal support from the federal government.

By this time, the success of the Parachute Project at Ninemile received the attention of the military, and in the spring of 1943 the project trained 25 people from the U.S. Coast Guard, the Canadian Air Observers and the U.S. Air Force for para-rescue operations – again a tradition that continues today. That year the project also expanded to other FS Regions: McCall on the Payette, Idaho, and Cave Junction on the Siskiyou, Oregon. Each receiving a squad of jumpers from Missoula.

The CPS Smokejumper program was increased the following year to 110, with each participant region expanding its contingent proportionally and, in effect, removing the Parachute Project from trial basis. With that, the U.S. Forest Service officially adopted the Smokejumper Project in 1944. Resulting in a number of National Forests in the northwest feeling confident to reduce the strength of their ground firefighting forces – a testament to the effectiveness and subsequent success of a program that a few stalwart pioneers had envisaged and worked so hard to achieve.

With the Smokejumper Project becoming official in 1944, and the remarkable twin-engine, Army Air Corps Douglas C-47[*] more available for civilian use toward the end of the war, the stage was set for the program to advance and further prove itself with better

---

[*] Developed from the 1935 Douglas DC-3 airliner, the C-47 Skytrain (Dakota to British Commonwealth countries), was the preeminent aerial workhorse of the Allies during WWII. Used famously during the Pacific campaign and during D-day and Arnhem, and for delivering cargo to China over 'The Hump', the Himalayas, from India. 10,000 were produced, a small number of which are still in use today. 'Dakota' being an acronym for Douglas Aircraft Company Transport Aircraft.

equipment, more powerful and larger capacity aircraft, and an uninterrupted supply of experienced personnel.

During the latter stages of the war Eagle could no longer keep up with the high demand for parachutes (200,000 parachutes had been requested by the air force alone in '41), and the manufacture of specialist smokejumper parachutes thus fell to Irving Air Chutes Company,[*] the world's first ever major parachute company. Irving manufactured parachutes largely to Frank Derry's specifications, incorporating his two 7-foot Derry slots, 7 gores apart, on a 28-foot flat circular canopy. A parachute that went on to provide excellent service, albeit with hard landings, until 1954.

As the war in the Pacific inexorably drew to a climax, the Japanese became ever more desperate to protect their beleaguered homeland and they attempted to set aflame the great forests of the northwest by using fire bombs attached to balloons that floated on the eastern winds. To counter this frantic attempt to create mayhem on the continental U.S., 300 members of the 555th Battalion of Black Paratroopers, The Triple Nickel, were trained in timber jumping and firefighting at Pendleton, Oregon, by instructors from Missoula. Although the balloon tactic was always doomed to fail, the 555th nevertheless made 1,200 jumps onto 36 fires throughout the west in what became a severe fire year – even without Japanese intervention.[†]

Not a year after the war's end the CPS program was stopped and, instead, the 164 jumpers in Region One were mainly made up of war veterans, with the remainder being college students. With more resources and increased funding available after the war, 1947 saw the start of an expansion in smokejumper bases, with Regions Four and Six developing their own training centers, instead of

---

[*] Leslie Irvin started the company in 1919 but a typist inadvertently added a 'g' to his name, leading to Irving Air Chutes.

[†] The 555th sustained the first ever smokejumper fatality during a fire jump when Malvin L. Brown fell while performing a letdown from a tree on August 6th, 1945.

relying on Missoula, and a base was established to serve the Gila National Forest in Deming, New Mexico, thereafter a particular favorite destination for jumpers of Region One.

Smokejumpers finally received justified national attention in 1949 when four Missoula smokejumpers flew to Washington D.C. in a Ford Tri-Motor for a demonstration jump on the White House lawn. Sadly, however, 1949 would be remembered more for tragedy, after 12 smokejumpers and a district guard were fatally burned in a fast moving grass fire in the hills of Mann Gulch on the Helena National Forest in Montana. Bringing to the fore the inherent risks of wildland firefighting and forever changing how firefighters would fight fires in the future. Up to that point the risks of parachuting onto remote mountainsides to fight wildfires were understood but not fully realized. It would be 45 more years before smokejumpers again saw such a tragedy, on the steep Gambel oak slopes of Colorado's Storm King Mountain.

Smokejumpers new and old, men and women, of all creeds and cultures, in bases throughout the country, can thank those early smokejumper pioneers. Without their risks, endeavors, hardships and tragedies, all those who have followed those fragile early steps could never have experienced what many only dream of. Not least of which is being a member of an elite specialized group of diverse individuals doing a job they love in countryside teeming with history, outstanding beauty and abundant wildlife.

Thanks to ongoing research and testing, the modern ripstop nylon parachute is a safe, efficient and altogether pleasant mode of transport for those disposed to use it, and far away from the bone-shattering, gut-wrenching, silk systems of yesteryear. The jumping organization has also benefited from vast improvements and capabilities in fixed-wing aircraft, especially since the adoption of one of the world's most respected aircraft; the rugged and versatile Turbine DC-3. These refurbished turboprop Gooney Birds quickly became the pride of the fleet during the mid-80s, and continue to prove their longstanding and legendary reliability as they cast a renowned, albeit fleeting, shadow over a variety of terrain. Their performance thankfully betters many wartime pilots' affectionate dubbing; "a collection of parts flying in loose formation."

Helicopters, a fantasy in those early heady days, have brought unparalleled efficiency, covering a multitude of tasks to modern firefighting. The over 400 smokejumpers available today, on bases throughout the western Lower 48 and Alaska, are indeed lucky humans. And thanks to continuous innovations in protective gear, modern aircraft, advanced parachutes and fire training, most are able to stay luckier for longer.

It is inherently human that those stalwarts of yesteryear brag about their lives and work being harder and they being tougher than anything comparable today. In the case of smokejumping this statement appears to be more true than most. Early smokejumper equipment and tactics demanded uncommon rigors in the face of an uncertainty that today's jumpers are thankfully not accustomed. However, all jumpers still maintain an athletic level of fitness to do any job assigned, at anytime – and do so with unselfish vigor not because of the government, but in spite of it.

CROSS-TIE RIDER IN THE SKY

Concocted over a beer or two by Pat and Scott

The tree were tall, the spot was, small, his asshole puckered shut,
The spotter signaled to the lad, come back here and HOOK UP!
He flung himself into the air and flipped o'er the top,
He rode his yellow cross-tie, down to the tiny spot.

Yippee yi yo,
Yippee yi ya,
Cross-tie rider in the sky.
Dumb, da dumb, da dumb, da dumb, da dumb.

The view was great, the steering sucked, the chute swayed and bucked.
He knew his fate, he was too late, he'd run clean out of luck,
His chute took off out of control and headed for the trees,
Then our fearless rookie, was not so very pleased.

He hit the trees with such a force the limbs began to break,
The rookie thought his jump today would be his last mistake.
He hung so high above the ground, he feared for getting down,
But foremost in his muddled thoughts, was Walter's angry frown.

Walt's eyes were red, his jaw was clenched, his arm was almost raw,
He grabbed the rookie by the throat and laid down the law.
Now listen to me rookie and heed what I say,
Or you'll be pounding fires for very little pay.

Now Steve was sad and feeling bad, his future still in doubt,
But don't you cry and don't you fret and don't you even pout.
The Crowley and the Straley were noted for the same,
And though they're not jumping, their still known for their fame.

USDA'S ANTI-DISCRIMINATION STATEMENT

Prepared by people who make a lot of money

> *The U.S. Department of Agriculture (USDA) prohibits discrimination in all its programs and activities on the basis of race, color, national origin, sex, religion, age, disability, political beliefs, sexual orientation, and marital or family status.*

With the added disclaimer, in small print:

> *Not all prohibited bases apply to all programs.*

Meaning the statement should, instead, read:

> *The U.S. Department of Agriculture (USDA) actively promotes discrimination in any program and activity that it chooses and on any basis that it chooses.*

Justification by Jack Ward Thomas, Chief of the Forest Service – 12/4/95:

> *It has nothing to do with an individual's ability to accomplish the job at any age.*

But:

> *A younger firefighting force is more desirable.*

Except when:

> *Individuals are free to continue to fight fire under temporary appointments at any age.*

347

ABOUT THE AUTHOR

Robert D. Hubble grew up to be a farmer, leaving his London school at the first opportunity to do so. Immediately after college, however, when life forced a change, as it so often does, Robert became a Sapper and served as a Combat Engineer in Britain's renowned Corps of Royal Engineers. Then, still with a desire to farm, he left England to help run a mid-west dairy farm among the frozen lakes of northern Minnesota. Another life changing experience led Robert to the wilds of central Idaho where he immediately fell in love with the magnificent mountains and the dirty physical work of fighting wildfires. A job which eventually enabled him to experience many terrific years as a U.S. Smokejumper in the wonderful Rocky Mountains of Montana. Where he now lives with his wonderful wife Christina, who has twice nursed Robert back from the edge and allowed him time to scribble three books.

ALSO BY ROBERT D. HUBBLE

Inside The Great Game

The Great Game continues. In its long and bloody history there have been periods of relative peace and tremendous violence. Through all, the subtle intrigue has remained, often coming violently to the fore when national interests are at stake. As is the case now, with one major superpower vying for influence against many smaller nations, rich and poor, for the only truly valuable commodity left in the world. Oil.

For this, countries still send their soldiers. But now under the guise of consultants and advisors, instead of travelers and tradesmen. The present struggle is no longer limited to the mountains of Central Asia, but is fought worldwide. And neither is it fought solely by nations. Individuals drawn into this fight are still abandoned by fickle national and corporate policy and few are ever remembered for their efforts. When the instigators give up and wash their hands soldiers die. All so their masters can have a continued role in the Great Game.

Churchill's Gold

In March 1941, nine months before America entered the Second World War, President Roosevelt sent a battleship to collect a shipment of gold bullion from South Africa as part of the 'cash & carry' agreement between a beleaguered Great Britain and an isolationist United States Government. An agreement that, through Roosevelt's pressure in enabling the 1939 Neutrality Act, finally allowed the United States to sell war matériel to Britain and its allies. But the system was bankrupting the British Government by having to pay for everything it was using to sustain the war; Churchill said, "we are not only to be skinned, but flayed to the bone." A few days afterwards the Lend-Lease Bill was passed by the Senate, which effectively ended America's neutrality.

Did this gold ever reach the United States? It is surrounded by conspiracy, largely thanks to Churchill's notion that: "In wartime, truth is so precious that she should always be attended by a bodyguard of lies." Some took this literally and went in search of the truth. What they found, after half a century of searching, took their breath away.

This is one man's tale of those events.

Made in the USA
Lexington, KY
10 May 2015